PRISON OF FOOD

PRISON OF FOOD

Research and Treatment of Eating Disorders

Giorgio Nardone
with
Tiziana Verbitz and Roberta Milanese

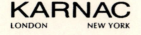

KARNAC
LONDON NEW YORK

First published in 2005 by
H. Karnac (Books) Ltd.
6 Pembroke Buildings, London NW10 6RE

British Library Cataloguing in Publication Data

A C.I.P. for this book is available from the British Library

ISBN 1 85575 367 7

Edited, designed and produced by The Studio Publishing Services Ltd, Exeter EX4 8JN

Printed in Great Britain

10 9 8 7 6 5 4 3 2 1

www.karnacbooks.com

CONTENTS

ABOUT THE AUTHORS

Giorgio Nardone is Director of Centro di Terapia Strategica (Strategic Therapy Centre) and of the Post Graduate School of Brief Strategic Therapy Centre in Arezzo. He is also Professor of Brief Psychotherapy at the Post Graduate School of Clinical Psychology, University of Siena, Italy. He has published numerous articles and several books, translated into many languages. He is renowned as one of the most creative therapists and authors in the field of brief strategic therapy and strategic problem-solving: his systematic and effective models for treating phobic–obsessive disorders and eating disorders are followed by many psychotherapists all around the world. He has published many books, details of which can be found at: http://www.giorgionardone.it/bibliography.asp

Roberta Milanese is an associated researcher at Centro di Terapia Strategica of Arezzo and an official, affiliated psychotherapist in Milan.

Tiziana Verbitz is an associated researcher at Centro di Terapia Strategica of Arezzo and an official, affiliated psychotherapist in Udine.

PREFACE

I am very pleased to present another of Giorgio Nardone's books. I greatly appreciate his work as well as his personality, and I truly treasure our long-lasting relationship.

I met Giorgio Nardone when he first came to our Institute in Palo Alto, many years ago, to study the Mental Research Institute's approach to therapy. A year later I supervised his first research project of the treatment of phobic–obsessive disorders, and it was then that I came directly in touch with his creativity and inventiveness as a therapist—especially his rigorous and system-orientated way of applying advanced research methodologies.

Soon after, we began to collaborate, and this gave me the opportunity to observe directly his techniques in their practical applications, which surprised me by their elegance and effectiveness.

What I want to stress specifically is the rigorous complexity of the non-ordinary logic and the apparent simplicity of the strategies he employs in order to solve complicated and complex problems.

In this book the author applies his model to eating disorders—one of the most difficult pathologies to treat effectively. As usual, he starts his approach on the basis of the results obtained from empirical and experimental research, and then applies and concentrates the most powerful strategies in order to obtain improvements.

I believe the reader will be impressed by the clarity of the description of specific interventions used by the author to bring about change.

Moreover, I am convinced that the reader will find it very interesting to see how Nardone and collaborators, concentrating on effective solutions rather than theoretical explanations, have reached an entirely new concept of the evolution of eating disorders in the course of their work during recent years.

By "getting to understand a problem through the discovery of its solution" they have acquired an empirically-based understanding of these disorders and a simple, clear account of the most effective ways to treat anorexia, bulimia, and vomiting syndrome.

In my opinion, this book is essential reading for anyone interested in knowing more about eating disorders and their effective treatment, as well as about advanced application of the Mental Research Institute's therapy model.

Paul Watzlawick
Mental Research Institute

CHAPTER ONE

From descriptive to operative diagnoses

> Words ordered differently produce different meanings; and meanings ordered differently produce different effects.
>
> Blaise Pascal, *Pensées* (1670)

> The educated philistee assigns unconditional perfection and objective validity to a few principles and methods, so that, having found them, he can use them to judge any event, to approve or reject it.
>
> Arthur Schopenhauer, *The Art of Controversy and Other Posthumous Writings* (1896)

Defining problems from an operative perspective

The first problem for clinical researchers is how to define the subject of their research. The configuration of the subject is a matter closely connected with a researcher's theory of reference. Consciously or not, researchers filter the observed reality through their personal interpretive lens. Modern constructivist epistemology has emphasized the problem of the observer's influence on the observed phenomena (Arcuri, 1994; Heisenberg, 1958; Rosenthal & Jacobson, 1968; von Foerster, 1987; Watzlawick, 1981), and pointed out how every action carried out in the search of knowledge places at the centre of its reflection not only the object under observation but also the subject who observes it.

Although this epistemological paradigm is now an important part of all scientific fields, including physics, most clinical psychologists and psychotherapists still believe that it is possible to obtain a pure objective description of studied phenomena. This is contrary to the constructivist point of view that there is no single reality, but many different realities that change according to one's perspective. *How* and *why* we know establishes *what* we know (Salvini, 1988). Thus, we have different realities and different ways of conceptualizing problems for each different point of view. This is particularly evident in the study and solution of mental and behavioural problems, a complex field that is characterized by an increasing number of contrasting theories and corresponding therapeutic approaches.

This concept is best illustrated by metaphor (Nardone, 1998):

> Once in Southern Italy, on a very hot day, a father and his little son started out on a journey with their donkey to visit some relatives in a distant town. At first, the father rode on the donkey while the son walked beside them. As they passed a group of people, the father heard them say: "See that cruel father! He rides the donkey and makes his little boy walk, on such a hot day!". So the father dismounted and let his son ride the donkey. After a while, they passed another group of people. The father heard them say: "Look! On such a hot day, the old father has to walk while his young son rides comfortably on the donkey. What's the world coming to?" When he heard that, the father decided that it would be best if they both rode the donkey. As they continued their journey, they passed another group of people. The father heard them say: "See, how cruel! Those two have no pity for that poor animal, which has to carry so much weight on such a hot day!". So the father dismounted and made his son do the same. They continued their journey on foot. After a while, they passed another group of people and heard them say: "Look at those two fools, walking on such a hot day when they could be riding their donkey . . ." [Nardone, 1998, pp. 9–10]

Obviously, this story could go on for ever. It illustrates how there can be very different opinions and perceptions of the same reality and how people's reactions change accordingly. It is interesting, for example, to observe how many different causal descriptions of food disorders there are based on scientists' different perspectives.

Psychiatrists of the biological school believe that there must be a specific gene for each food disorder. Authors who subscribe to the theory of repressed memories believe that 90% of women who suffer from food disorders have undoubtedly suffered some sexual abuse in the past.[1] Psychologists who take a psychodynamic perspective believe with absolute certainty that food disorders are connected with a failure to overcome archaic complexes, particularly (since more women than men suffer from food disorders) the Electra complex. More up-to-date researchers, such as those who adopt the relational perspective, see mother–daughter dynamics or parental conflicts as playing an obvious role in the formation of food disorders. (Zerbe, 1993). In the past few years, a theory that classifies eating disorders with dependency disorders such as alcoholism and drug addiction has become increasingly popular, leading to the foundation of Overeaters Anonymous (OA) (Malenbaum, Herfog, Eisenthal, & Wyshak, 1988). Their basic assumption is that anorexia and bulimia cannot be cured, only managed through self-help groups.

However, apart from such parochial, self-validating, theoretical, and practical propositions, most researchers seem to agree that eating disorders are "a sort of functional adaptation to a reality that is perceived as unmanageable" (Bateson, Jackson, Haley, & Weakland, 1956; Costin, 1996).

The strategic–constructivist perspective (Maturana & Varela, 1980; Nardone, 1991; Von Foerster, 1973; von Glasersfeld, 1981, 1995; Stolzenberg, 1978; Varela, 1981; Watzlawick, 1977, 1981) does not rely on any theory about "human nature", nor, consequently, on any definitions of "normality" or "pathology", but considers human problems as a product of interactions between the subject and reality. It is a non-normative model that sees human problems as the result of a complex process of retroactions between the subject and reality, where a person's efforts to change actually contribute to maintaining the problematic situation.

According to this viewpoint, a problem persists because of the *solutions attempted*[2] by the subjects and the persons around them in order to resolve the problem. When those attempts fail, they retroact upon the problem and complicate it (Nardone, 1994; Nardone & Watzlawick, 2000; Watzlawick, Weakland, & Fisch, 1974).

This leads to the formation of what we call a pathogenic "system of perceptions and reactions",[3] which expresses itself as an obstinate perseverance in using supposedly productive strategies that have worked for similar problems in the past, but that now, instead, make the problem reverberate (Nardone & Watzlawick, 1990) Indeed, the redundant repetition of failed attempts to solve the problem actually increases the problem instead of solving it, leading to the formation of an autopoietic cybernetic system of attempted solutions and persistence of the problem.[4] This circular dynamic of interactions maintains the stability and equilibrium of the system despite the fact that it is dysfunctional for the subject.

The objective of strategic interventions, therefore, is to interrupt the vicious circle established between the attempted solutions and the modes of persistence of the problem. Using specific manoeuvres that have the power to subvert the pathogenic equilibrium of the system, such interventions aim to induce changes in the modalities by which these persons have constructed private, dysfunctional realities in the relational, cognitive, and emotional organization that underlies their disorder.

In order to solve a problem, we need to understand how the system of perception and reaction towards reality functions in the person's *here and now*. In other words, we must try to understand *how* the problem *functions*, not *why it exists*. In that sense, we leave behind the search for knowledge based on *why* for a search of knowledge based on *how*—going from a search for the causes of a problem to a search for its modes of persistence. This allows the resolving process to evolve from slow, gradual solutions to rapid and effective interventions.

Applied research on this subject (Fiorenza & Nardone, 1995; Nardone, 1993, 1995a; Nardone & Watzlawick, 1990) has enabled us to detect a series of specific models of rigid interaction between the subject and reality. These models lead to the formation of specific typologies of psychological disorders that are maintained by reiterated dysfunctional attempts to solve the problem. Such attempts actually increase the problem that they are supposed to solve (Nardone & Watzlawick, 2000).

The evolved model of the strategic approach goes beyond the nosographic classifications of psychiatry and clinical psychology[5] by adopting a model of categorization of problems in which the construct "perceptive–reactive" system replaces the traditional categories of mental pathology.[6]

This goes against the current tendencies of many therapists who, having initially rejected the usual nosographic classifications, now seem to want to resume their use. This is the case, for example, of Selvini Palazzoli, Cirillo, Selvini, & Sorrentino (1998), who divide anorexics into four typologies that correspond to four personality disorders listed in *DSM-IV*: dependent, borderline, obsessive-compulsive, and narcissistic. From our point of view, classification is just another attempt to force the facts to make them fit one's theory of reference, because it turns out to lack any concrete value from the operative point of view.

In light of these theoretical–epistemological assumptions, it seems essential to make what we call an "operative" diagnosis (or "diagnosis–intervention") when defining a problem, instead of a merely "descriptive" diagnosis. Descriptive perspectives such as that of the *DSM* and most diagnostic manuals, give a static concept of the problem, a kind of "photograph" that lists all the essential characteristics of a disorder. However, this classification gives no operative suggestions as to how the problem functions or how it can be solved.

By operative description, we mean a cybernetic–constructivist type of description of the modalities of persistence of the problem, i.e., the problem *how* feeds itself through a complex network of perceptive and reactive retroactions between the subject and his or her personal and interpersonal reality (Nardone & Watzlawick, 1990).

From an operative point of view, the models of persistence of a particular typology of problems are identified through applied, empirical–experimental research with the objective of preparing solutions that guarantee increasingly effective and efficient interventions.

According to this mode of research, which we call "research–intervention", external observation does not allow us to understand how a problem functions; for that, it is necessary to try to change the way it functions. Indeed, observing how the system responds to the introduction of change is the only way to reveal its previous functioning. The basic premise of this mode of research is therefore *"to know by changing"*.

This methodology is perfectly in line with what Kurt Lewin defined as *action-research* in social psychology (Lewin, 1946), i.e., a research that studies the phenomenon in the field, empirically and experimentally, producing changes in events and observing the effects of those changes. Along the same lines, we also have modern cybernetic–constructivist epistemology, effectively expressed by von Foerster (1973) in his aesthetic imperative—"If you want to see, learn to act" and by von Glasersfeld (1981)—"Man can know only what he does", and again, "Action constructs knowledge".

On that basis, we maintain that it is possible to know a reality by intervening on it, because the only epistemological variable that we can control is our strategy, i.e., our "attempted solution" that, when it works, enables us to understand how the problem persisted and maintained itself. The logic of our research–intervention is therefore based on the construct "Knowing a problem through its solution" (Nardone, 1993), i.e., knowing a reality through the strategies that are capable of changing it.

If we transpose this construct into clinical research, it follows that a successful solution strategy, repeated on a large sample of subjects with the same type of disorder, enables us to reveal the model of functioning of the disorder.

The method of *"knowing by changing"* is analogous to a chess game in which each player discovers his adversary's strategy by observing the moves made in response to his own. However, neither player will gain actual knowledge of the other's strategy until the game is done or won, because only a successful strategy can reveal the adversary's strategy. In later, similar games, the player will have available an already experimented successful strategy and be able to reach checkmate more easily and with fewer moves.

It is possible to operate in the same manner in the study of a psychological pathology: the therapeutic game opens with manoeuvres that, however minimal, are capable of introducing an initial retroactive effect. We then proceed step by step, adjusting the strategy on the basis of the patient's responses while trying to lead him or her to change the perceptive, emotional, and behavioural modalities that are maintaining the presented disorder.

With all the necessary adjustments to the patient's particular personal and contextual situation, the same strategy can be applied to pathologies that are isomorphic to the typology for which the strategy was constructed, thus increasing the efficiency and effectiveness of the therapeutic intervention. As a consequence, this intervention is not based solely on the therapist's artistic creativity, but mostly on a strategy that has proved to be predictive as far as it effects are concerned.

This way of conducting the therapy as a *systematic process of research* also leads to a more advanced understanding of the modes of persistence of those specific disorders. This in turn leads to further improvements of solution strategies, in a sort of evolutionary spiral nourished by the interaction between empirical interventions and epistemological reflections, which leads to the construction of specific, innovative strategies (Nardone & Watzlawick, 2000).

In our study of the various forms of eating disorders, this methodology turned out to be an important instrument of knowledge from an operative point of view, as it had been in our previous study of phobic disorders. In fact, the data gathered during our research intervention not only enabled us to devise an effective psychotherapeutic model for the rapid solution of these problems, but also led us to produce an epistemological and operative model of their formation and persistence.

This methodology, whose primary aim was the devising of an effective and efficient clinical intervention, thus enabled us to acquire further information on the disorders in question, and opened new perspectives of knowledge. At the same time, the new knowledge that emerged based on the effects of our interventions served as a guide for progressive adjustments to the interventions, thus enabling a continuous process of self-correction based on the interaction between the solution and the problem.[7] In view of these theoretical and methodological considerations, the following exposition will discuss not only the change and solution of eating problems, but also their formation and persistence.

Before examining the results of our research–intervention, it may be useful to review the classification of eating disorders as it appears in *DSM-IV*, despite the above-mentioned limits of this approach. This will enable us to make references to internationally recognized and applied diagnostic definitions of psychological disorders. We believe it is important to use a conventional language familiar to all clinical researchers in order to communicate based on common diagnostic criteria and reduce the possibility of misunderstandings when exchanging information with scientists who choose different theoretical and practical approaches.

The classification presented below should therefore be considered a communicative "sleight of hand" for addressing the scientific community familiar with this type of language.

The diagnostic classification of eating disorders[8]

Anorexia nervosa

Diagnostic criteria

A. Refusal to maintain body weight at or above a minimally normal weight for age and height (e.g., weight loss leading to maintenance of body weight less than that expected or failure to make expected weight gain during period of growth, leading to body weight less than 85% of that expected).[9]

Weight loss is primarily obtained by reducing the total quantity of food eaten. Although the calorie restriction may initially be limited to the exclusion of foods that are thought to contain too many calories, in most cases these subjects eventually adopt a diet that is rigidly restricted to a small number of food categories. There may also be purging behaviour (such as self-induced vomiting, or misuse of laxatives or diuretics) or excessive physical exercise with the objective of losing weight.

B. Intense fear of gaining weight or becoming fat, even though underweight. The fear of becoming fat is unmitigated by weight loss; in fact, weight-related worries often increase as real weight decreases.

C. Disturbance in the way in which one's body weight or shape is experienced, or undue influence of body weight or shape on self-evaluation, or denial of the seriousness of the current low body weight.

Anorexic subjects present an altered self-image of their body shape and dimensions, with distorted perception and the values attributed to physical appearance. Some subjects feel that their whole body is excessively fat; others admit to being thin, but perceive some parts of their bodies (usually the abdomen, glutei and thighs) as being "too fat". Self-esteem is excessively influenced by weight and body shape. Weight loss is seen as an extraordinary conquest and an indication of an indomitable self-discipline, while weight gains are experienced as an unacceptable loss of control. Although some may be conscious of their thinness, subjects with this disorder typically deny the severe consequences of their emaciation upon their physical health.

D. In postmenarcheal females, amenorrhea, i.e., the absence of at least three consecutive menstrual cycles. (A woman is considered to have amenorrhea if her periods occur only following hormone, e.g., oestrogen, administration.)

Amenorrhea usually follows weight loss, but may precede it in a minority of subjects. In premenarcheal females, the disorder may lead to a delay in the appearance of menstrual cycles.

Subtypes

Based on the presence or absence of regular bingeing or purging during the current episode, the following subtypes are used:

(a) *Restricting type*: During the current episode of anorexia nervosa, the person has not regularly engaged in binge-eating or purging behaviour (i.e., self-induced vomiting or the misuse of laxatives, diuretics, or enemas). Weight loss is obtained primarily by dieting, fasting, or excessive physical activity.

(b) *Binge eating and/or purging:* During the current episode of anorexia nervosa, the person has regularly engaged in a binge-eating or purging behaviour. Most subjects with Anorexia Nervosa who binge also engage in purging behaviour through self-induced vomiting or the misuse of laxatives, diuretics or enemas). In some cases, the subject does not binge, but engages in purging even after consuming modest quantities of food.

Manifestation and associated disorders

When subjects with anorexia nervosa are significantly underweight, they may experience depressive symptoms such as depressed moods, social isolation, irritability, insomnia, and sexual disinterest. They also often present significant obsessive–compulsive symptoms that may or may not be related to food (food preoccupation, collecting recipes, food hoarding, etc.) Other symptoms often associated with anorexia are discomfort when eating in public, feelings of inadequacy, a need to control one's surroundings, mental rigidity, reduced spontaneity in interpersonal relationships, and an excessive repression of initiative and the expression of emotions.

Bulimia nervosa

Diagnostic criteria

A. Recurrent episodes of binge eating. An episode of binge eating is characterized by both of the following:

1. Eating, in a discrete period of time, (usually within a two-hour period) an amount of food that is definitely larger than most people would eat during a similar period of time and under similar circumstances.
   A single episode of bingeing does not necessarily happen within a single context, and continuous "snacking" on small amounts of food cannot be considered as bingeing. Although the type of food consumed during the binge varies significantly, it usually includes high-calorie foods such as ice-cream or cake. In any case, bingeing appears to be characterized above all by the anomaly of the amount of food, rather than a compulsion towards a specific type of food. Bulimic subjects are typically ashamed of their pathological eating habits and try to hide them, so that bulimic crises happen in solitude, as secretly as possible. Episodes may be more or less planned, and are usually but not always characterized by the rapid ingestion of food. The binge often continues until the subject feels "so full as to feel sick". It is precipitated by dysphoric moods, interpersonal stress, intense hunger following a dieting restriction, or by dissatisfaction regarding weight, body shape, or food. During the binge there may be a temporary reduction of the dysphoric state, but depressed moods or merciless self-criticism often follow.

2. A sense of lack of control over eating during the episode (e.g., a feeling that one cannot stop eating or control what or how much one is eating). The subject may experience a feeling of extraneity during the binge, especially in the early phases of the disorder. Some describe the binge as an experience of dissociation. In later phases of bulimia nervosa, the subjective sense of acute lack of control during the crisis may subside, and there may instead be an inability to resist the impulse to binge or to interrupt the crisis once it has started. The loss of control associated with bingeing is not absolute: the subject may continue the binge despite a ringing phone, but may interrupt it abruptly if someone enters the room unexpectedly.

B. Recurrent inappropriate compensatory behaviour in order to prevent weight gain. The most common method adopted in order to neutralize the effects of the binge is self-induced vomiting following the binge (80–90% of subjects). Vomiting reduces the feeling of physical discomfort as well as the fear of gaining weight. Subjects may use different stratagems to induce vomiting, by using their fingers or other instruments. In the advanced phases of the illness, they are generally able to vomit at will. In some cases, the vomiting itself is the desired effect: the person binges in order to vomit, or vomits even after eating small amounts of food. Other purging behaviours are the misuse of laxatives (one-third of cases), diuretics, or other drugs. Enemas are rarely used immediately after the binge, and are never the subject's only purging behaviour. Other compensatory measures are fasting in the days following the binge, or excessive physical exercise. (Physical activity is considered excessive when it interferes with other important activities, when it occurs at unusual times and places, or when it is practised despite precarious health conditions.)

C. Binges and compensatory behaviour occur twice a week on the average for three months.

D. Levels of self-esteem are unduly influenced by body weight and shape.

E. The disturbance does not occur exclusively during episodes of anorexia nervosa.

Subtypes

Based on the presence or absence of regular purging behaviour to compensate for bingeing, the following subtypes are used:

(a) *With purging behaviour*: During the current episode of bulimia nervosa, the person has regularly engaged in self-induced vomiting or the misuse of laxatives, diuretics, or enemas.
(b) *Without purging behaviour*: During the current episode of bulimia nervosa, the person has regularly used other inappropriate compensatory behaviours, such as fasting or excessive exercise, but has not regularly engaged in self-induced vomiting or the misuse of laxatives, diuretics, or enemas.

Manifestations and associated disorders

Subjects with bulimia nervosa are usually within normal weight parameters, although some may be slightly underweight or overweight. These subjects typically reduce their consumption of food in between binges, giving preference to low-calorie foods and avoiding foods that they believe can make them fat or give impulse to a binge. These subjects have a high incidence of depressive symptoms (for example, low self-esteem) or mood disorders (which in most cases follow the development of bulimia). There is also a higher frequency of anxiety disorders and symptoms (for example, a fear of social situations) that frequently recede after treatment for bulimia nervosa. Substance abuse (particularly of alcohol and stimulants) occurs in approximately one third of subjects. The use of stimulants often starts as an attempt to control appetite and weight.

Eating disorders not otherwise specified

This category includes eating disorders that do not meet the criteria of a specific eating disorder. Examples include:

1. For females, all of the criteria for anorexia nervosa are met except that the individual has regular menses.
2. All of the criteria for anorexia nervosa are met except that, despite significant weight loss, the individual's current weight is in the normal range.

3. All of the criteria for bulimia nervosa are met except that the binge eating and inappropriate compensatory mechanisms occur at a frequency of less than twice a week or for a duration of less than three months.
4. The regular use of inappropriate compensatory behaviour by an individual of normal body weight after eating small amounts of food (e.g., self-induced vomiting after the consumption of two biscuits).
5. Repeatedly chewing and spitting out, but not swallowing, large amounts of food.
6. Binge eating disorder: recurrent episodes of binge eating in the absence of the regular use of inappropriate compensatory behaviours characteristic of bulimia nervosa.

In its appendix, *DSM-IV* lists the following research criteria for binge eating disorder:

A. Recurrent episodes of binge eating. An episode of binge eating is characterized by both of the following:

1. Eating, in a discrete period of time (e.g., within any two-hour period), an amount of food that is definitely larger than most people would eat in a similar period of time under similar circumstances;
2. A sense of lack of control over eating during the episode (e.g., a feeling that one cannot stop eating or control what or how much one is eating).

B. The binge eating episodes are associated with three or more of the following:

1. Eating much more rapidly than normal;
2. Eating until feeling uncomfortably full;
3. Eating large amounts of food when not feeling physically hungry;
4. Eating alone because of being embarrassed by how much one is eating;
5. Feeling disgusted with oneself, depressed, or feeling very guilty after overeating.

C. Marked distress regarding binge eating.

D. The uncontrolled eating behaviour occurs, on average, at least two days a week for six months.

E. The binge eating is not associated with the regular use of inappropriate compensatory behaviours (e.g., purging, fasting, excessive exercise) and does not occur exclusively during the course of anorexia nervosa or bulimia nervosa.

Main results of the research–intervention

Our research–intervention on eating disorders led to the preparation of specific protocols of treatment that are particularly effective and efficient for these types of disorders and improved our knowledge of the reality that we were treating, i.e., the typical perceptive–reactive system of persons with eating disorders.

The first decidedly surprising result of our research–intervention was a new definition of the problems being studied. Even at the earliest phases of our research, the actual reality of eating disorders turned out to be somewhat different from the ways it is described in psychiatric literature. Aside from the two pathologies listed in *DSM-IV* (anorexia nervosa and bulimia nervosa) we began to observe the existence of a third type of eating disorder, which we named "vomiting syndrome" or simply "vomiting". This type of disorder involves compulsive eating and vomiting several times a day. Current psychiatric literature classifies this symptom as a subtype of anorexia and bulimia ("subtype with purging behaviour").

On the contrary, our empirical–experimental analysis shows that the symptoms of vomiting make up a distinct pathology with its own characteristics of persistence, characteristics that are completely different from those of anorexia and bulimia. The vomiting disorder originates with bulimia or anorexia but, once established, it becomes what biologists call an "emerging quality", i.e., something that has lost all significant connections to what initially produced it, in the same way that a molecule of water is something very different from hydrogen and oxygen. As we will see in Chapter Five, when vomiting establishes itself as an actual disorder, it produces a cybernetic model with its own very specific modes of persistence, losing the aspects of an eating problem and taking on the characteristics of a food-based "perversion".

Based on the above, some readers might conclude that the construct of vomiting introduced here coincides with the classical construct of bulimia nervosa. However, there is one essential difference between the two constructs. *DSM-IV* defines self-induced vomiting as one of several types of purging typical of bulimia nervosa and attributes it to anorexia as well as bulimia. This reduces vomiting to a mere symptomatic expression of those clinical frameworks.

We do not consider the vomiting as a symptomatic expression, but as a separated syndrome. We believe that persons who present this disorder are characterized by an uncontrollable impulse to eat *in order* to vomit, as opposed to an uncontrollable impulse to binge that is followed by vomiting as the necessary mode of elimination of the food just consumed. Over 100 interviews conducted during our research showed that what makes the typical compulsion of vomiting so uncontrollable is the pleasure derived from the whole sequence of eating and vomiting, which should therefore be thought of as a model of pleasure-seeking.

In the traditional definition of bulimia nervosa, the main emphasis is placed on the bingeing, and self-induced vomiting is considered as a secondary symptom equal to other forms of purging. In contrast, our definition of vomiting emphasizes the complete process from the preliminary fantasy through the food binge and on to the final purge—a sequence characterized by intense feelings of pleasure.

Our classification of vomiting as an autonomous disorder is based on our finding that the intervention techniques that had proved effective on anorexia and bulimia[10] were ineffective when applied to subjects with the symptoms just described. In the course of our research–intervention it therefore became necessary to devise an *ad hoc* intervention for this disorder that would enable its solution and reveal its modes of persistence and self-nourishment.

Moreover, vomiting currently appears to be the most significant and widespread eating disorder (approximately sixty-five per cent of our cases),[11] leading us to consider it a predominant disorder as opposed to an accessory disorder or subtype of the two traditional forms of eating pathologies. Its high frequency may be explained as a sort of "technological advancement" of eating disorders, where an initial attempted solution with the objective of losing weight or avoiding weight gains eventually leads to a completely different problem, independent of the problem that initially produced it.

It appears, then, that eating disorders are rapidly evolving, especially towards an epidemic diffusion of the vomiting pathology. It is therefore necessary to have available evolved forms of treatment that can continuously be adapted and updated. In order to stay effective and efficient, a model of intervention needs to be able to evolve by adapting itself to the characteristics of the problem to which it is applied.

A second important finding of our research–intervention is that eating disorders have a higher complexity than, for example, the phobic–obsessive disorders that were the focus of our previous research. In order to maintain the efficacy and effectiveness of the treatment, it became necessary to introduce variations within our treatment protocols for the three types of eating disorders. As our research–intervention proceeded, it emerged that the modes of persistence of these disorders are more variable than those of phobic disorders. While only one or two variations of intervention per disorder were necessary in order to unblock the symptoms of phobic disorders, we found that eating disorders required at least three variations. Our observation of several variations within the same syndrome led us to distinguish between different types of anorexia, bulimia, and vomiting according to their different characteristics of persistence.

The presence of different "types" within the same pathology indicates a higher complexity of eating disorders with respect to other types of pathologies. This aspect may help explain their particularly strong resistance to change. Because of the higher differentiation in their modalities of pathogenic homeostasis, eating disorders require more therapeutic variations, and a significant ability on the part of the therapist in determining the typology of persistence of the problem and (perhaps even more importantly) the most appropriate form of relationship and communication for each particular case.

This peculiarity of eating disorders probably explains why the efficacy and effectiveness rates of our therapeutic protocols for these disorders are lower than those for phobias and obsessions. In particular, it would explain the much higher number of unchanged or little improved cases within these typologies.[12]

In the following chapters, after a few clarifications regarding our methodology, we shall describe the specific modalities of persistence of each food disorder (including its variants) and the typology of treatment devised for it, with examples drawn from our clinical practice.

CHAPTER TWO

The construction of treatment protocols

"The obscurity that envelops us cannot be dissipated. Still, stretch by stretch, the lights of intelligence illuminate a part of the road long enough that we are able to continue. Thus, a car cleaves the night, speeding continuously into the short beam of light that it projects from itself"

Ugo Bernasconi, *Parole Alla Buona Gente* (1988)

From the general model of brief therapy to specific treatment protocols

In 1985, the Centro di Terapia Strategica in Arezzo initiated a research project with the objective of producing an evolution of brief therapy from a general model to a specific model of intervention on specific disorders. The definition of brief strategic therapy developed by the Mental Research Institute (MRI) in Palo Alto (Watzlawick, 1981; Watzlawick, Weakland, & Fisch, 1974) was the starting point for our research, which eventually led to the construction of specific treatment protocols for different forms of mental problems, such as phobic-obsessive and eating disorders (Nardone, 1993, 1995a; Nardone & Watzlawick, 1990, 2000).

The Palo Alto model of brief therapy was essentially based on focused interventions aimed at breaking the redundant interactive sequence between patients' attempted solutions and the persistence of their problems. This therapeutic approach described its intervention from a general perspective, in terms that could be applied to problems of different origins and contexts.[13] Over thirty years of empirical experience and clinical experiments have demonstrated the fruitfulness of the empirical construct "attempted solution that maintains the problem", which was formulated by the MRI researchers as a clinical tool. Our studies showed that this construct is also a fruitful research tool, both for gathering knowledge about the models of persistence of mental pathologies and for devising advanced therapeutic strategies.

Our intent was to produce an evolution of brief therapy, from a general model to a model that would include specific protocols of intervention constructed *ad hoc* for specific types of problems (Nardone & Watzlawick, 2000). In other words, we wanted to advance from a general theory of the formation and solution of problems (Watzlawick, Weakland, & Fisch, 1974) to specific formulations on the functioning of specific mental disorders and their rapid solution.

Our basic methodology of research is the same as the one used in sciences such as physics and biology (Popper, 1972) for the development of advanced systems of management of the realities that are the object of study. This method is structured in three phases:

1. Study the specific characteristics of a problem or a group of problems;
2. Determine what solutions have already been attempted;
3. Replace the dysfunctional solutions that maintain the problem instead of solving it with other solutions that have experimentally proved capable of producing the desired effects (Nardone & Watzlawick, 2000).

We first applied this empirical/experimental methodology to the study of phobic and obsessive disorders. Through direct experimentation on hundreds of cases, we developed five specific protocols of therapy for the different types of generalized phobias. These protocols were applied with success to thousands of cases (Nardone, 1993, 1995a; Nardone & Watzlawick, 1990).[14]

In 1993, we began our research–intervention on eating disorders. As previously done for phobic–obsessive disorders, we proceeded from a study of the characteristics of the problem in terms of class/structure (Whitehead & Russel, 1910–1913), to determine which redundant attempted solutions repeat themselves for each individual disorder. In other words, we tried to determine which elements tended to maintain these structures of problems and which strategies were most efficacious and effective in resolving them. As we explained in Chapter One, our focus was not on how the problems may have originated (their "causes") but on how they were maintaining themselves (their persistence). If we wish to produce a quick and effective change, we need to break the persistence of a problem, not reconstruct its causes in a past that, in any case, cannot be changed.

We began by studying a limited number of cases, using systematic and rigorous empirical experiments to determine which interventions were effective and which redundant attempted solutions were being stopped. We initially applied the techniques we had available, some drawn from writings on those specific problems and others derived from the treatment of disorders that appeared to be similar, such as obsessions and phobias. This was the first phase of the construction of our treatment protocols.

We then proceeded to a second phase of observation and elimination of techniques that proved to be inefficient, choosing those that had proved themselves capable of producing effective changes. We also invented some completely new techniques.

Whenever a solution "fit" the problem and produced effective results, we tried to adapt and repeat that same solution on a higher number of cases. Only the techniques that continued to produce changes when repeated on several problems of the same type were considered empirically effective.

By this method, we gradually tried to select the most appropriate techniques for the specific types of problems under study, included those techniques in a predetermined sequence, and hypothesized possible variations so as to optimize the effectiveness and efficiency of our interventions. By gradually refining, adding and eliminating a number of manoeuvres, we arrived at the construction of the first ordered sequence of possible moves and countermoves: in other words, a strategy, or a specific clinical model for the type of pathology under study. This strategy, composed of specific tactics and techniques and organized in a progressive sequence of therapeutic stages with specific objectives, is the *treatment protocol* of the specific disorder being studied.

Readers who are expert at logic will recognize in this methodology the basic criteria for a specialized branch of mathematical logic called Strategic Logic (Da Costa, 1989a,b; Elster, 1979, 1985). Within that discipline, the construction of models is not based on descriptive and prescriptive theories (as are most models of psychiatry and psychotherapy) but on the specific characteristics of the problem at hand and predetermined objectives to be reached. In other words, the strategy is constantly adapted to the problem and the objectives, without being influenced by previous, deterministic theories (Nardone & Watzlawick, 2000). Each treatment protocol is, therefore, a problem-solving model that has been constructed *ad hoc* based on the redundant patterns that form the structure of the problem. The protocol must, however, be adapted to the unique characteristics of each person and context.

To respect the uniqueness of each individual, protocols must include the principle of self-correction, i.e., foresee the possibility of different variants. A protocol is not made up of a rigid sequence of moves, but leaves space for different possibilities of operation according to the responses of the person we are seeing.

Based on each patient's specific responses to prescriptions, the therapist chooses the most productive among several possible paths. What guides each step of the therapy (i.e., the choice between several options of successive moves) is always the patient's reaction. A second element of self-correction, which completes and amplifies the first, is the therapist's ability to change the strategy if the current one is not working.

The therapy thus takes the form of a strategic problem-solving process where the therapist tries to foresee the patient's possible reactions to each single manoeuvre, and plans possible tactical or technical variations on the initial strategy based on its observed effects (Nardone & Watzlawick, 2000). The treatment protocols are thus *predictive*, i.e., able to anticipate the possible developments of the therapeutic interaction, bringing about a constant and continuous self-correction of the model of intervention based on the effects observed at each stage.

By including principles of self-correction for each move and stage of the intervention, strategic therapy presents itself as a systematic research process characterized by phases of discovery followed by phases of cognitive organization, as opposed to a process of validation of *a priori* theories.

This is made possible by using the most advanced theories of mathematical logic, such as "paraconsistent" and "non-aletic" logic (Da Costa, 1989a,b; Grana, 1990) that go beyond the traditional Aristotelian logic of "true or false" and lend logical rigour to the use of interventions based on contradiction, paradox, and self-deception. This makes it possible to proceed in a manner that is both creative and systematic, making proficuous use of the contributions of empirical experience as the basis for a predictive structure of interventions guided by advanced logical and epistemological criteria, in a constant circularity of retroactions between the operative perspective and the epistemological perspective that safeguards us from "self-immunizing" rigidities (Popper, 1972) and keeps the model in a constant state of self-corrective evolution (Nardone & Watzlawick, 2000).

Another self-corrective criterion regarding therapeutic communication is a principle derived from persuasive rhetoric and Ericksonian hypnotherapy, which makes therapists adapt their language and logic to those of the patient and adopt the latter's personal world-view.

Thanks to these principles, the application of the protocols to each particular case becomes something unique and unrepeatable, while the protocol's guidelines remain unchanged. In other words, while the strategy and the usual "attempted solutions" that maintain the problem remain the same for each type of disorder, the communication and therapeutic relationship change for each case, so as to adapt and fit in with the originality of each individual human system, situation, and context.

Thus, our therapeutic protocols include a planned sequence of technical procedures that can be adapted and corrected based on the evolution of the intervention (Fiorenza & Nardone, 1995). Our therapeutic work is therefore systematic and rigorous in structure, but also flexible in its direct application.

Criteria for evaluating the results

Once a protocol for intervention has been prepared, the subsequent phase is one of rigorous verification of its *efficacy* and *effectiveness*. To that end, the protocol is applied to at least one hundred subjects who present the specific disorder being studied. We consider an intervention to be valid in terms of "therapeutic efficacy"[15] only if the efficacy rate is higher than seventy per cent, in other words if at least seventy of the treated cases recover as an effect of the intervention. This result must also prove to last over time; to that end, we follow up with the patient at three, six and twelve months after the end of the therapy.

The evaluation of effects obtained through a therapeutic intervention is undoubtedly one of the most thorny subjects in psychotherapy. This difficulty is due to the fact that different schools of psychotherapy use different criteria to evaluate the efficacy of therapies. These criteria are strictly dependent on different, often opposite, theoretical and practical perspectives.

For example, Freudian psychoanalysts consider a treatment to be efficacious when it leads the patient to overcome the Oedipus complex. For Jungian analysts, the treatment is efficacious when patients have reached personal "individuation". For behavioural therapists, a therapy is successful when behavioural symptoms are "extinguished". Moreover, different personality theories include different objectives, which in turn require different ways of evaluating the results of the therapy. Differing theoretical concepts of "human nature" determine the criteria for evaluating what is normal and what is pathological, and consequently also the concept of what a "cure" consists of, as well as many different concepts of treatment efficacy.

Nevertheless, according to Sirigatti (1988, p. 230) there seems to be some agreement that a treatment can be considered efficacious when it leads to: symptomatic improvements, increased work productivity, improved interpersonal relationships, increased ability to deal with common psychological conflicts and to react to daily stress factors.

As explained in our previous works (Nardone, 1991, 1993; Nardone & Watzlawick, 1990, 2000), the strategic approach to therapy is not based on any theory that defines the concepts of normality and abnormality in some definitive way, nor on any theory on human nature that defines its characteristics in some absolute way. Because strategic therapy is a non-normative model, its concept of healing is not that of reaching some hypothetical and improbable state of total absence of problems. In strategic therapy, healing consists in the overcoming of the specific problem experienced by the subject in that particular moment and context of his or her life. Based on this theoretical perspective, the efficacy of a particular intervention is, therefore, represented by the solution of the specific problem presented by the patient/s (Nardone & Watzlawick, 1990, pp. 112–113).

The second criterion that we use to evaluate the treatment protocols is *efficiency*. We consider this a fundamental criterion, in that it represents the ability of a model not only to solve a problem but to solve it quickly. Otherwise, we would not have obtained anything really new and clinically important, since many long-term models of therapy have already proved to be efficacious.

The time limit that we set ourselves for reaching our pre-set objective—i.e. the complete resolution of the problem presented by the patient and the absence of recurrences within one year after the end of therapy—was twenty sessions, within a maximum of six to eight months.

In the field of psychotherapy the evaluation of effectiveness, i.e., the cost–benefit ratio, is regrettably one of the aspects that receive the least consideration and study (Garfield, 1981). Careful consideration of the effectiveness of clinical work is an important factor of study when we wish to analyse and evaluate the real power of intervention of any therapeutic model.

Indeed, having established that a therapy is efficacious, it should be considered the more positive the more it is effective. The time needed to obtain results is an important factor in evaluating the result because the cost–benefit ratio of an intervention is more positive the shorter the cure that obtains the effective and permanent resolution of the presented problems (Nardone & Watzlawick, 1990, pp. 116–117).

Moreover, from our perspective, the limited time frame also makes it possible to verify the real efficacy of an intervention, because if a change is observed within a limited period of time, that change is very probably the product of a focused therapy. The same thing would be extremely difficult to prove in long-term therapies, where so-called "intervening variables"[16] (Salvini, 1993) actually seem to be even more important in determining changes than the therapy itself (Sirigatti, 1988, 1994).

Despite the fact that the problem of "intervening variables" is of fundamental importance in clinical research, it is often underestimated by most researchers in our field. This is true, for example, of the research by Selvini Palazzoli, Cirillo, Selvini, and Sorrentino (1988), where the authors attribute to their own therapeutic intervention the well-being of patients who received a follow-up after an average of thirteen years (from a minimum of eight years to a maximum of twenty-four years) from the end of their treatment. If we consider that family therapies conducted on the average thirteen years earlier consisted, for half the cases, of a number of sessions between one and three, and were in some cases limited to only one session, these conclusions seem hasty, to say the least. If we also consider that 54.6% of patients later received individual therapy and that twenty-five per cent were hospitalized after family therapy, the decision by Selvini Palazzoli *et al.* to attribute the resolution of the patient's disorder to their therapy is clearly doubtful.

Selvini Palazzoli *et al.* apparently do not consider that the numerous changes that intervened in their patients' lives over this long period of time have undoubtedly had an enormous influence on the evolution and resolution of their disorder—as much as, or maybe more than, the family therapy they received.

CHAPTER THREE

Efficacy and effectiveness of the therapeutic model: results

"The best proof of a theory is its application"

George C. Lichtenberg, *Libretto di Consolazione* (1981)

Our protocols for eating disorders were applied to 196 cases from 1993 to 1997. This group included persons from all regions of Italy; its significance is therefore not limited by cultural differences related to restricted areas of origin. The sample included a wide range of social classes, from low to very high. However, most of our patients belong to the higher middle class. This may simply be due to the fact that ours is a private centre of therapy.

The first remarkable fact that emerged from an analysis of our case sample was, as expected, a marked prevalence of the disorder that we have called vomiting syndrome or vomiting. While this pathology is usually defined as bulimia nervosa in international literature, we consider the latter to be a very unsatisfactory descriptive criterion for this emergent and highly complex eating disorder.

Many researchers have observed a significant evolution of eating disorders in the direction of vomiting (American Psychiatric

Association (APA), 1994; Costin, 1996; Faccio, 1999; Selvini Palazzoli, Cirillo, Selvini, & Sorrentino, 1998) and a concurrent decrease in the number of pure "anorexics", which, in our sample, represented only nine per cent of all cases. These results evidently confirm our remarks in the previous chapters on the evolution of eating disorders (Table 1, Figure 1).

Efficacy of the treatment

Two parameters were used to evaluate the efficacy of our treatment (Nardone & Watzlawick, 1990, p. 114):

1. *The proven efficacy of the implemented treatment*, i.e., the evaluation of the final result of the therapy. At the end of the therapy, had we reached the objectives agreed upon at the beginning with the person who came to us for help?
2. *The efficacy of the treatment over time*, i.e., did the results attained at the end of the therapy last over time? Were there any recurrences? Did other disorders replace the original ones? To measure this factor, we conducted three follow-up interviews

Table 1. Treated cases

Disorder	No. of patients	Percentage
Anorexia	18	9%
Bulimia	55	28%
Vomiting	123	63%
Total	196	100%

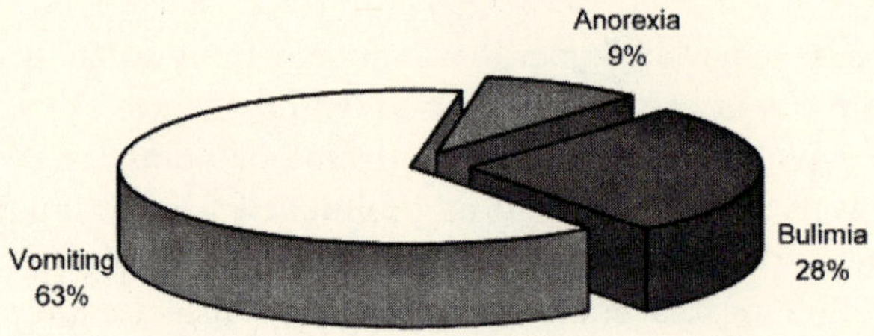

Figure 1. Treated cases.

with the patient and his/her family or partner. The follow-up interview was structured according to the guidelines cited by Sirigatti (1988) and the specific objectives agreed upon at the beginning of the therapy.

It is important to note that our follow-up interviews were carried out by meeting the patient at our centre, and not by telephone. Unfortunately, telephone interviews seem to have become very common in follow-ups within the systemic tradition as well as in other schools of therapy (see, for example, Selvini Palazzoli, Cirillo, Selvini, & Sorrentino, 1998). We consider the value of phone interviews to be doubtful because there is ample evidence that this type of interview yields a high percentage of untruthful answers (Paguni, 1993; Sirigatti, 1988, 1994). We believe that it is absolutely necessary to follow up in person with patients and their families.

We consider a case resolved and a treatment successful only if both the above-described criteria are met, i.e., when the absence of symptoms and problems at the end of the therapy lasts over time, without recurrences or replacement symptoms.

Based on these methodological criteria, we evaluate the effects of a therapy according to the following five categories:

Resolved cases: cases where the problem was completely resolved at the end of the therapy, with no recurrences within a year.

Highly improved cases: cases that show a complete remission of the symptoms at the end of the therapy and still show a net improvement of their situations at the time of the follow-up, but with some sporadic, light recurrences that are, however, quickly brought under control.

Slightly improved cases: cases that show a partial reduction of symptoms at the end of the treatment and that report, at the time of the follow-up, having frequent moments of crisis and recurrences of symptoms, even though the subjects describe such critical moments as being much less severe than before the therapy.

Unchanged cases: cases where the treatment did not lead to any change in the patient's problematic situation within ten sessions. In such cases, the treatment is interrupted after the tenth session, because of our conviction that if we have been unable to change anything in ten sessions, it is very improbable that we will succeed over a longer period of treatment.

Worsened cases: cases where the treatment led to a worsening of the patient's situation.

We also consider it very important to evaluate the efficacy of an intervention in relation to the different problems treated. In other words, in order to have a better evaluation of the efficacy of a model of therapy, we need to measure its *differential efficacy*, i.e., how efficacious the model is on different problems (Nardone & Watzlawick, 1990, p.115). The data below is therefore presented in terms of both the general efficacy of a model and its efficacy when applied to different categories of disorder.

The data in Table 2 and Figure 2 show how our research–intervention led to the preparation of concretely efficacious treatment protocol. Indeed, if we adopt the international criterion for "efficacy", which considers *resolved* and *much improved* cases as successful therapies, we can say that our work had an efficacy of eighty-one per cent.

It is also significant that most of the cases that appear as "unchanged" refer to therapies that we interrupted after the tenth treatment because we saw no improvement. It is our practice to set

Table 2. Efficacy of treatment protocol

Assessment	No. of patients	Percentage
Resolved cases	144	74%
Highly improved cases	14	7%
Slightly improved cases	16	8%
Unchanged cases	22	11%
Worsened cases	—	—
Total	196	100%

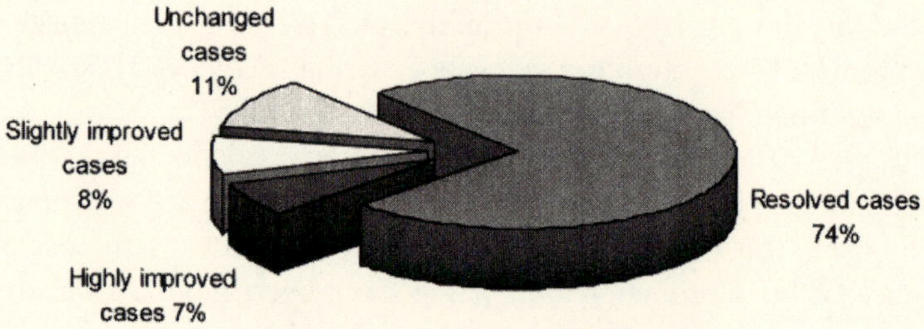

Figure 2. Treatment efficacy.

a time limit of ten sessions for working on the persistence of the problem; if we have not produced any significant change within the tenth session, we prefer to discontinue the therapy rather than taking the risk of becoming accomplices of the problem.

A differential analysis of the efficacy of each specific protocol shows even more significant results. Table 3 shows clearly how different the results are when the protocol is applied to different types of problems, and how a presentation of data that showed only general averages would be misleading for a concrete evaluation of results.

Anorexia

Mental anorexia appears to be the disorder most resistant to change: only fifty-six per cent of our cases had positive results. At first, we decided not to present the specific treatment protocol for anorexia, since it did not satisfy the research criteria described above (as the reader may recall, we adopted a minimum efficacy rate of seventy per cent in our research for the preparation of treatment protocols).

However, when we compared our results for mental anorexia with the results reported in international literature on the subject, we realized that our work might still be deemed significant, because the average number of successful treatments internationally is lower than our results.

The APA's guidelines for the treatment of eating disorders (cited in Costin, 1996, p. 20) show the following results for hospitalized

Table 3. Differential efficacy

	Anorexia		Bulimia		Vomiting	
	No.	%	No.	%	No.	%
Resolved cases	10	56%	46	84%	88	72%
Highly improved cases	—	—	2	4%	12	10%
Slightly improved cases	—	—	7	12%	9	7%
Unchanged cases	8	44%	—	—	14	11%
Worsened cases	—	—	—	—	—	—
Total	18	100%	55	100%	123	100%

anorexics: four years after the appearance of the disorder, approximately forty-four per cent of all cases obtained good results (weight within the recommended limits and regular menstrual periods); twenty-four per cent obtained slight results (weight below the recommended range and absent or sporadic menstrual periods); twenty-eight per cent reported intermediate results. Hsu (1987), in an overview of five studies on this subject, reports the average percentage of successful treatments of anorexia as forty-four per cent.

In a follow-up study on 143 cases of anorexia treated between 1971 and 1987 at their Centre, Selvini Palazzoli, Cirillo, Selvini, & Sorrentino (1998) report success rates that varied according to the therapeutic method adopted: 66.7% for the paradoxical method, 48.9% for the invariable series of prescriptions, and 37.5% for the "revealing" of family games. Their average general success rate is thus fifty-one per cent , although this is not explicitly declared by the authors.

Finally, according to a study by the National Association of Anorexia Nervosa and Associated Disorders (cited in Costin, 1996, p. 20) only between thirty per cent and forty per cent of anorexics recover completely, while twenty per cent continue to enter and exit hospitals. Moreover, between five and ten per cent of anorexics die within ten years from the appearance of the disorder, and 18–20% die after twenty years.

These scarce results are generally explained in literature by making reference to a particular resistance to change that supposedly characterizes anorexia in comparison to other psychological disorders, an aspect that would confer a generally unpromising prognosis on this pathology. This tendency seems to be characteristic of all orientations that Popper (1972) has defined as *self-immunizing propositions*, i.e., statements that cannot be denied in that they legitimize themselves whether they succeed or fail (Nardone, 1994, p. 13). Based on these premises, if a disorder seems difficult to cure, the reason lies in its particular forms of resistance to change rather than in the lack of efficacy of the therapeutic method that is used to resolve it.

For example, Selvini Palazzoli, Cirillo, Selvini, & Sorrentino (1998, p. 33), analysing the data that emerged from their follow-ups, conclude that bulimic anorexics have a worse prognosis than restrictive anorexics, and therefore that suffering from one of the two types of anorexia should be considered a "predictive factor" regarding the outcome of the disorder.

Thus, the different rates of recovery found for the two different variants of anorexia are mistakenly attributed to characteristics believed to be inherent in the nature of the disorder rather than to a different level of efficacy of the therapeutic method used to treat the two typologies. In this case also, we have a reading of the data in light of a heavily *a priori* theory to the detriment of facts, giving a tendentious interpretation of results that is both logically and methodologically incorrect.

Moreover, the supposedly worse prognosis for bulimic anorexics as opposed to restrictive anorexics is denied by the results of our research–intervention: to the contrary of the findings by Selvini Palazzoli, Cirillo, Selvini, & Sorrentino (1998), "restrictive" anorexia was the most difficult disorder to resolve for us, compared to a high efficacy for vomiting.[17]

However, we do not wish to say that our scarce efficacy on "restrictive" anorexia compared to the other two disorders should be considered an effect of an intrinsic higher resistance to change in this disorder; we simply consider it due to our scarcer ability to construct a specific model of intervention compared to what we were able to do for the other two disorders.

Probably, as Sirigatti has suggested (1997, personal communication), our higher ability with bulimia and vomiting is due to the fact that the strategies and stratagems used for these disorders have a similar logical structure to the strategies and stratagems that we successfully developed for treating phobic–obsessive disorders in the decade preceding our research on eating disorders.

In the case of anorexia, we also need to note the presence of a high percentage of improvements that we might call "intermittent", i.e., cases where the patient shows a good compliance with the therapy and also some significant improvements. However, such improvements are always followed by recurrences of symptoms, in a continuous alternation between improvements and recurrences, causing a prolonging of the therapy. Unfortunately, in most of these cases we were unable to exercise any deep influence on the pathology's dysfunctional balance, which tends to regain ground after several attempts. In other words, we were only able to produce "first order" changes and not "second order" changes (Watzlawick, Weakland, & Fisch, 1974).[18] These results seem to correspond to those reported in international literature, where approximately one third of all cases of anorexia show a tendency to become chronic.

This is the reason why our case study on anorexia does not present any *much improved* or *little improved* cases, but only *resolved* or *unchanged* cases (Figure 3). We cannot consider something that will later lead to an equally severe recurrence of a pathology to be an improvement. This aspect definitely separates anorexia from bulimia and vomiting, for which we have a group of *much improved* and *little improved* cases, since with these disorders it is possible to obtain results of reduction of symptoms that persist over time.

The difference we have found between bulimia and vomiting on the one hand and anorexia on the other is similar to another difference that emerged from our previous research–intervention between strictly phobic disorders (agoraphobia, panic attacks) and phobic variants with a more marked obsessive structure (obsessions, hypochondriac fixations) (Nardone, 1993; Nardone & Watzlawick, 1990). The latter disorders show results similar to anorexia (where the obsessive component is also of fundamental importance): we either obtain a complete resolution of the disorder, or intermittent improvements followed by a complete restructuring of the pathology. On the contrary, our treatment of phobias has resulted in several degrees of improvement just like bulimia and vomiting.

Bulimia (Bulimia nervosa without purging behaviour)

The treatment protocol for bulimia[19] proved to be the most efficient of all, with positive results as high as eighty-eight per cent. As the

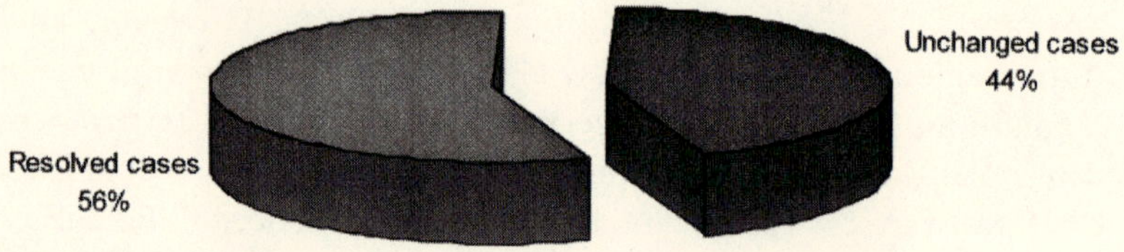

Figure 3. Efficacy in cases of anorexia

reader will have the opportunity to observe in the pages that follow, we believe that our success is due to a higher compliance of bulimic patients compared to the other two types, i.e., a lower resistance towards following the therapeutic prescriptions. In devising a protocol for this disorder, a re-adaptation of some of the techniques and tactics used for the treatment of obsessions and compulsions, without too much creativity, was sufficient to obtain extremely encouraging results.

The high compliance of bulimic patients also explains why this type of disorder also finds efficacious solutions in different forms of therapy (behavioural, cognitive–behavioural, or sometimes even consulting a dietologist).

Finally, it is of note that none of our cases of bulimia or binge eating was *unchanged* (the same observation was made of agoraphobia in our previous research–intervention): the intervention always produces some small improvement (for example, the person may succeed in losing some weight, although not as much as she would have wished).

Much improved and *little improved* cases are, however, significantly fewer than those found to be *completely resolved* (Figure 4).

Vomiting (bulimia nervosa with purging behaviour)

We believe our most important results were achieved by our treatment of vomiting, because of its epidemic diffusion in the last few years (it is currently the most common eating disorder) and because most therapies are scarcely efficacious on this type of disorder.

The results of treatments of vomiting ("bulimia nervosa" in psychiatric literature) are usually calculated in terms of average percentage reduction of binges and vomiting episodes rather than in terms of a complete disappearance of the bulimic symptoms.

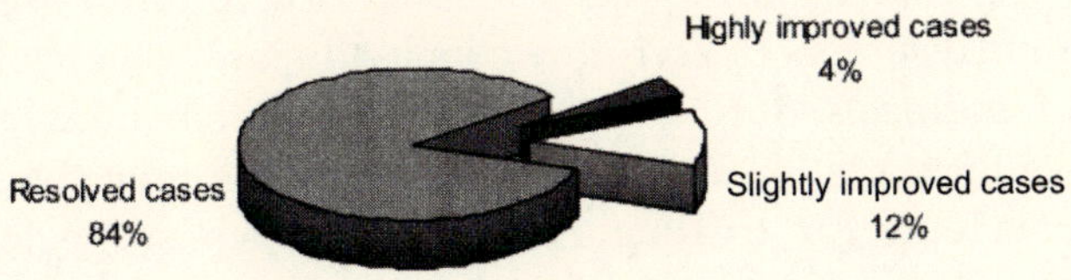

Figure 4. Efficacy in cases of bulimia.

Costin (1996) reports an average reduction of seventy per cent in bulimic subjects whose treatment is considered to be concluded. As far as hospitalized bulimics are concerned, several studies found that three years after the end of treatment, twenty-seven per cent binge and vomit less than once a month (this is considered a good result); thirty-three per cent binge and vomit daily (considered a poor result), while forty per cent present intermediate results.

In a survey of several studies, Wilson and Fairburn (1993) found between seventy-three per cent and ninety-three per cent average reduction rates for binges, with 51%–71% complete remissions.[20] Tridenti and Bocchia (1993, p. 287) in an overview of the main studies completed during the 1980s, report reductions varying between fifty-two per cent and ninety-seven per cent for bulimia nervosa (vomiting). However, the authors note that if we consider the disappearance rates of bulimic symptoms (i.e., complete absence of binges) instead of their average reduction, the results, varying between nine and forty-five per cent are anything but satisfactory. Similarly, Abraham, Mira, and Llewellyn-Jones (1983) report remission rates between twenty-nine per cent and forty-two per cent, while Keel and Mitchell (1997) surveying eighty-eight studies, report average rates as being approximately fifty per cent.

The results of using the latest generation of antidepressant drugs (SSRI) also seem rather disappointing (Walsh, Hadigan, Devlin, Gladis, & Roose, 1991), since they produce an estimated remission of symptoms of 20–33% (Costin, 1996).

As the reader can see, our positive results for eighty-two per cent of cases are significantly higher than those presented in international literature. But, as we shall see, what makes this result even more important is the fact that it is obtained in a relatively brief period of time (see the section on effectiveness).

The fact that vomiting has a similar structure to obsessive–compulsive disorders (for which we devised highly efficacious and effective protocols during our previous research–intervention) undoubtedly made it easier for us to select appropriate strategies and stratagems for treating it; however, such strategies and strategems had to be created *ad hoc* because the vomiting disorder is not based on fear but on pleasure (Figure 5).

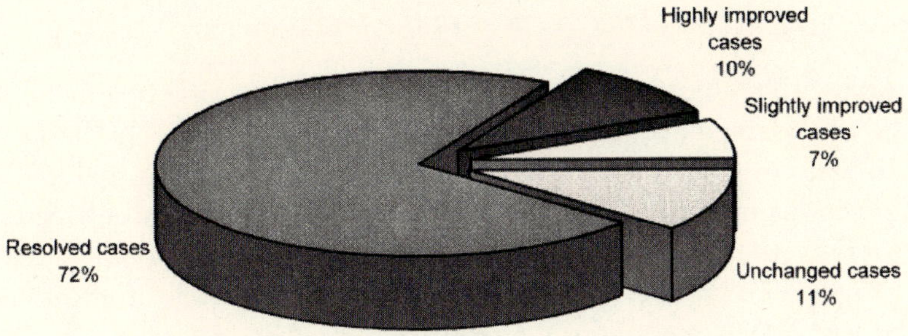

Figure 5. Efficacy in cases of vomiting.

It should be noted that, in clinical literature, treatments for this type of disorder are usually strictly linked to treatments of anorexia. For us, this represents a major difference: as we mentioned earlier and will explain in more detail further on, we believe that vomiting, with its rigid structure, is an "emerging quality" with respect to the disorder that it originates from (mainly anorexia). Therefore, the vomiting pathology requires an intervention that fits its specific structure, not that of the disorder that it might have originated from and then evolved into a new and different organization.

Conclusions on efficacy

In synthesis, we can state that in terms of efficacy, the results of our work are decidedly significant both from a general and a differential perspective, because these results are markedly higher than those reported in international literature.

Moreover our results proved to be lasting: as in our previous research–intervention of phobic–obsessive disorders: follow-up interviews conducted three, six, and twelve months after the end of the therapy showed a minimal presence of recurrences and the absence of symptom replacements.

We should not underestimate a final important aspect, i.e., the fact that it is our practice to discontinue the therapy if we see no results, or to continue it for a few more sessions at the most if there are intermittent results. This is the only way to avoid prolonging the therapy and running the risk of having the treatment become a factor of complicity with the persistence of the problem.

Effectiveness of the treatment

Apart from efficacy, we consider the effectiveness of a treatment to be a fundamental criterion for the validation of a model of therapy. To measure effectiveness, we ask how fast an efficacious therapy is in producing results. There is, indeed, quite a difference between a therapy that proves efficacious in five years and a therapy that proves efficacious in five months. Thus, the measure of effectiveness validates the measure of efficacy.

Moreover, as noted earlier, from a methodological point of view it is very difficult to measure the concrete efficacy of an intervention that lasts over a long time, since the "intervening variables" in the patient's life outside therapy are definitely out of the researcher's control. On the other hand, when a therapy lasts only a few months, it is possible to have almost total control of its efficacy, since it is highly probable that the results are produced by the current intervention and not by casual events in the patient's life (Nardone, 1994; Salvini, 1993)

As shown in Table 4 and Figure 6, seventy-nine per cent of our cases received a therapy that lasted less than twenty sessions (about 6–7 months). Of the approximately twenty per cent that lasted longer than twenty sessions, most were "slightly improved" or showed intermittent improvements until their final resolution It should also be noted that the longer therapies were for "restrictive anorexia", the incidence of which, as we have already mentioned, is significantly decreasing. We consider this lower effectiveness a consequence of our having less therapeutic influence on this disorder compared to the other two duration lengths.

We get an even more precise evaluation if we carry on our analysis from a global study of the duration of therapy to measur-

Table 4. Therapy duration.

No. of sessions	No. of patients	Percentage
1–10 sessions	71	36%
11–20 sessions	84	43%
21–30 sessions	35	18%
31–43 sessions	6	3%
Total	196	100%

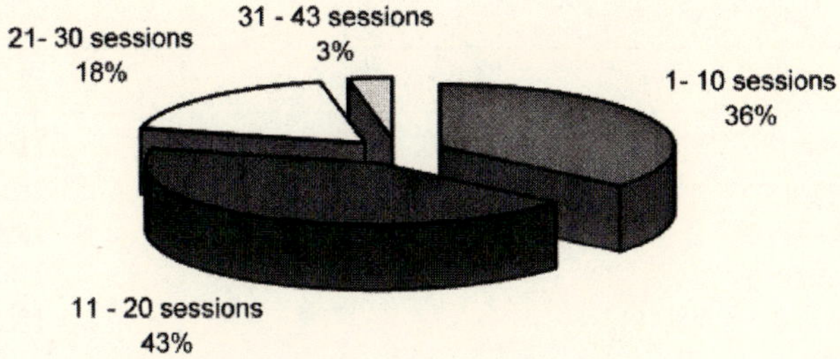

Figure 6. Duration of therapy.

ing real effectiveness, taking only those therapies that had successful outcomes into account. We measured effectiveness in terms of the average duration of treatment in cases with successful outcomes, i.e., completely resolved or much improved cases (Nardone, 1993; Nardone & Watzlawick, 1990). In any case, as the tables show, we were amused to find that the percentages remained almost completely the same

The data in Table 5 and Figure 7 show how the majority of successful treatments lasted less than fifteen sessions. It should also be noted that in most cases the remission of severe symptoms occurs within the first ten sessions, i.e., during the first few weeks of therapy. After this remission, the remaining therapeutic effort consists of working with the patient to construct the new psychological balance that is necessary in order to avert the reappearance of the same or similar problems.

This is an important aspect of our approach, which distinguishes it from other historical models of brief therapy, such as those of Palo Alto (Watzlawick, Weakland, & Fisch, 1974; Weakland, Fisch, Watzlawick, & Bodin, 1974), Washington (Madanes, 1981, 1984, 1990), and Milwaukee (de Shazer, 1985, 1988, 1994), which consider a therapy to be successful when it leads to the remission of symptoms. In other words, a doctrinaire reliance on systems theory has led to the assumption that once the balance of a system has been broken, this system will naturally reorganize itself in a new equilibrium (the self-organization of living beings). Thus, the remission of a disorder (considered as a sort of equilibrium within a system) should spontaneously lead to a non-pathological self-organization of that system.

Table 5. Effectiveness.

No. of sessions	No. of patients	Percentages
1–10 sessions	49	31%
11–20 sessions	75	48%
21–30 sessions	29	18%
31–43 sessions	5	3%
Total	158	100%

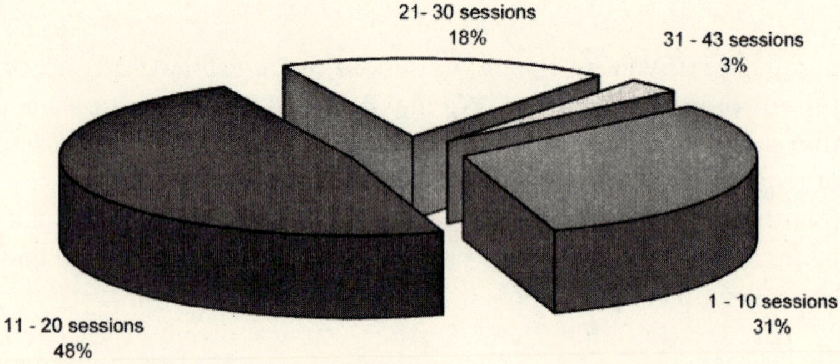

Figure 7. Effectiveness of the treatment.

To us, this perspective seems empirically incongruent, particularly when working with heavily incapacitating and long-lasting pathologies such as severe forms of eating disorders and phobic–obsessive disorders. We believe, therefore, that once the symptoms are in remission, it is necessary to help the person construct a new dynamic balance, using all the resources that she is starting to rediscover beyond the symptoms that were blocking them.

The last part of the therapy is therefore usually the longest, especially for patients whose disorders lasted for years or even decades and who, once the disorder has disappeared, find themselves having to make a concrete effort to reconstruct their personal identity.

Anorexia

Apart from being the disorder most resistant to our type of intervention, Anorexia also compelled us to provide longer therapies, even though most remissions of symptoms, when the therapy worked, occurred within the first ten sessions.

Bulimia (bulimia nervosa without purging behaviour)

Most of these cases are in remission within the first five sessions. After that, we often continue the therapy with one monthly session in order to follow the patient's slow and gradual weight loss. When it is a matter of losing 60 lbs, the process of losing weight should not happen in three months, but needs to be more gradual.

Vomiting (bulimia nervosa with purging behaviour)

In this case, about fifty per cent of cases are in remission within the first five sessions; the remaining cases achieve this result between the fifth and the tenth session. As usual, we continue with a number of sessions, focusing on the reorganization of a functional mental balance.

Conclusions on effectiveness

Based on the results presented here, we may state that our research intervention has led to the preparation of highly effective treatments. Indeed, if we compare our treatments with the usual time employed to obtain remission of disorders as presented in international writings on the subject, which usually report years of therapy, it seems clear that interventions that last an average of 5–6 months, with a good percentage of even shorter therapies, represent a truly significant contribution.

CHAPTER FOUR

Anorexia: formation, persistence, change

"He would like to be nothing but fog, so that no one could find him"

Elias Canetti, *La Rapidità dello Spirito: Appunti da Hampstead* (1996)

The formation and persistence of anorexia

Anorexia is undoubtedly the best known of all eating disorders. It appears to mainly afflict young women—often adolescents—but also a number of men (5–10% of cases reported in scientific publications and two per cent of our cases studies were men).[21] Although anorexia is still the eating disorder most frequently studied in scientific literature on this subject, the number of "pure" anorexics seems to be decreasing.[2]

As already mentioned, in the course of our experimental study we observed the existence of several variants among eating disorders, and devised different protocols of treatment for such variants. Our research indicates that there are two distinct types of anorexia, which we have named *sacrificial* and *abstinent*.

Sacrificial anorexia

This is the most well known type of anorexia. It has been very well described in the literature of the systemic tradition, particularly by the Milan school (Selvini Palazzoli, 1963). Whenever anorexia is mentioned, it is almost always safe to assume that what is being referred to is the sacrificial type.

The young women who are "candidates" for sacrificial anorexia typically start experiencing difficulties and developing symptoms in conjunction with particular family situations. In these cases, the family presents a "pathogenic" sort of energy, with one member usually assuming the whole weight of the problem by developing some psychological disorder, for example some form of delirium, psychosis, or phobia—in other words, not necessarily an eating disorder.

These persons also derive some secondary advantages from their disorder because, thanks to their symptoms, they become the most important member of the family. For example, if a young woman who has very demanding parents and talented siblings is not being appreciated for her own worth, she may discover that she can obtain just as much or more attention because of her disorder. Or a young woman may be caught in a situation of constant conflict between her parents, and her disorder keeps the parents together by providing them with a common enemy.

Costin (1996) calls this latter type of anorexic "*the scapegoat*" because the parents shift their focus from their marital conflicts to their daughter's problem, gaining a sense of unity from their shared effort to defeat the disorder. Another type of anorexic is defined by Costin as "*the family hero*". Living within a chaotic family system, without any strong figures of reference, this type of anorexic takes on the whole the family's responsibilities, becomes precociously independent and develops an almost perfect degree of self-confidence and self-control. In such cases, the anorexic symptoms may be interpreted as the ultimate form of self-control imposed by the subject upon herself.

Before presenting our treatment protocol for the *sacrificial* anorexics, we again need to emphasize that, despite its important place in scientific literature, this variant is decreasing in comparison with that of the *abstinent* anorexic. As we noted earlier, eating disorders are in constant and rapid evolution.

The abstinent anorexic

This is the most frequent form of anorexia (over sixty per cent of our cases). Abstinent anorexics are usually very intelligent but also extremely sensitive, psychologically fragile persons who have great difficulty in controlling their emotions. These persons (predominantly women) see reality through a deforming lens that magnifies everything to gigantic proportions, so that all problems seem enormous, difficult, and exceedingly worrisome. Their attitude towards reality is characteristically expressed by constant feelings of dissatisfaction, insecurity, and fear of failure. This despite the fact that anorexics belonging to this group tend to be quite successful, both academically and professionally.

Finding it impossible to control their emotions, abstinent anorexics learn by chance (in other words, without intentional choice), that they can obtain some relief from their extreme emotions by concentrating on something else, such as the ability to deny themselves food. Through abstinence, prolonged fasting, and weight loss, these young women gradually succeed in anaesthetizing their emotions and perceptions.

We might say, metaphorically, that abstinent anorexics don a medieval armour that protects them from their extreme sensitivity, but that eventually becomes a prison. Abstinence becomes the *attempted solution* that seems impossible to give up, because if they took off their armour, they would be unable to manage their emotions. Their self-denial is not limited to food, but is extended to all potentially disturbing experiences, especially those induced by pleasurable stimuli. These young women are not afraid to work hard and make sacrifices: they show an incredible endurance at work or at school, but are terrified of any concrete emotional experience that might give them pleasant stimuli, because of their fear of losing control.

In the course of our research–intervention, we observed how the specific system of perceptions and reactions of abstinent anorexics is characterized by a tendency to avoid eating as well as other enjoyable experiences. Weight loss becomes a means to anaesthetize emotions. Since abstinent anorexics cannot imagine any personal balance better than their own, they are extremely resistant to change.

Moreover, when young women lose weight by abstaining from eating and their weight settles below a certain point, there is a very important physiological effect. As Win Moley, former director of the Eating Disorder Centre of the Mental Research Institute in Palo Alto has excellently described, the emission of certain neurotoxins produces drug-like states similar to the effects of cocaine and amphetamines. This is very evident in anorexics, who express extreme forms of excitement and an inexhaustible energy (as well as an apparent imperturbability) similar to the attitudes observed in some drug addicts.

Apart from the anaesthesia of feelings and emotions that in our view is the most important aspect of this disorder, the fact that the anorexic is able to refrain from eating also gives her a feeling that she is somehow better than other people, having succeeded at something that most people find very difficult. In a society where more or less everyone is battling with weight and diets, the abstinent anorexic is able to control herself without any effort.

As we mentioned, secondary advantages are found in the special attention and affection that the anorexic receives from her family because of her disorder. In other words, she has achieved a kind of exclusive success, which she fears she may not obtain in other, non-pathological, fields, although she constantly aspires to it.

Apart from individual solutions attempted by the abstinent anorexic, the solutions attempted by the system that surrounds her (particularly her family) are also very important. Family members tend to make all kinds of efforts to help the subject by insisting that she eat, keeping her company, constantly checking on her, etc. Many of these attempted solutions complicate the problem instead of solving it. Indeed, worrying about someone's health may be the strongest possible declaration of affection, love, or importance. While the relationship system within the family may not be a determining factor in formation of the disorder (as it is for *sacrificial* anorexics), none the less it seems to play a fundamental role in the persistence of the problem.

Among the attempted solutions that complicate and maintain the problem, the fundamental one seems to be the anorexic's individual strategy of managing her frail emotions and relationships by abstaining from food and anything else that is potentially disturbing. In addition, there are all the dysfunctional solutions attempted by others, especially the family, with the intent of helping the anorexic, and the consequent secondary advantages that the anorexic person obtains by virtue of her disorder.

The treatment of anorexia

We normally administer a "mixed systemic" type of treatment for anorexia. In other words, we work on the person who has the symptom and on her system of relationships. In order to break the rigid persistence of the anorexic system of perceptions and reactions, we must work both on the young woman's attempted solutions and on the solutions attempted by the family.

We usually see the whole family in the first session and the young woman alone at the following sessions. If this is not possible, we try to see the family at a later session—at least once in the course of the therapy. As mentioned, anorexia is a disorder that entangles other people, and there are always direct or indirect attempts by the family to make the patient eat. We therefore need to enlist family members as co-therapists. We use different prescriptions in the course of the therapy to guide them, with the goal of blocking all the usual attempted solutions (asking the person to eat, checking on her, etc.).

Sometimes, persons suffering from anorexia, like those suffering from vomiting disorders, refuse to go into therapy. In such cases, it is often sufficient to see their parents and persuade them to stop all their attempted solutions. Out of 196 cases of eating disorders included in our study, we treated twelve cases indirectly through their families, without ever seeing the young women themselves. Our method of indirect treatment is described in Chapter Five.

More frequently, after a few sessions with just the family, the young woman decided to come into therapy personally because she was irked by the changes in her parents' behaviour.

On the other hand, a family's refusal to see the therapist may indicate a wish to sabotage the therapy. To counteract such cases, we try to reinforce all the subject's personal resources in order to enable her to deal with her family and its attempted solutions on her own.

Treatment protocol for the sacrificial anorexic

In our experience, sacrificial anorexics have proved to be the easiest to treat, because we often obtain a swift improvement by administering a few simple manoeuvres in the course of the first few sessions. With a few modifications, the models of treatment developed by the Palo Alto school (Watzlawick, Beavin, & Jackson, 1967; Watzlawick, Weakland, & Fisch, 1974) and the Milan school (Selvini Palazzoli, 1963) have proved very effective with this type of anorexia.

Particularly in the early phase of treatment, our intervention is essentially a systemic family therapy that focuses on reorganizing the communication within the family. Later, depending on the subject's response to these early manoeuvres, we either move on to a swift conclusion of the therapy or, if necessary, continue the treatment according the protocol for abstinent anorexics.

First stage

Our first intervention with *sacrificial* anorexics is to give a *positive connotation to the sacrifice* (Selvini Palazzoli, 1963; Weakland, Fisch, Watzlawick, & Bodin, 1974). This manoeuvre is intended to provoke a reaction from the patient. It consists of a positive reframing of the role played by the young woman's disorder within the family. During the whole session, based on the cues that have emerged in the therapist's interaction with the family, the therapist repeatedly presents the idea that the anorexic is making a sacrifice for the sake of the rest of the family. The therapist congratulates her, saying that she is doing something very important for her family, and that she must continue to do it because it is thanks to her that all the others are well, and who knows what would happen if she weren't there?

"Congratulations. You're making a splendid sacrifice for the sake of your family. Thanks to your having this problem, everyone else around you will stay healthy. So please keep it up—actually, try not to change anything, because if you change, everyone else will fall to pieces."

The therapist's assertion that the anorexic is actually making a sacrifice for her family's sake is strongly provocative, and usually leads to a swift improvement of the symptoms. The recommendation that she try not to change and continue not to eat is an example of "prescribing the symptom". As the systemic–strategic tradition has shown,[23] this paradoxical technique makes it impossible for the patient to follow the prescription, because it prescribes a symptomatic behaviour that is the patient experiences to be spontaneous and uncontrollable. Provided that the therapist does not exaggerate in delivering the provocation, and the insistently mentioned sacrifice is seemingly plausible, this manoeuvre plays a fundamental role in unblocking the *sacrificial* anorexic's symptoms.

Selvini Palazzoli, Cirillo, Selvini, and Sorrentino (1998) also report a high rate of effectiveness for the paradoxical method in treating anorexics. According to their data, its effectiveness (66.7%) is definitely superior both to that of invariable prescriptions (48.9%) and to the unmasking of family "games" (37.5%).

Second and third stage

With this type of anorexic patient, the *positive connotation of the sacrifice* has such a disruptive effect that it can sometimes produce a complete unblocking of the anorexic symptoms by itself. In such cases, the therapist gives the family a short set of instructions, after which the therapy may be considered complete. In most cases, however, we find that an *abstinent* anorexic was hiding behind the structure of *sacrifice.* Through their sacrifice, these young women have also constructed a pattern of abstinence. They have gradually isolated themselves from the rest of the world by spending more and more time at home, avoiding contact with others. It is extremely difficult for them to re-establish interpersonal and social relationships. These anorexics differ from "pure" *abstinents* in that they are conscious of wearing an armour that imprisons them, and not knowing how to free themselves.

In such cases, we continue the therapy according to the protocol for *abstinents.* After unblocking the symptoms by awarding a positive connotation to the sacrifice, it is extremely important to establish a very intense emotional relationship with the young woman, and proceed with interventions that stir up her emotions, such as the *nightly letter-writing, the aesthetic report card, massage with lotion,* etc., during the second stage. In the third stage, we start working directly on her relationship with food. These two stages are described in the treatment protocol for *abstinents.*

Fourth stage (final session)

At this stage, our goal is to consolidate the patient's personal autonomy by explaining in detail the therapeutic process and the strategies we have used so far. We point out that the change has been produced thanks to a systemic, scientific intervention (and not thanks to any "magic power" held by the therapist), and emphasize how, by her constant efforts, the patient has played an essential, active part in the solution of her problem. We underline the fact that the change has occurred thanks to the patient's personal abilities. The therapist's role was merely to activate those abilities without adding anything that wasn't already there. We also emphasize that she has now acquired the ability to overcome other problems that may arise in the future.

These final manoeuvres are essential for the consolidation of the person's autonomy and self-esteem.

A clinical case example of sacrificial anorexia

P was referred to the Centre for Strategic Therapy in Arezzo by a colleague in one of our branch offices. Our colleague had found that, after several months of therapy, the situation had reached an impasse. P was thirty-five years old; she lived with her aged parents in a remote village. Her job offered very few opportunities for contact with other people, and she had no social life apart from her work. After a very long history—more than fifteen years—of anorexia and failed therapies, her appearance was truly shocking. She was extremely thin, emaciated, with oedematous legs and wrinkled skin, her teeth ruined. At first sight, it was very difficult to tell whether she was a man or a woman.

Session one

In the following exchanges P is the patient, T the therapist, M the patient's mother, and CoT is a cotherapist.

> P: It took me more than fifteen years to realize that I was anorexic. Until then, I hid it inside me. I mean, I thought I was getting fatter and fatter,

and didn't realize how skinny I really was. I was indifferent towards life . . . It was like vegetating, not living. Now I've decided that I want to come out of it, but I don't have the incentive or the will to do so . . . I have many doubts and uncertainties. Whenever I say "I want to come out of it", there's something inside that stops me.

CoT: How did you realize that you had this problem?

P: Partly because I see my parents suffering because of it; my mother's always asking, "Can't you see what a state you're in?" And partly because I'm getting weaker. People stare at me. But to tell you the truth, I'm more motivated by my parents asking "Can't you see what a state you're in?" Personally, I'm not all that interested in life because I don't have any incentives to continue. On the one hand, I'm happy to be alive; I make plans . . . on the other hand, I'm not interested. There are moments when . . . things are sometimes good, sometimes bad.

CoT: What do you do in life? Do you have a job?

P: Yes, I work in a preschool. I don't like it . . .

CoT: How long have you been working there?

P: Eight years. I used to work in a store where I had contact with other people, and I was fine there. Later, I worked in the school kitchen for four years. Then they transferred me to the laundry department, where I'm basically on my own.

T: (*To the patient's mother*) Now, Mrs _____, what can you tell us about your daughter's problem?

M: I'm sorry, because . . . yes . . . I don't know the reason why she made this decision.

T: What decision?

M: The decision not to eat, not to sit at the table . . . to be alone rather than in company . . .

T: When did all this start?

M: More than fifteen years ago.

T: (*to P*) How old are you now?

P: 35 . . . I mean, 36.

T: And you live with your family?

P: Yes.

T: And who are the members of your family?

P: My dad, her and me. I have a married sister.

T: Now, what have you and your husband done to try to help her?

M: I'm the one who's trying to help her, telling her to go places, saying, "Take a holiday, find some company, take a trip . . ." But she won't. She won't. She says "I'm happy at home." I've told her, "You shouldn't be alone all the time. Go, don't worry about us." "No, I'm fine here." My husband isn't as involved in this as I am, because he's been very sick.

T: How so?

M: He has a heart disease, he's had an operation. He has diabetes. It's really bad, he can't walk . . .

T: Do you help your father?

P: Yes, I help them both. I'm very close to both of them. For a while I thought about going to live alone, but to tell you the truth, I can't. I fight with her sometimes, and sometimes she tells me: "Either you leave this house or I go", but that doesn't solve my problem. We won't solve anything by my running away, or her running away. We're trying to fight it. I tell her, "Don't say anything if you don't see me eating, or if I eat just a little. It's enough for me. The moment will come when I eat more."

CoT: And what does your mother do instead?

P: Instead, she might keep quiet for a couple of days, and then she starts again: "Haven't you looked at yourself in the mirror? You're disgusting. I can tell you're getting worse." That kind of thing makes me feel really confused in my mind, because she doesn't understand me. I'm not a drug addict that can take a pill and get well. It's already hard to put it into my head that I have to get well . . .

T: So if I understand this right, you, Mrs. _____, follow her, check on her, try to tell her to eat, "Be like other people! Make an effort! Life is beautiful", and she says "No!" She won't do it.

M: She won't. She won't.

T: She won't.

P: And I get upset, because even when I do eat the little I eat, she says "I never see you eat . . . you make me this . . . you make me that." Then I get angry and have a crisis.

M: But how many times have you deceived me . . .

P: Yes, I have, in the sense that I said "All right, I'll eat at the table" to make her happy. But I can't stand sitting at the table, I feel blocked here, so I say, "Isn't it better that I eat when I want and what I want, rather than sitting down at the table, eating, and vomiting in the bathroom."

T: Do you usually vomit?

P: No, not now, not the little I eat now. I used to in the beginning. I felt bad because deep inside I'm also afraid that I may become bulimic.

T: What small amount of food are you able to eat and retain?

P: Maybe two or three wedges of processed cheese a day. That's enough for me. Two cups of coffee and some tea. That's enough.

T: So, processed cheese . . .

P: Yes, processed cheese. I eat vegetables, ham . . . not too many things.

T: Do you always eat the same things, or does it change?

P: No, it changes. Sometimes I eat some rice, sometimes a piece of processed cheese . . .

T: When you eat those things, do you feel scared?

P: No, not now.

T: Do you enjoy it?

P: Yes.

T: Can you feel the taste?

P: At first I couldn't, but now I can. I like tasty things, seasoned with herbs. For example, I love pizza. I fight with my mum because I can't eat melted mozzarella yet. So I eat pizza without the mozzarella, and she asks, "But why?"

M: She goes to the pizza place and orders pizza without oil, without oregano, just tomato.

P: Yes, but if that's how I feel like eating it, that's how I want to eat it.

T: OK, so there's a conflict between you on this.

P: Yes, she does that and blocks me . . .

T: And your father says nothing?

P: No.

T: Who are you most worried about, your husband or your daughter?

M: My daughter, because she has her whole life ahead of her. We're already old.

T: Right. How old did you say you are?

P: Almost thirty-six.

T: And do you have any relationships with other people, or not?

P: I do now. I care about myself now, but there was a time when I was seeing Dr . . .. Can I speak about Dr _____?

T: Certainly!

P: I know I deceived him, and I'm very sorry about it. But apart from deceiving him, I also deceived myself. I saw him for a year and a half, but anorexics are liars, as you know; they hide . . .

T: I'm perfectly aware of that. I don't expect you to tell the truth, you know!

P: But I am telling the truth!

T: But I don't expect you to tell the truth. On the contrary, I think the best way to tell the truth is to lie, because when you lie, you think you can deceive people. So lie! That will help me understand your truths much better than if you were trying to tell me the truth. Lie as much as you can. The more you succeed in lying, the more I'll be able to understand you.

P: Ever since I started with Dr ____ . . . I misled him . . . I don't know why. I had a beautiful relationship with him. He was like a friend to me.

T: You [anorexics] are very good at that, aren't you?

P: He helped me. I used to neglect my clothing and my personal appearance, and he told me "Why don't you take care of yourself?" So I stopped focusing on my illness. I became careful about my appearance, I started talking to people, and was starting to feel calmer. I left my illness behind, so to speak. But then I said to myself: "No, I'm deceiving everyone this way." During my last session with Dr ___ I told him "I know I've been lying all this time. Can you give me another chance?" He said no, and I agreed to come here.

T: That's right, because you were so good at deceiving Dr ____ until the very end.

P: My mother came along just for the last two sessions, and she also asked Dr ___ to give me a last chance, and he said no. I was glad he made that decision, although it hurt me very much.

T: You were too good at duping Dr ___.

P: Too rude.

Therapeutic double bind

T: Too *good* at making his intervention fail. That's why I'm telling you not to try to tell the truth. I wouldn't believe you anyway. Lie! It's more helpful to me. Good. And your social relationships are non-existent, right? And I assume there are no young men in the picture . . .

P: No.

T: From that point of view, your life stopped at age twenty. You anaesthetized yourself completely, because life outside is so dangerous . . . it's better to stay within your own family and think about dad; better to protect oneself from the external world and one's own emotions.

P: But I don't want to escape any more. I want to grow up.

Reframing through metaphor[24]

T: But you have no emotions left. You anaesthetized them all. You donned an armour which, like all medieval armours, protected but also imprisoned you. Now you don't know how to take it off.

P: But I've got to take it off.

T: But I don't know if you'll be able to do it.

P: But if my real self wants it, I must!

T: You know, duty often conflicts with two things: often with pleasure, but mostly with fear. You've been wearing an armour for so many years that who knows if you'll be able to take it off. And if you do take it off . . . You know you're fragile. Anything can wound you. As long as you wear this armour, nothing can hurt you. You're walking on a cloud, other people can't touch you, all your emotions are anaesthetized, and so are your physical senses.

P: Yes, but this is no life.

T: But if life is so scary . . .

P: That was all fine until now, but not any more.

T: OK, but if life is so scary . . .?

Therapeutic double bind

P: That's why I'm asking you to help me grow up and take off my armour. Where should I start?

T: First of all, we'll have to see if you're actually able to take off your armour. Otherwise it would be better to say "Keep it! Keep it on! You can't do it!" We'll have to see. You've already been so good at making my very good student and collaborator fail.

P: If I was good at making Dr ____ fail, I can be just as good at taking the armour off. I think it's a personal thing.

T: Of course. But you take off your armour and . . . Aaargh! You begin to feel the terror: "I have no defences; any dart can wound me." Who knows . . . Of course, even with the armour, you might die under some conditions: in the heat, under the sun. Those armours used to be like cremation ovens. Some knights drowned if they fell into water . . .. But you avoid both the sun and the water. Who knows?

P: That way, I also avoid the pleasure of living well.

T: Of course! But if one is convinced that one wouldn't make it anyway . . . or if one is so scared of one's emotions and sensations, scared of losing control . . . Who knows?

P: I've got to make it.

T: We'll have to see if you can do it.

P: But I'm asking you to help me, since, as you put it, I'm in an armour and afraid of coming out. I do have impulse . . . the instinct . . .

T: Good. Are you prepared to do anything?

P: Yes.

T: Really?

P: Yes.

T: Good. We'll give it a try, but I don't know if you'll be able to do it. Actually, I'm afraid you won't be able to do it. We'll see. We'll start by giving you some homework. First, I'm going to give some to your mother. (*To the mother*) Since you've been very good at keeping after your daughter for the past fifteen years, helping her and insisting that she eat, I'm hoping that you'll be even better at following the instructions that I'm about to give you. All right? Actually, I'm sure you'll do a great job. From now on, I want you to promise not to say anything at all to your daughter about food. You must completely avoid mentioning her problem. And there's more: I think you need to start to undermine the importance of her problem. For example, stop setting a place at the table for her. Stop telling her to come to the table. Stop taking any interest in what she eats. And, from now until we meet again, I want you to tell your daughter at least three times a day: "Be careful about what you eat, because it might be bad for you. If you gain weight too fast, you might get scared!" Morning, noon and night, you are to repeat this formula to your daughter: "Have you been careful about what you eat? If you gain weight too fast, you might get scared!"

M: All right.

T: Apart from that, you are to avoid speaking about food. Don't set a place for her at the table. Set the table for yourself and your husband. "Don't eat too much. If you gain weight too fast, it will become a problem. You might lose control. You might become bulimic. You might get really fat. You might have too many emotions." Remind her three times a day. All right?

M: All right.

Prescribing the "smallest but concrete change"[25]

T: And to P, I say: if you want to get rid of your armour, I want you to think about the following, every day. What would be the smallest but meaningful concrete thing I could do to prove to myself, and to that sceptic down in Arezzo, that I can take off the armour? The tiniest, most minimal, but concrete thing. We'll see if you can do it. Every day. OK?

P: And should I write it down?

T: Yes, write it down. Well . . . I'll see you in fifteen days.

P: That'll be hard. It's not that I want to escape, but I live so far away . . .

T: That's your problem, not mine . . .

P: Couldn't you prolong . . .

M: Would it be possible to check her into a hospital here?

T: For women like your daughter, sending them to a hospital amounts to giving them the upper hand. She'll gain five kilos, go home, and lose seven. So what you should do, and I know you'll be good at it, is what I've just told you. It's very, very important. I must see her every fifteen days until I see some results, if there are any. Who knows? Who knows if you'll be able to take the armour off . . .

P: Fine. Not to do it would be like running away.

T: I see that you can play along if you want to, but I'm still sceptical.

Session two

P. enters alone.

T: Well?

P: Well, I was supposed to write, but I didn't.

T: I knew it.

P: No, it's that I can't express myself in writing. I'd rather talk, OK?

T: We'll see.

P: I've been thinking that one concrete thing that would help me get of it would be to become part of society again. I mean, I need to grow up. I was blocked. My age and body have grown, but inside I'm still a little girl, afraid to face the world. I don't know how to put it. In the past fifteen days I've been struggling so much because I've still got so many ifs and buts inside me. But I'm trying to accept what life is offering me, whatever happens to me, without looking at my body. My body's disgusting, so I'm ignoring it. I know I need to get well mentally in order to begin, and it's a long fight for me. There are days when I can't do it. I get blocked.

T: In what?

Unblocking of the anorexic condition

P: I tell myself I can't go on. Then I go for a walk and tell myself "But I've got to make it!" I know that walking is part of the disorder, but I don't do it to lose weight. I do it to get some fresh air and think better. It helps a lot. As for becoming part of society again, I try to deal with my problems at work without running away. I tell myself that those problems are part of life. My parents let me do whatever I want; I have to say I feel inspired to eat more. I've actually gained half a kilo. You can ask my mother; it's not something . . .

T: Did your mother manage to avoid telling you to eat?

P: Yes, she's good at that. And I have to admit I understand her. All she wants is to see me gain weight. I tell her: "Look, I need to get well inside . . ."

T: How did you manage to gain half a kilo?

P: I eat what I like, whenever I want. It doesn't bother me . . . it's a normal part of life . . .

T: But I didn't ask you to do that.

P: No, but I like it, because it's part of life. When I feel like eating . . . it's true, I don't eat much, but the little I eat . . . then slowly . . . it's hard, because I still have guilt feelings sometimes and tell myself: "maybe I'm doing this wrong, maybe I'm doing that wrong, what am I doing?" But . . . I know I have to make it.

T: Who knows if you'll succeed.

P: But I want to.

T: But I already told you last time that it's extremely improbable that you'll make it.

P: What? We'll see about that! Let's give it some time. I'm not saying it's hard because I want to go back. I have to go forward!

T: Yes, but you've seen that you're so good at deceiving yourself, and at deceiving others . . . So, let me be sceptical and free of illusion . . .

P: Yes. Everyone has their own way of thinking.

T: I doubt that you'll make it.

P: I think I will, because I believe in myself now. Until now, I wasn't interested in life. I lived fifteen years like that . . . I didn't really live those years. I was practically in a cage, in a . . . what did you call it?

T: An armour that protects and imprisons.

P: But I'm slowly loosening the screws.

T: But will you be able to live without your armour?

P: Yes.

T: We'll see who's right in the end, me with my pessimistic predictions, or you with your optimistic predictions.

P: We'll see.

T: You didn't write to me. Tell me what you would have liked to write.

P: That I see something solid in myself; that I understand what it means to live.

T: In just fifteen days? You didn't understand it for fifteen years, and now you've understood it in just fifteen days?

P: That's because I wasn't interested. I've told you, I want my life back, even if it's hard to continue. What's the use of being a vegetable? I don't want that any more.

Considering the type of patient being treated, the therapist continued to use a therapeutic double bind, aiming to provoke desirable reactions from the patient without asking for them directly.

This excerpt is an example of a paradoxical intervention. This kind of intervention is useful in situations where the anorexia appears to be functional to a homeostatic condition characterized by aspects of both "abstinence" and "sacrifice". The same type of intervention can be an effective manoeuvre with patients who have already "devoured" several therapists, i.e., the type of patients that we have defined *contrary* or *oppositional* patients (Nardone & Watzlawick, 2000).

Treatment protocol for abstinent anorexics

As we noted above, *abstinent* anorexics are distinguished by a state of anaesthesia produced by extended periods of abstinence, which enables them to control their extreme sensitivity and emotionality. Considering this particular mode of perception and reaction, our goal for the first and second stages of treatment is to interrupt the patient's state of anaesthesia by performing direct or indirect therapeutic interventions that help the patient recover her ability to experience enjoyable feelings without being completely overwhelmed. Only later, during the third stage of treatment, do we start working directly on her relationship with food if necessary.

Another essential goal for the first two stages of treatment is to put a stop to the family's attempted solutions. The specific manoeuvres used for this purpose will be thoroughly described in the following paragraphs.

According to our theoretical and practical premises, we begin the therapy with suggestive manoeuvres and stratagems that lead to a number of unconscious changes in the patient. Later, we provide cognitive explanations of the process that has just occurred. This order of actions allows us to overcome our patients' marked, often declared, resistance to therapeutic change.

First stage (first/second session)

The first meeting with the anorexic patient and/or her family is crucial to the whole rest of the treatment. If the first meeting is not well conducted, the therapy will very probably be abandoned before it even starts.

As we have already mentioned, patients with eating disorders often refuse any therapy at first, claiming that they have no need for it. Seventy-one per cent of our cases entered therapy only because they were directly or indirectly forced to by their families, while nine per cent were treated indirectly.

Therefore, the initial phase of the therapy requires us to "capture" the patient with the use of suggestion. The therapist needs use some specific manoeuvres and communication techniques to establish a verbal and non-verbal alliance with the young woman, constructing a relationship that has the flavour of exclusiveness. It is essential that the therapist learns to use the anorexic patient's particular logic and language. During the whole first session, the therapist replicates[26] the young woman's modes of perception and expression, emphatically boosting her personal vision of reality.

For example, if she complains of being ugly and uninteresting, we can gently reply at an analogical level: "That's true. You're a blot that needs to be deleted and started all over again."

We completely avoid trying to persuade her to eat. On the contrary, we show respect for her choices and appreciation of her skills. Only if she perceives that the therapist does not blame or condemn her, but accepts her view of the problem, will the anorexic patient be motivated to continue the therapeutic effort. It is therefore necessary to give a positive connotation to everything she says, avoiding all negative formulations, since the latter would only increase her resistance.[27]

It is likewise necessary to establish an alliance, a trustful relationship, with the family so that all its members will accept and collaborate with the therapist throughout the different stages of therapy.

In the first session, we carefully explore the nature of the problem and identify the dysfunctional solutions so far attempted by the young woman and her family. The therapist then performs the first direct therapeutic manoeuvres, usually (1) the *nightly letter-writing* prescription; (2) the *miracle fantasy* prescription; and (3) *reframing and stopping the family's attempted solutions.*

1. *Nightly letter-writing.* As mentioned, the treatment of *abstinent* anorexics is essentially based on upsetting their emotional anaesthesia by establishing a kind of seductive therapeutic alliance with the young woman. At the end of the session, we give her the following prescription:

> From now until the next time I see you, each night when you go to bed, on your pillow, the last thing you do before going to sleep . . . you'll need to buy some stationery (preferably a pretty kind) . . . write me a letter. There's only one prerequisite: it has to start with 'Dear Doctor'—that's me. After that, you can write anything you want, even that I'm mean or stupid . . . But it must start with 'Dear Doctor'. When you've finished the letter, sign it, put it in an envelope, seal it, and bring me all your letters next time. This will help me understand you and get to know you—better than a lot of talk.

Although we present it as part of a diagnostic investigation, the letter writing is useful for giving the patient–therapist relationship a connotation of emotional intensity ("The last thing you do on your pillow before you go to sleep . . ."). Thus, we apply the ancient Chinese stratagem of "sailing the sea, unbeknown to the sky".[28]

The letter written on the pillow evokes exchanges of love letters. Somehow, this seems inconsistent with the words "Dear Doctor". This apparent incongruity fosters a certain level of intimacy while maintaining a "safety limit". It is a classic form of therapeutic double bind (Watzlawick, Beavin, & Jackson, 1967).

What mainly interests us, therefore, is the process of perturbation set off by the letter-writing exercise. This manoeuvre is also an effective instrument for promoting communication, because the young woman feels free to write things that she would probably find it difficult to say in person.

At the next session, we ask: "What did you write in your letters? Did you write anything that you would have found it very difficult to say? Now you can talk about it too, since you've already written about it."

The *nightly letter writing* is a first step in establishing an intensely emotional relationship with the therapist. This manoeuvre starts a process of emotional subversion in the *abstinent* anorexic. After that, we proceed to the next stage, where we lead the patient through several experiences that disrupt the rigidity of her perceptions and reactions.

2. *The miracle fantasy*. At the end of the first session, we generally add a second prescription to the letter writing:

> This task involves a fantasy that you will engage in every morning, from now until we meet again. Every morning, as you wash, get ready, get dressed, I want you to have this concrete, magical fantasy. Imagine that you walk out of this room, as you will walk out of this room today, and that you close the door behind you, as you will close the door behind you today, and as soon as you're out of here, as if by magic, your problem disappears. It no longer exists. What would immediately change in your life? What other problems would you need to take care of? Have this fantasy every morning, imagining that you're beyond the problem.

This prescription is based on a reorganization of what Paul Watzlawick has called the *as if* technique (1990), and on the well-known *miracle question* technique devised by Steve de Shazer (1988). Its goal is to induce a positive, solution-orientated self-deception where the fantasy of having overcome the problem becomes a self-fulfilling prophecy. This manoeuvre has two effects: it introduces a positive suggestion that takes advantage of the "logic of belief" (Nardone, 1998; Nardone & Watzlawick, 2000), suggesting that the "miracle" can happen, and more importantly, shifts the person's attention away from the present symptom to a future free of the disorder.

This change of perspective, obtained through suggestion, is therapeutic in itself, because it opens new horizons and projects the person beyond the problem. Truly "magical" effects are often obtained in this way as we observe a swift improvement of the symptoms as early as between the first and second session. Moreover, even in cases where it produces no other effects, the *miracle fantasy* can help us discover the possible secondary advantages of the problem and thus be useful to our diagnostic examination, helping us identify our objective and correct the focus of our intervention.

The *miracle fantasy* is one of the most useful and least hazardous manoeuvres available to us, because even when it does not work, it produces no resistance. It is also very useful in revealing different aspects of the problem, enabling the therapist to improve the focus and direction of successive interventions. Therefore, this prescription is also generally used as an opening manoeuvre in the therapy of the two eating disorders discussed later in this book as well as for a wide range of other disorders treated by us.

3. *Reframing and stopping the solutions attempted by the family.* At this stage, it is extremely important that the family, or at least the patient's mother, participates in the therapy. As we have already mentioned, direct or indirect attempts by the family to make the daughter eat paradoxically increase her tendency to deny herself food, and ends up complicating the problem instead of solving it. To ensure a good beginning of the therapy, the therapist must therefore intervene directly on the family's communication system by giving prescriptions that put a stop to the most common attempted solutions.

To that end, the therapist asks the young woman to leave the room and then requests that the family starts a *conspiracy of silence*, i.e., that they stop intervening or even mentioning the problem. In giving this prescription, it is very important to avoid any criticism of past actions, or any implication that the family is somehow guilty. Instead, we must use injunctive language, give positive connotations and above all avoid negative formulations, praising the parents for having been so good, patient, and dedicated in their attempts to help their daughter.

> Since you have been so patient and so good at helping your daughter, being there for her, guiding her, working to avoid a worsening

> of the situation . . . I am now going to ask you to make an even greater effort for her sake. Although it may seem strange, you must now start observing without intervening. I want the whole family to maintain a *conspiracy of silence* concerning your daughter's problem. In other words, you must absolutely avoid talking about the problem. All right? You need to get very good at not speaking about it. Just think that every time you talk about it, you make the problem worse. I don't know if you'll succeed in doing that, but consider that every time you mention the problem and try to do something about it, you're making it worse. So please help me help your daughter by observing without intervening, and keep me informed on what happens.

When followed, this prescription completely stops the usual solutions attempted by the family. This often leads to surprising improvements in the anorexic symptoms. The manoeuvre is effective because it interrupts a retroactive vicious circle between the family and the young woman, which had been nourishing the problem. In strategic logic, this is called "to throw a brick to get jade in return".

In order to ensure that the family follows this prescription, it is essential that the therapist communicate it in a language that is consistent with the parents' logic, appealing to their desire to help their daughter, to their sense of sacrifice, turning them into co-therapists. The parents will only be prepared to follow a request that goes against the course of action followed so far if they are praised and asked to help—not if they are blamed and made to feel guilty about their past actions.

Second stage (from the second or third session to the fifth)

In this phase also, the therapy essentially proceeds along two lines, with an intervention that aims to stir the anorexic patient's emotions and prescriptions to the family.

1. *Intervention for a recovery of the patient's femininity.* Having established a relationship of "exclusive alliance" with the patient through the letter writing, we continue our efforts to produce a stirring of emotions by concentrating on the patient's rediscovery of her own femininity. We start by focusing on her ability to be seductive, encouraging her to "toy" with being seductive in her style of

dress, mode of speech, hairstyle, etc. Anorexic women tend to enjoy this theatrical aspect very much.

These interventions aim to give the patient some pleasant perceptions and emotions by indirectly bolstering her sense of desirability as a woman so that, as she begins to "feel" something somewhere, she will want to have feelings in other places as well. However, we must perform this stimulation without asking too much of her, taking advantage of small things in order to start the process of change.

The young woman needs to feel that she's "working on the problem", but within a margin of safety. It is as if we were teaching her how to jump, but with a parachute! Such small changes tend to have a snowball effect, becoming larger and larger as they roll, until they turn into an avalanche.

During this stage, we continue the nightly letter writing, but gradually tell the young woman only to write if she wants to. We also prescribe the *aesthetic evaluation in front of the mirror*:

> Every day, after a relaxing bath, place yourself naked in front of a mirror, with pen and paper. I want you to give a grade, based on aesthetics, to every part of your body. I want to see the report, with grades from 0 to 10, from your hair to the tip of your toes, front and back, and a written motivation for each grade. Place the report in an envelope and don't look at it again. Bring me all your evaluations at the next session.

At the next session, we add the prescription to apply *body lotion* to her whole body after the bath, also in front of the mirror, "So that you can really feel your body. You need to get to know your body." Looking at oneself in a mirror and massaging oneself with lotion, touching and observing, produces a gentle erotic quality that gradually transforms the anorexic person's perceptions, reviving her contact with her own body by feeling instead of just watching it.

The *aesthetic report* and *massage with lotion* are useful for producing emotional experiences in the young woman, for provoking feelings and emotions that have less to do with her contact with her own body than with her interaction with an "other" person, because she is doing it for the therapist. They are not, strictly speaking, physical interventions, but essentially stimulating interventions that aim to produce corrective emotional experiences, starting a process that leads to the person's rediscovery of her relationship with an "other". Thus, we lead the abstinent anorexic to gradually lay down the armour she has been wearing to protect herself from her extremely sensitive feelings, and gradually revive her desire for relationships.

Seductiveness plays a great role in these manoeuvres—not in the erotic sense, but rather in the communication between the therapist and the patient (*therapeutic double bind*). While it is true that a male therapist might induce an emotional stirring, a female therapist can be a seductive behavioural model that the young woman can imitate. Consider, for example, the considerable "seductive" qualities of therapists such as Virginia Satir, Mara Selvini Palazzoli, and Cloé Madanes, to name just a few.

Through the above-described prescriptions, the therapist gradually stimulates the young woman to strengthen her femininity, by asking her to dress as femininely as possible, daring her to assume the attitudes of a *femme fatale* ("let's see if you can do it!"), and so on, thus guiding her to recover feelings and emotions primarily connected with pleasure, "being liked" and "liking oneself".

At the same time, we work directly on interpersonal attitudes by applying a particular version of the *as if* prescription:

> Every morning, while you wash, get dressed and get ready to go out, I want you to ask yourself the following question: "What would I do differently today if I thought other people considered me desirable?" Among all the things that you think you might do, choose the smallest, tiniest one, and do it. Do one small but concrete thing every day *as if* you felt desirable. Choose a different thing every day. Next time, bring me a list of the things you did.

Like the *miracle fantasy*, the *as if* technique (Watzlawick, 1990) is a positively orientated technique that aims to introduce a minimal change in the person's daily actions. Although minimal, this change can have a butterfly effect (Thom, 1990) analogous to those observed in the theory of catastrophes, according to which the flutter of a butterfly's wings can start a hurricane many miles away. If we succeed in changing the attitude that has led a person to construct a dysfunctional reality—even just once a day, in a seemingly unimportant context—we produce a *corrective emotional experience*. This experience can easily be expanded by developing further *as if* actions and attitudes, until a new, functional reality has been constructed and replaces the previous one. Small but concrete *as if* actions gradually overturn the usual interaction between the person and her reality, eventually leading her to experience a real sense of being courted and desired.

This experience derives from an induced form of self-deception that changes the direction of the "self-fulfilling prophecy", completely overturning the latter's effect on the person's experiences. This concrete change of experience also gradually leads to a change in her beliefs and perceptions of reality (Nardone, 1998, Nardone & Watzlawick, 2000). This technique has the added advantage of leading the person to construct her own solution, not one delivered by the therapist.

At the following sessions, we increase the *as if* prescription to two, three, four small actions a day, until the person starts to behave spontaneously as if she felt desirable.

2. *Prescriptions to the family*. The therapist proceeds in the direction established at the first session, asking family members to continue *observing without intervening*, but also to amplify and exaggerate their daughter's problems in different ways, for example by not setting a place for her at the dinner table ("you're not going to eat anyway"), reminding her to be careful not to eat too much because she might gain weight and it might be bad for her, and so on. We must gradually lead the parents to stop all their dysfunctional attempted solutions, and also to discredit all the patient's attempts to start eating again. For example, the therapist might tell the mother:

> From now on, I want you to make an effort to discredit your daughter's problem. So please stop setting a place for her, stop telling her to come to the table, stop showing any interest in what she eats. In fact, from now until I see you again, I want you to remind your daughter three times a day, morning, noon and night: "Mind what you eat, because it might be bad for you. If you gain weight too fast, you might get scared!" Morning, noon and night, you must repeat this formula to your daughter: "Have you been careful about what you eat? If you gain weight too fast, you'll get scared!"

Thus, we use the logic of paradox to make the parents adopt the opposite of their usual attitude and behaviour towards their daughter's disorder, until they begin to frustrate and discredit her symptoms. This type of paradoxical communication within the family has disruptive effects on the anorexic symptoms, as the patient often begins to eat again at this point. Of course, the parents will only accept to follow this kind of prescription (which may seem absurd and contrary to common sense) if the therapist has skilfully "captured" them and engaged them as co-therapists.

By the end of the second stage, the young woman is usually eating again and gaining weight. Having broken the dysfunctional system that maintained the problem, thus opening new possibilities of perception and reaction for the patient, in the third stage we perform interventions aimed at consolidating these changes and producing new ones, gradually restructuring the anorexic person's system of perception and reaction.

Third stage (from the fifth/sixth session on)

During the third stage of therapy, our central aim is to help the patient acquire new repertoires of perception and reaction towards reality, and thus a new and more flexible psychological balance and a definitive solution of the presented problem. Therefore, this phase requires more time than the prior ones do.

As we have seen, we rarely speak directly about what the young woman should eat, or about her problem with food, during the first two stages of treatment (however, this does not mean that we absolutely avoid mentioning it). In the third stage, if necessary, we work directly on the patient's relationship with food, guiding the young woman towards a more correct perception in this context, as we did earlier for other types of feelings. We might, for example, help her recover the pleasures of taste.

Once their symptoms have started improving, anorexic persons often find themselves in the situation of wanting to eat and gain weight, but being unable to do so. The reason is often that they think they are eating an adequate amount of calories per day, while they are in fact eating much less. These young women have a considerable ability to deceive themselves in their perception of what they eat. It's as if they were wearing deforming lenses that magnify everything. In such cases, we can teach them to weigh "with their eyes" and then with a scale, so that they eventually abandon their deforming lenses for more functional means of perception.

A direct intervention on the anorexic person's relationship with food is also necessary when she has regained some weight and her menstrual cycle has started again, but her relationship with food remains difficult (for example, if she is afraid to sit at the dinner table, or is still eating a very limited amount of food). Since they want to be perfect and in control, these young women assume rigid attitudes towards their diet and do not allow themselves any transgression at all. In such cases, we teach them *the small disorder that keeps order* with the following reframing:

> Behind every boundary, there's a transgression. The more rigid your boundaries are, the more you are tempted to transgress. If, instead, you construct an order that includes disorder, you will no longer feel a need to transgress, because that one small disorder saves you from a huge disorder and keeps your system balanced and in constant evolution. A small piece of chocolate, a little transgression, means that you don't feel the need to transgress in big matters at other times. One has to allow oneself something. *If you allow it, you can do without it; if you don't allow it, it will become irresistible.*

The therapist emphasizes the importance of well-organized nutritional habits and decides with the patient what would be a correct and balanced diet for her ("Who knows better than you?"). However, the therapist also introduces the idea that a healthy, balanced diet needs to include a small disorder that keeps the order, because we need a small disorder in order to be orderly.

To avoid losing control, we need a small transgression. The therapist therefore prescribes *one small food transgression* every day (a piece of chocolate, a biscuit, etc.)—something different every day, but it has to be really transgressive and tasty. The therapist says: "If you can do that, it will help you avoid losing control over the rest." This manoeuvre is essential when the young woman continues to be obsessed with food even though she is no longer abstinent.

Fourth stage (last session)

At the last session, we follow exactly the same procedure as for *sacrificial* anorexics.

Clinical example (abstinent anorexic)

Session one

In the following exchanges P is the patient, T is the therapist, M is the patient's mother, and F is the patient's father.

(*The patient and her parents enter*).

Defining the problem

T: Here I am. So what's the problem that you've come to see me for?

M. (*points to her daughter*)

T: Oh, so this time . . .

M: [. . .] Mine is almost a non-problem at this point.

T: (*To the patient*) What's the problem that [your mother was] pointing her finger at?

M: Let her say it! What's her problem? Anorexia!

T: Then maybe I'd better talk with her alone. If I need you, I'll call you both in, all right?

M: Maybe that's better . . . I think.

T: I'll see what's best, OK?

M: Maybe we can meet later to say goodbye.

T: Yes, yes. We'll think about it.

(*The parents leave the room*)

T: Now, what's the problem?

P: I don't know. I don't think I needed to come here. I didn't have any problems . . . then . . .

T: So they forced you to come here?

P: No, no, maybe it was my own decision. I suddenly realized a few days ago that I've become a slave . . . ever since I started following this diet . . . I've lost eighteen kilos. I thought I was fine, but it wasn't true, because I kept feeling cold, but I told everyone I was fine. Then, at the interpreter's school where I study they had a lesson about anorexia, and I recognized myself in several things that the teacher described. I felt ashamed like a dog, but again I said to myself, "No, it's got nothing to do with me! It isn't true." But for the past few days I've been realizing that I've truly become a slave of what I eat. Every evening I have to count the calories. If I've exceeded the limit by ten or twenty calories, I have to punish myself by eating less the next day. Meanwhile, I keep losing weight. I don't know . . .

T: How much do you weigh now?

P: Fifty-one or fifty-two kilos.

T: And you keep losing weight? At what rate?

P: One kilo every two or three weeks.

T: Are you making an effort to avoid losing more weight, or are you basically happy about it?

P: When I stand on the scale and see that I've lost another kilo, on the one hand I get worried and think, "Oh God, how is this possible?"

Investigating the patient's system of perceptions and reactions and her attempted solutions

T: On the other hand, you feel happy about it.

P: On the other hand, I do my best not to regain the weight I've lost. I mean, I really find it impossible to eat.

T: What do you eat? Only vegetables? Do you avoid . . .?

P: No, I eat a bit of everything. I don't avoid sweets, because I have a sweet tooth, but if I have an ice cream one day, I'll have only vegetable soup that night.

T: Exactly. Do you ever vomit after eating, or do you avoid that?

P. *shakes her head.*

T: You can't do it?

P: No.

T: Or you don't like to do it?

P: No. I realized I shouldn't start it, and that was that. I did it a couple of times.

T: Fasting is enough for you.

P: Well, not really fasting. It's just that it bothers me to have to plan everything. I mean, I won't deny myself a good dinner, but if I plan to go out to dinner one night and have pizza and ice cream, then I have to eat a lighter breakfast and lunch, and if I happen to exceed the limit, I start feeling guilty and get mad at everybody.

T: I see. What else?

P: I don't know what else to say.

Investigating her system of relationships

T: Do you have a boyfriend?

P: Yes.

T: What's your relationship like?

P: Well, it hasn't been going very well lately, but last week I told him about [the problem]. He was glad I did. He said "I knew it anyway. You didn't have to tell me. I'm just happy that you've realized it yourself." Things are going better now.

Investigating the solutions attempted by others

T: What about the people around you? What are they doing to help you? Are they telling you to eat, eat, and eat?

P: Yes, so I react by doing exactly the opposite.

T: Who does it most? Your mother?

P: My boyfriend's mother.

T: Your boyfriend's mother? Why, do you often eat at their house?

P: Lately I've been avoiding it, because I'm afraid.

T: What do you do at home?

P: Well, I eat with them, but they've got to leave me alone, because otherwise I lose count of the calories. I'm afraid they might add some extra olive oil, because . . .

T: And do they just sit there and observe, or do they talk about it?

P: My father often asks "Did you add some oil, did you put some sugar in it?" But often they keep quiet because they're afraid of my reaction, I think. Because I tell them off. But I know that they'd be pleased if I ate the foods I used to eat with them. It's beyond my control. I have to use a scale in order to count how much pasta I can eat. I can't judge just by looking at it any more. If I do that, I'm always afraid I might eat too much, so I put some back. But if I have a scale, I eat a hundred grams of pasta. I've stopped buying products that don't show the calorie content on the box, because otherwise I can't calculate. It's become an obsession and it's driving me crazy.

T: So all you think about the whole day is the calorie count. How many calories a day do you allow yourself?

P: At the moment it's 1,500.

T: But are you sure it's 1,500?

P: Well, I always round it off.

T: If one food is 50 calories, you count it as 200.

P: No, not that much.

T: What's your name?

P: M.

T: M., you don't lose one kilo, or even half a kilo, by eating 1,500 calories per day. Someone like you would keep the same weight by eating that much.

P: Well, right now I actually weigh about fifty-one or fifty-two kilos, but I'm not sure about the 1,500 calories. I mean, I do round them off.

T: Then here's what I'd like to know. You spend your days thinking about controlling your food intake, but are you trying to do something to improve the situation, or are you truly a slave of this demon?

P: Some days I think "OK, I'll do something about it"; other days I convince myself that I'm just fine, and that it's a convenient situation. I don't know, it's like the little devil and the little angel.

T: OK.

P: Sometimes one prevails, sometimes the other.

T: Well, well. Apart from food, are there any other problems that bother you?

P: My parents' behaviour, a bit, but I suppose that's normal.

T: Why? What bothers you about their behaviour?

P: Well . . . they fight sometimes . . . they're nervous.

T: Do they fight with each other?

P: And often . . . I don't know . . . especially my father. I feel kind of oppressed by him . . . I don't know . . . "Did you add this? Have some sugar!" If I'm having a bad day and he says "have some sugar", I won't have any even if I intended to.

T: So, of the two it's your father who's a bit more insistent.

P: Yes, but maybe because my mother's a bit scared. I don't know, maybe she thinks I'll get angry with her. She's scared . . . I don't know . . .

T: So you've decided to come to me.

P: Yes, it was my decision.

T: Or did they choose?

P: Well, we'd been talking about it for a while, but . . .

T: But I'm also talking about the choice of coming to me, in particular.

P: Well, at that point I thought "Mum was happy with him . . . it's someone I know, someone I can . . ."

T: OK, good.

P: . . . someone I can trust . . .

T: Good. Would you like some candy? Chewing gum?

P: (*shakes her head*)

Agreement upon the manner of treatment. Therapeutic double bind

T: I knew it. (*They both smile*). So you already know that I have some very peculiar methods; that I don't talk too much and don't make anyone else talk too much either; that I give tasks, and those tasks may sometimes seem strange and illogical, funny and grotesque, but they must be carried out to the letter. I do give explanations, but always afterwards.

P: (*nods*)

T: Another rule is that I only allow myself ten sessions to see if there are any results. If I don't see any results, I suspend the therapy at the tenth session. If at the tenth session we see that there have been some changes, but we still haven't finished, we'll continue. If everything goes as usual, the problems will be solved by the tenth session, but I don't know if that will happen in your case.

P: Let's try it.

T: Fine. I think I've got some good methods for solving your problems, because this is a problem I've worked on many times, on which we've done some special research, and for which we've devised specific models, but I don't know if it will work for you.

P: Is it that serious?

T: It depends on how good you are at carrying out what I ask. There are two things I want from you. I'm also going to ask your parents to do something that you'll like. Now, here's the first thing. Do you have any letter stationery?

First prescription: nightly letter writing

P: (*nods, looking perplexed*)

T: Every night when you go to bed, as the last thing you do that day, I want you to take some sheets and an envelope and write me a letter. The only prerequisite is that it should start with "Dear Doctor"—that's me. After that, you're free to tell me that I'm dislikeable, stupid, an idiot . . . Write anything that comes to mind. When you've finished the letter, sign it, and bring them all to me next time. All right?

P: Anything . . .

T: Anything's fine. Whatever comes to mind. It'll help me to get to know you, better than a lot of talk. OK? But every night, with your head on the pillow, the last thing you do.

Second prescription: miracle fantasy

The second thing I'm going to ask you to do is to imagine a sort of magic fantasy every morning when you wake up. As you get dressed and ready for the day, try to imagine that you walk out of here, just like you'll be walking out of here today; that you close the door just like we 're going to close the door today, when we walk out of here; and that as soon as you walk out of here, "Puff!"—by some kind of magic, your obsession disappears. You're no longer obsessed with food.

P: I wish!

T: What would immediately change in your life? What other problems would you have to solve after this one? In order to answer that question, I need you to project yourself into that situation, so you have to make up an image, a tangible emotion. You walk out of here, close the door, and as soon as the door is closed, "Puff!"—the problem's gone. What problems would come next? What would immediately change in your life? Bring me the answers. The tasks are to remain a secret between you and me, OK?

P (*nods*)

T: Now, please wait while I call your parents and give them their homework.

(*The parents enter*)

Third prescription: conspiracy of silence

T: Hello. Please sit down. So . . . first of all, the problem's very clear. The problem can be solved, on condition that all three of you do everything that I ask you to do to the letter, all right? Good. I've already given M her homework, and that will remain a secret between me and M, OK? You're going to have to commit to something that won't be easy, something that will require some effort: you must absolutely avoid speaking about the problem. There must be a conspiracy of silence on this subject. No one may mention the problem of anorexia, and no one may say "Eat!". On the contrary, if you see that M starts to eat excessively, you must warn her that she's going to regret it. "M, be careful. If you eat too much you're going to regret it." But you must absolutely avoid telling her to "eat this, eat that, eat more" because that just increases the problem.

M: But I've never said that. He does it more. (*She points at her husband.*)

T: But we're not here to place the blame on anyone.

M: No, but the fact is that she needs to be . . .

T: She already told me that. But what we're saying here is that all members of the family must avoid speaking about the problem, and everyone must promise to avoid telling M to eat. I know it's difficult to watch this girl get thinner and thinner and eating less and less every day, but keep in mind that every time you say it, you increase the pathology and start a power struggle that just makes her want to eat less, and this will help stop it. Inform everyone around you that they must avoid speaking about the problem. No one should presume to say "eat".

P: So tell Teresa! (*She smiles*)

T: Tell everyone, all right? Because, with this type of problem, the zeal of those who want to help is the most dangerous thing. All right? And she's got her homework.

M: I understood it immediately, but sometimes . . .

T: It's not easy.

M: We don't know what to do, because we don't know how to give advice, so we keep quiet, with our heads in the sand like ostriches. We try to avoid . . . but sometimes she explodes . . . any little thing, and boom!

T: Well, I've already started to work with M. Now, I could see you next week, and in that case I need to see her every week for ten sessions, without skipping any sessions, because we're working on a little problem, OK?

M: OK.

Session two

T: Come in, M.

P: Here are the letters. There's one missing.

T: Only one missing? Sit down.

P: Yes, because I felt sick that night.

Redefining the effects of the first prescription: nightly letter writing

T: And you didn't write that letter, so we've got three letters. Good. What did you write in here?

P: Whatever I felt like. I didn't even revise them. There may be some mistakes. Otherwise I would have erased things.

T: (*Ironically*) So I'm going to make you underline them: "mistake, mistake, mistake". Tell me, since you said you wrote whatever came to mind, is there anything in here that you would have found it difficult to tell me verbally?

P: Yes, I think so. Actually, sometimes I didn't know what to write, so I wrote whatever came to mind, including some banalities.

T: Since you wrote some things that you might be afraid to say, or have a problem telling me directly, you can tell me now.

P: Now?

T: Start with them. What did you write that you might have a problem saying?

P: I don't know . . . a lot of things which I do now and didn't do before.

T: What are the things you didn't do before and that you do now?

P: Being interested in cooking, going to supermarkets, and always checking things.

T: Studying the calories.

P: Yes.

T: You don't buy anything if it doesn't have all the calories written outside. And what else?

P: And then . . . I don't know. I wrote about everything and nothing; even completely extraneous things and also things that made me feel bad.

Report about the past week

T: How have you been feeling these days? Better or worse than usual?

P: Well . . . the first night, I don't know, I was totally confused. I felt fine at first, walking around the city together with my parents. I didn't think about it at all. I was really able to follow your advice to the letter (*she smiles*). Then I got home and . . . I don't know, maybe because I was alone in the house, and the very thought of having to go back to my little village (*she smiles*) . . . I've noticed that when I'm in C I don't think about it as much, but when I'm at home . . . (*she sighs*).

T. You think about it more.

P: Yes, it really gets worse. When I'm away I sometimes think "Oh, I can make it", but when I'm at home . . .

T: Good.

P: And, actually, the fact that I'm going to C now makes me feel a little better.

T: Good. How did you behave with respect to your little problem in the past few days?

P: Well, as I said, better at first, but then on Saturday I felt terrible.

T: What do you mean by better?

P: That I tried to eat what I wanted . . . Well, after making the necessary calculations.

T: Of the calories.

P: But at least I ate what I wanted.

T: Yes.

P: In fact, after I walked out of here, I had an ice cream.

T: Really! Wow!

P: But it was part of my diet plan.

T: Well, of course, ice cream isn't bad for you.

P: But on Saturday I felt terrible . . . I don't know, I also wrote to you about it. Since I usually go out for a pizza with my boyfriend on Saturdays, I had a smaller breakfast than usual and didn't have any lunch. Then at night we went to a different place, and I don't know . . . I started dreading the pizza, because he had already told me the food was good there and that they used a lot of seasoning.

T: Oh.

P: I started feeling nervous. And the pizza had more seasoning than I had imagined.

T: Of course.

P: I ate it and felt ill afterwards. I don't know if it was because of some psychological reason, or . . .

T: Well, in any case, you felt ill . . . and what did you do?

P: Nothing. I had a crisis of nerves.

T: And then?

P: Well, I got a stomach-ache and they put me to bed.

Redefining the effects of the second prescription (miracle fantasy)

T: Did you do the morning task I gave you?

P: Yes, I tried.

T: What happened?

P: I don't know . . . when I'm in C I can do it. Friday morning I went out and felt like my old self again, back when I used to like going shopping—not in food stores (*they both smile*). So I walked around and looked at the stores, as if nothing were wrong.

T: Oh!

P: And everything was normal. But then, in the evening I went home and it started all over again.

T: So if I understand you right, there were some moments when it seemed as if it had disappeared—puff!—as if by magic.

P: And other moments when it came back multiplied by a hundred.

T: What was the tangible difference in the moments when you felt . . .

P: When I felt well?

T: Yes, as if it had all disappeared by magic.

P: Well, I don't know . . . My mood . . .

T: What?

P: My mood, yes. I feel that I really want . . . I don't know . . . I feel happy.

T: But if I understood you correctly, that means that this week, these past few days, something has started to move inside you.

P: Yes, but I had moments . . .

T: Good. That's important.

P: . . . when I felt better and moments when I felt worse. I noticed that the times I feel better always happen when I'm in C, and the worst times are when I'm at home at the weekends.

T: Don't you ever have any good moments while you're at home?

P: Sometimes.

T: Well, well.

P: Although I still count the calories when I'm in C.

T: Of course

P: But I feel less oppressed; instead, at home . . .

T: Well, well, well. Did you weigh yourself? Did you measure yourself?

P: Yes.

T: Good.

P: Yes, I did on Saturday, but then I told myself, "That's enough until next Saturday."

T: "I won't weigh myself." Did you find that you had gained some weight, or were things as usual?

P: I lost weight (*she smiles*)

T: You lost weight again?

P: About half a kilo.

First prescription: continue the letter writing every night

T: Well, OK. I simply want you to keep writing me every evening, and include everything that comes to mind, OK?

P: Yes, I feel better when I write.

T: Good.

P: At first I never feel like starting because I'm a bit lazy (*she smiles*) but then, when I start writing, I don't know, it's a way . . .

T: Good.

P: . . . to get things out of my system.

Second prescription: one small thing every day as if the problem didn't exist

T: And I want you to continue with the morning fantasy, but focus on the day ahead this time, changing the question to something like this: "If by magic there had been a miracle, OK? What would I do differently today? What would I do differently from what I do now, if I didn't have this problem any more?"

P: When I think about it, I remember the way I used to be!

T: You know, no one can go back in time, we can only go forward.

P: I know that, but it's as if I had this great wish to go back to being like . . .

T: And ask yourself: "How would I behave today if I didn't have my problem any more? Among the things that come to mind that you would do if the problem were gone, I want you to choose the smallest, the tiniest, most imperceptible thing, and put it into practice, OK?

P: I hope I've understood you correctly.

T: You already did that spontaneously this week, right?

P: Yes.

T: I want you to look beyond your relationship with food, and look especially at your moods, OK? The question is " What would I do if I didn't have the problem?"

P: But, yes, I've noticed that even if . . . I never stay well the whole day. Especially at night, after dinner, I'm overcome by moments of . . .

T: Sadness, melancholy . . .

P: Sadness, confusion.

Third prescription: aesthetic evaluation in front of the mirror

T: Tell me about that in your letters, OK? And one more task: from now until I see you again next week, after you take a bath or a shower . . . do you usually take baths or shower?

P: I shower.

T: Good. Twice, leaving a few days in between, I want you to . . . do you have a full-length mirror where you can see yourself in C?

P: Yes.

T: Go to the mirror without your clothes on, OK? Take a pen and a sheet of paper. I want an aesthetic report, from the tip of your hair to the tip of your toes.

P: I already do that.

T: Front and back, with grades from 1 to 10, and motivations for the grades you give, OK? I know you're already doing it, that's obvious, but this time you'll do it for me and bring it to me.

P: I'm supposed to write a kind of report card?

T: That's right, an aesthetic report card on every part of the body, with grade points and motivations for every part of the body. Each time you do the report card, put it in the envelope for that night, and don't look at it again the next time, OK? Let's see what happens, OK? I'll see you next Monday. What time are your trains? Have you checked the timetable?

(*The session ends as they set up the next appointment.*)

Session threee

Redefining the effects of the first prescription (nightly letter writing)

T: How are things going? I see you've brought me some more letters.

P: The two last ones . . . I don't know . . . I wrote them in the morning instead of in the evening. Does it matter?

T: How come?

P: In the morning . . .

T: You felt like doing it.

P: Yes.

T: Did you do it out of a sense of duty, or did you really want to?

P: No, I just feel that I do things better in the morning.

T: Good.

P: In the evening I don't feel like it. It's laziness on my part.

T: Fine. What did you write about this time? Are there any more things that you would have been too embarrassed to tell me personally?

P: Maybe.

T: What are they, since I'm going to be reading about them anyway?

P: I can't remember now.

T: Oh, OK, fine. I'll just read them. (*They both smile.*)

P: They're things that come to mind as I write. I don't re-read any of my letters, to avoid reconsiderations.

Report on the past week

T: How have things been going this week?

P: I thought the weekend was going to be bad, but it went a little better.

T: How?

P: Well, with respect to my moods, perhaps.

T: Were things bad when you went home?

P: Yes. I expected it to be disastrous, like last week, but things actually went better with my boyfriend and my parents.

T: How did you notice that things were better?

P: I was calmer. Maybe I answered them less rudely.

T: Really? And what else?

P: I feel calmer, a bit less agitated.

T: Oh.

P: Apart from occasional moments.

T: And how did you behave regarding your little problem?

The young woman says she is still losing weight despite the fact that she is eating 1,500 calories per day. She attributes her weight loss to the fact that she exercises intensively. The therapist suggests the possibility that although the patient believes that she is eating 1,500 calories, she is probably eating much less than that. In order to prove to the patient that her perception of the quantity of food she eats is subject to a "deforming lens" without making her feel guilty or openly contradicting her, he asks her to examine together with him a standard daily menu that she believes to contain 1,500 calories. In the end, the patient has to admit that her daily menu usually contains approximately 1,100 calories, never more.

T: Listen, I'm not blaming you. I know perfectly well that a slightly deformed view of things and a tendency to increase calorie content is part of your problem, OK? . . . Because you're concerned about overeating.

P: Yes. For example, if I'm at 750 calories, I think "OK, let's say 800."

T: Listen, I'm already happy about what you're eating—I mean about everything you've been doing since I first met you, very happy. But what I want to teach you now is let's measure things more accurately. I'm not saying "do more". You already know what you need to do.

P: Yes, I know.

T: And I'm certainly not going to push you. What I'm saying is that I'm very happy, you're doing a good job, OK? But you're the one who's weighing yourself, and you know what it means. Good.

The session continues with a discussion of the effects of the other two prescriptions ("As If the Problem Were Gone", and "The Aesthetic Report Card". The young woman says she's been unable to do anything differently "as if" the problem were gone, but that she has nevertheless noticed some changes (exceptions to the problem). She also says she that felt very embarrassed in doing the aesthetic report card.

The therapist ends the session by repeating the letter-writing prescription (not as an obligation, but as an opportunity if the patient wants it) and the aesthetic report card in front of the mirror. He also replaces the "as if" prescription with the task of noticing exceptions to the problem:

Looking for exceptions to the problem.

T: Instead of asking yourself "how would I behave differently?", I'd like you to notice if there's any sign, anything that happens without any inducement from you, anything spontaneous that makes you think it's a sort of exception to the problem, something different with respect to your life with the problem. Look for some moment of different behaviour, attitudes, or feelings that are separate from the problem, OK?

Session four

The patient reports that she has finally realized that she is too thin, and that she wants to gain weight by following the prescriptions of a dietician. The therapist reframes this intention, stressing the importance of a balanced food intake that will allow her to gain weight gradually until she reaches her ideal weight and is able to maintain it without the risk of gaining too much weight.

T: Apart from that, what have you been doing?

P: I wrote down the different things you told me to notice, and . . . nothing . . . I felt a bit more cheerful.

Redefining the effects of looking for exceptions to the problem

T: So you noticed the exceptions among the exceptions. You're more cheerful.

P: Yes. I mean, my friends noticed it too. I started making jokes again. I didn't do that before. And then there's something that may sound a bit ridiculous: I tried sleeping without a water bottle.

T: That's not ridiculous, it's something real.

P: . . . Because, well, it had got to the point that if I didn't have a water bottle . . . I don't know, I felt cold. I tried to make the cold go away.

T: Hmmm.

P: That's also what often used to keep me from going out, because I was scared of feeling cold. So I've been going out more.

T: Good.

P: So I had some distractions. Otherwise I would have stayed at home thinking "I'd like to eat now but I won't". Instead, I went out and, oh . . . once I tried . . . but it was a fiasco (*she smiles*) . . . usually when I go home to see my parents, I bring my own food. Last week I tried not bringing it. I thought "I'll eat whatever's there", but we had a small misunderstanding. My mother hadn't cooked anything for me, because she said "I knew you always bring your own food!" (*She smiles.*)

T: Oh! She hadn't cooked anything for you.

P: So, for once that . . . Oh, well. (*They smile.*)

T: You did a lot. So there are quite a few small, important exceptions.

P: Yes, but, well, I had some moments of crisis too.

T: Oh, well, you've got to expect that! You can't think . . .

The therapist emphasizes the importance of extending the "conspiracy of silence" to her boyfriend, in order to avoid encouraging the problem. The young woman restates her wish to gain weight even though she admits that it makes her happy to hear others comment on her thinness.

Redefining the effects of the aesthetic evaluation in front of the mirror

T: Listen, how did it feel to stand in front of the mirror and writing the aesthetic reports?

P: Oh, God!

T: Didn't it bother you? Or did you like it?

P: It depends on the day, and . . . It depends.

T: Did you like what you saw or not?

P: No, not above this point. On the contrary, I'm worried about the summer approaching. When I put on a swimsuit, all you see is bones. But below this point I . . . I don't think I look thin. I try telling myself "I'm thin!"

T: No, stand in front of the mirror and give yourself points like we said. And I want you to keep writing the letters.

P: Do I have to do it every . . .

T: Every day.

P: Because sometimes I can't think of anything to write.

First prescription: write letters when she wants to

T: No, wait. It's an opportunity now, not an obligation. Write when you feel like it.

P: Right.

T: Whenever you feel like it, grab pen and paper and write, and bring me the letter.

Second prescription: continue to look for exceptions

T: Keep on looking for exceptions. Look for things that happen spontaneously during the day and make you think "Hey, I'm feeling better!"

Third prescription: massage body in front of mirror

T: And instead of doing the report, I'd like you to go to the mirror—but you have to do it every day, OK?—and use a good body lotion.

P: I've already done that.

T: How did it feel?

P: Bony.

T: Bony? Good, that's what I want. But you have to love that body of yours.

P: But the thing is I ashamed of it.

T: I can believe that . . . Now, I want you to do that every night. You feel ashamed, right?

P: I feel ashamed, especially with my boyfriend, very ashamed. He makes an effort to say, "It's OK, I like you anyway," but I know it isn't true. So I don't know . . . I'm ashamed of myself. But I'd still rather be like this than how I used to be . . .

T: What you need to do now is simply to say "I have to do this task because I need to start making contact with my body again", OK? Every night, massage yourself from head to toe even if you feel bony, or fat.

Session five

The patient says she still has not made an appointment with a dietician, and that she has not been able to regulate her food intake the way she wanted. Nevertheless, she has been eating normally at times.

T: Now, help me understand this; did you continue weighing yourself?

P: I only weighed myself once—yesterday.

T: Have you lost weight?

P: No.

T: You've stayed the same?

P: Yes.

Redefining the effects of the manoeuvres

T: You haven't gained weight either. So you've done really well. Did you do the homework I gave you?

P: Sometimes I did, sometimes I didn't.

T: Hand them over.

P: Oh, the homework . . . the letters?

T: Yes.

P: Oh, the letters. I didn't write any this time.

T: What else did you sometimes do and sometimes not?

P: The body lotion. Sometimes . . . I don't know . . .

T: What do you mean?

P: I don't feel like it. The more I look in the mirror, the more depressed I get, so . . .

T: What do you mean?

P: I don't know, I'd rather avoid seeing myself . . . in order to feel, to convince myself that I'm well.

T: And if you look in the mirror, you can't convince yourself?

P: (*shakes her head.*)

T: So now you avoid looking at yourself?

P: (*nods and starts to cry.*)

T: So you're trying to avoid doing what I asked you to do, also because you've understood why I asked you to do it. Here. (*He hands her a paper tissue.*)

P: Thank you.

T: But it's also true that if I don't make you acknowledge it, you'll never change, you know? Right?

P: Yes, I know. That's what makes me so unhappy—the fact that I know. I mean, part of me knows, but there's always that other bad part.

T: Oh, but we both know that there's a duel going on between those two parts, and we both know that last time you came here and told me "I want a diet that'll make me gain weight" simply because when you stood in front of the mirror and put on lotion, you saw yourself differently.

P: Yes.

T: Differently from when you're wearing your deforming lenses, right? With the deforming lenses, you always see yourself as fat. But at those other moments, you don't have them on. It's as if I made you take off those lenses. That's why I want you to do it.

P: Like letting my boyfriend touch me.

T: Of course, because he doesn't have the deforming lenses on either!

Since the young woman is uncertain whether or not to consult a dietologist, the therapist decides to agree with her on a diet.

T: Do you remember that we had agreed on a diet, and you told me, "Yes, I'll eat this"? Then we made the calculations and saw how self-deceptions work?

P: I'm the first to deceive myself.

T: Of course you're deceiving yourself, and when you run into something that frees you from self-deception, such as the prescriptions I've been giving you, you follow them, but then they make you suffer and you stop following them. But if you want to keep your commitment to get rid of this problem, there's only one way, OK? If you want to succeed in doing the things we agree upon, then going to the mirror and massaging yourself with lotion has to become a daily appointment, otherwise you won't be able to do what you want, because if we can't make you see the deforming lenses you have in your eyes, it will always be a problem, OK? All right? Good. As I told you once, I don't think it requires any big things, do you understand? We mostly just need to follow your current eating habits, so what are your eating habits at the moment? The habits you're able to follow without too much effort?

The young girl tells the therapist about her eating habits. The therapist agrees with her on a "dissociated" diet and prescribes that she weigh the foods she eats in order to "re-educate her eyes" for a more accurate perception of the quantity of food she actually eats.

First prescription: take measurements

T: You can't trust your eyes, because your eyes have deforming lenses. So in order to re-educate your eyes you're going to have to do something very boring that we usually prescribe for bulimics, OK? Weigh yourself.

P: Weigh myself—my favourite thing.

T: Don't worry, OK? I don't want to know your weight, because you're already checking that; I want your measurements, OK? Like a top model.

P: I've never done that, so . . .

T: This time you'll have to do it. Every area of your body. I'll see you again next Thursday.

Second prescription: continue massage with lotion

T: Apart from that, continue as usual; I want you to stand in front of the mirror and massage yourself with lotion after showering or taking a bath, OK?

P: All right.

T: Don't skip even one day. Bye, see you soon!

Session six

The therapist asks the patient to continue taking her measurements; to follow a diet that will enable her to gain half a kilo a week and to introduce one small transgression per day within that diet.

Session seven

T: So, M, how have things been going for you?

P: I think I'm starting to gain weight.

T: Oh, dear.

P: But I don't know. It happened on Saturday. Not this Saturday, but last Saturday.

T: Can I tell you something? You look better when you're tanned.

P: Thank you.

Seductive shake-up of emotions and reinforcement of the patient's confidence in her own beauty

T: You're much prettier.

P: But I don't know . . . I don't know what to do about measuring myself, because sometimes . . .

T: I'm one way . . .

P: Sometimes, I'm one way, sometimes I'm another.

T: Maybe you're doing it wrong.

P: I've been thinking: maybe sometimes I place the measuring tape higher, sometimes lower. But I've noticed that I'm getting bigger in places where I don't want to.

T: Oh, no! Where?

P: Maybe around the waist, which is the only part that's average. The rest is all wrong, I've realized that . . .

T: Show me your current measurements.

P: Well, currently my waist is 64 [cm], I'm 79 here, and my hips are 84.

T: So the only good measurement is this one, and it's increasing?

P: But how come? First it was 62, now it's 64, and my breasts have grown from 70 to 78. My hips get slimmer one time and fatter the next.

T: It depends on where you place the measuring tape—maybe you place it higher or lower over the buttocks.

P: That's right.

T: But there seems to have been an increase of a few centimetres.

P: Yes, and that's why I don't know whether I did the right thing or not. Last time you told me to increase the portions again, but the measurements I told you last time were from Saturday, so I only had one day with the increased portions. Then I re-measured myself, and . . .

T: You did the right thing when you decided to keep the portions as before.

P: I asked my dad's advice too . . .

Motivating the patient by praising her proven capacity

T: You did very well, very well, because if your weight increased with the earlier portions, there's no reason to increase them further. It would be too much effort.

P: Was it an increase, or not?

T: If what you're telling me is true, then yes. Your waist measurement has increased by two centimetres, your breast measurements one centimetre, and we don't know exactly what's happening with your hips because it's difficult to take precise measurements there.

P: And to tell the truth, I also stepped on the scale . . .

T: Oh, you did? How much weight have you gained?

P: Well . . . about half a kilo.

T: Good.

P: But I've measured myself since then, and there have been no more . . .

T: Variations?

P: Variations.

T: That means you've done some things well.

P: What do you mean?

T: You've managed to find a threshold and stop there.

P: That's right, I haven't increased any more, but I was waiting to hear what . . .

T: Perfect. You also need to consider that the hips and stomach are the first things to grow simply because that's where the food goes first.

Later it gets distributed, so it's normal that in the first few weeks you see a greater increase at the waist, OK? It will get distributed later.

P: I also measured my thighs, my ankles and everything.

T: And they stayed the same?

P: Yes.

T: Good. So, how have your moods been?

P: My mood was . . . Well, apart from a few moments . . . but I've always been like that, losing my temper easily, so things are pretty much like they used to be normally, according to what other people have told me . . .

T: What people?

P: My parents, my boyfriend, my friends.

T: Do they feel that you're better now?

P: They've told me that . . . there's really a difference.

T: In what way is there a difference?

P: There's no comparison between how I am now and how I used to be.

T: But do you see a lot of difference?

P: Well, I do because other people tell me, and I see it too, but . . . I think there's a difference, but it's not as . . .

T: . . . Marked as other people think.

P: But still a significant one.

The therapist stresses the importance of continuing to gain half a kilo per week, as they had agreed in the previous session.

P: And should I use the scale?

T: You've been doing it anyway!

P: I do it anyway (*smiling*).

T: But not more than once a week.

P: No, never.

T: When you take your measurements, you can step on the scale too, but I want you to start learning that your measurements are what really counts.

P: That's right. I've realized that they're a bit off.

T: Because if one really wants to look good, weight is not important. What matters is how the weight is distributed—the proportions. It's important to be chubby in the right places, not in the wrong places, so we also need to think about how to fill in the areas that are too empty, [not] those that are too full . . .

P: That's what I'm worried about. I'm afraid I'll increase only in those places . . .

T: Stop! First try to re-join the female world, OK? Then we'll worry about shaping you. We can't start shaping you until you're back in the female world, OK? Then we'll shape you, but you have to come back first. There's nothing easier than shaping a young girl's body, even though you think it's so hard. Of course, if all you do is get thinner, there's nothing to shape—in fact, you lose your shape, just as if you just gained weight. How's your boyfriend reacting?

P: He's happy.

T: What made you decide to change your hair colour?

P: I've always done that.

T: Now and then, you change your hair colour.

P: Yes. Actually, when I was ill, I stopped doing that, and people told me "You're not the same! Where's the girl who used to come as a red-head one time and with black hair the next?"

Praising the patient's appearance

T: Well, for a while you stopped paying attention, caring about your appearance, didn't you? I'm very happy, and I want you to pay as much attention as you can to your appearance, and try to be as feminine as possible. You look a lot better now; you're much more feminine, so that's what we need to work on, OK?

First prescription: continue massages

T: So continue with the massages . . .

Second prescription: one small thing every day to increase femininity

. . . and do one tiny thing every day to look more feminine. Ask yourself, "What can I do to day to look more feminine?" and do at least one small, tiny thing that has to do with what you wear, or something you do, or your attitude, how you dress or do your make-up. That's what we need to work on. It's really important now, and keep the food portions the same as we said last time.

P: That's 130 grams of pasta . . .

T: Exactly.

P: . . . 150 of meat, and the transgressions, and that transgression has to be calorie rich.

Third prescription: one small, enjoyable transgression every day

T: Who said that the transgression had to be food? It can be whatever you want—just something you like.

P: Sometimes I find myself in a predicament. Today, for example, I had breakfast very early, at seven, so I felt hungry again around eleven and had a fruit juice. I wouldn't have done that before, because I had to wait for lunch, but now . . . I've been thinking about this the whole day: can that be considered a transgression, or . . .?

T: That's a transgression.

P: So that's it for today.

T: Exactly. I want one small transgression every day—something that you enjoy. For you and your colleagues, as I call them, it's difficult to allow yourself something you enjoy. You are the abstinents.

P: Another thing I wanted to mention is that strangely, particularly at dinnertime and after dinner, I feel like eating continuously. I mean, I could just keep on eating without stopping, even though I feel full . . .

T: You know, once you start feeling pleasure, it becomes enjoyable.

P: It's never enough, I mean . . .

T: Oh, that makes me happy, even more than all the rest.

P: But not me.

Redefining the importance of experiencing pleasure in connection with food

T: I'm not saying you should abandon yourself to it! Do what we said. The important thing is that you're having those feelings.

P: But I used to feel that way before, too.

T: Yes, all anorexics are hungry as wolves, but they manage to sedate the hunger. Above all, they feel guilty about it. But when you tell me that you're hungry and want to eat, that's different. You're starting to perceive it as a pleasure, but one that you can control, since you have one transgression a day available!

P: But I control it. Only one a day.

T: That's right, and no more than one. And everything else we've mentioned. Pay attention to your femininity. Good.

P: All right.

Session eight

The patient says that she is still gaining weight.

Redefining the effects of the daily transgressions

T: What were your daily transgressions, apart from what we agreed that you would eat?

P: Well, it varied: always sweet stuff like chocolate, a piece of cake or some jam.

T: Good. Did you ever feel guilty about eating?

P: No, because I knew it was allowed, I mean that I was supposed to do it, so . . .

T: So you never thought: "Oh God, what am I doing, I'm losing control, oh God . . ."

P: No. I feel like that at the end of the day, when I've finished eating and feel that I'd like to eat more.

T: Even more.

P: But I tell myself no, I have to stop, I have to, I've finished eating [all I'm supposed to]. But maybe it's because I've got nothing to do. I don't know.

T: Has anyone else had the nerve to say "You look better"?

P: Yes.

T: Didn't that scare you?

P: No, but it depends on who says it. If it's my boyfriend or one of my friends, I'm happy about it, but I'm less pleased if it's my parents or my boyfriend's parents who tell me I look better. For them, my getting well only means that I eat more. I don't think they realize that it's not primarily a physical problem. But certainly, if people tell me I look better, logically that makes me happy.

Redefining the effects of paying attention to femininity

T: Good. And how are your efforts to be feminine proceeding? Better, I see.

P: It's going well.

T: Do you enjoy standing in front of the mirror and taking care of yourself, or not?

P: Yes, but I've always liked that.

T: You didn't seem to.

P: No. (*They both smile.*)

T: Well, maybe before, but now . . . It's true that on some days I think look better and other days I think I look worse, but I think that's normal.

P: I should say so! Do people compliment you for being more feminine, for paying more attention to your appearance, or not?

P: Yes. (*They smile.*)

T: That must scare you.

P: No, I feel pleased about it.

T: It doesn't bother you?

P: No.

T: Not at all?

P: No. Before, if anyone told me "You're disgustingly skinny", it made me happy. Now I've realized that it's better when people say "You look good", or "You look bad".

T: Really? And you feel calm about all this?

P: Yes.

First prescription: "weigh with eyes and scale"

T: Then do an experiment. Starting today, before you weigh the food, put some quantity of it on a plate, trying to make it as close as possible to the amount you have to weigh, OK? Then put the food on the scale and check the difference between your perception and what the scale says. Do that with everything.

P: Everything?

T: Yes, because I want to see how good you are at weighing with your eyes, because sooner or later we'll have to do without the scale, right? When you learn to look at something and see that that's more or less 100 grams of meat, more or less 120 grams of pasta, more or less 30, 50, 100 grams of bread, OK? Let's measure your ability, OK?

P: Still the same portions?

Second prescription: small daily transgression

T: Exactly. You're doing well. Small daily transgression.

Session nine

The patient reports that things are improving: she's taken up some hobbies and is increasing her efforts to be attractive. Her weight is also increasing gradually.

T: How are your measurements going?

P: My measurements increase, decrease . . . In any case, about the weight, I started at fifty kilos and now I'm at 52.5, almost fifty-three.

T: 52.5—does that scare you?

P: No, also because I can see that I look better.

T: Good.

P: I can tell from the clothes I wear . . . Some of them used to hang really loose . . . they still do . . . I realize that I was really in a bad state before . . . Am I gaining weight now because I eat more than I should, or because I eat normally, so my body is . . .?

T: You're eating normally, and your body is gradually recovering. OK?

P: Because that's what I'm afraid of now, that when I reach my ideal weight . . .

T: When I reach my ideal weight, will I lose control?

P: My problem is, when I reach my ideal weight and have to start decreasing my present portions in order to maintain it, I might start again . . .

T: On the contrary, you'll notice that you can even allow yourself a few more transgressions without gaining extra weight. Right now your body's like a withering plant: it's assimilating. When you reach your ideal weight, your body will be much more flexible, right? So it will be my job to prove to you that you can maintain a nutritional balance that also includes transgressions, as I've been teaching you, right? Without being fixated on it. It's useless for me to tell you this now. I'm making you conquer it.

P: Yes. I've also realized that I'm really good at judging the weight of food just by looking at it.

T: You're getting closer and closer.

P: It's true.

T: You're great at this! Well done.

We keep the prescriptions from the week before (weigh with eyes and scale, try to look and act in a feminine way, take measurements, small daily transgression).

Session ten

(The patient has called the therapist once during the week to tell him that her period has returned after one year of complete absence.)

T: So how are things going?

P: Well. We've become . . .

Reframing the important change that has occurred

T: Well . . . what does that mean? We've become . . . I heard your phone message and it makes me very happy. How does it feel to have joined womanhood again?

P: Good.

T: Is it better, among the females?

P: It's good.

T: This whole thing hasn't given you a shock?

P: I felt bad because I started having menstrual pains again and all that, but I really didn't care.

T: You were too happy to care?

P: (*nods.*

T: Well, well. And listen, during the following days you never felt scared again? Never thought "Now I'll get fat again, now I'll become ugly, now . . ."?

P: When it happened, I asked myself "And now, what's next? What do I do? Do I continue as before?" But I continued without any problems—well, I had a crisis now and then, but . . .

T: But that's part of life, isn't it?

P: It used to be, especially before all this happened.

T: Of course . . . So did your menstrual cycle return after you gained more weight, or from staying the same?

P: The same.

T: Wow. As we were saying, it was simply a question of accepting your femininity. What has changed for you now?

P: Well . . . I feel as if I've succeeded.

T: What does that mean?

P: That I don't feel sick any more.

T: Good.

P: I feel well.

T: You know that we had already reached this situation since a couple of months, although—how shall I put it?—a physical confirmation was still missing.

P: Another thing I'm happy about is that I haven't got any fatter.

T: OK, but that also seems obvious. One shouldn't pay the price of returning to the female gender by gaining too many kilos. You need to maintain a weight that makes you attractive and keeps you healthy. We've received a signal, right? If your period stops coming, it means that you're underweight, or at least that you've returned to a certain mental state. If your period stays regular, as I think it will, it means that you're calm.

Giving the patient credit for the change

T: Most importantly, this is something you've reached by slowly constructing it step by step, by yourself, and that's fundamental.

P: Now I'm a bit worried that my period might stop coming (*she laughs*).

T: Of course, but watch out, because, as you know, sometimes that happens when young girls get anxious after committing some peccadillo . . .

P: In any case my parents also think that my having my period again is a good sign . . . Then, if it starts being late or irregular . . .

T: Well, that's something you should expect!

P: Yes.

T: Don't think that . . .

P: After a year . . .

T: . . . that your menstrual cycle will be regular after such a long period of absence. It'll take a few months for it to become regular again.

Redefining the change

T: Listen, has this changed your feelings about yourself at all? The way you perceive yourself?

P: Well, no, I mean, lately . . .

T: Things had already been going well for a while.

P: Yes. Except some times, when someone says something wrong and I start thinking about it, but I can take it . . . I get nervous for a moment maybe, but I can take it.

T: Listen, did you have a family feast, did you celebrate the event (*he smiles*), or did it just go by?

P: No, my parents weren't there. I was at my boyfriend's house. I went to the beach. I don't know, maybe the sea air was good for me . . .

T: Or the fact that you were relaxed and, as we discussed, recently . . .

P: Well, I wasn't exactly relaxed . . . I did have a few crises those days. I was a bit nervous . . .

T: No, maybe I didn't express myself right. I wasn't talking about relaxation in a general sense, but about your relationship with him. In the past couple of months there was the danger of that girl, remember?

P: (*smiles*)

T: You have, as they say, released a lot of your sensuality, right? That's very important.

P: What should I do now? Continue with everything?

T: Let's see. Please remind me.

P: Should I keep on weighing everything I eat?

T: Do you still need that? Lately you've been doing it just with your eyes, right?

P: Yes, when I was at the seaside without . . .

T: Without a scale. Good. We've reached the time when, as you rightly said, you've succeeded. I think so too, so from now on you can just weigh with your eyes, OK?

P: (*nods*)

Final prescription: "as if" she had never had the problem

T: Weigh with your eyes, and let everything go. In fact, you should ask yourself "what would I do now if there had never been anything wrong with me?"

P: But what should I do to avoid getting fatter?

T: I think you've already discovered that in the past month, haven't you? And the month before. If you eat regularly, you'll neither gain nor lose weight.

P: So I basically just need to follow the same programme.

T: More or less

P: Making a rough estimate with my eyes.

T: Exactly.

P: So always lunch a certain way, dinner a certain way, and the transgression . . .

Let things go

T: That's right, the transgression—or change things around. Right now, you see, this thing needs to become more and more spontaneous, OK?

I believe that what you've been constructing all these months will come spontaneously now. The important thing is that you mustn't feel that you need to control everything. Let things go. You know, when you repeat an exercise for so many months, we start doing it spontaneously.

P: (*nods*)

T: You don't need to control and think "I have to do the same things". They'll come to you. You don't need to control the same things. Are you touched?

P: (*nods as she cries*)

Encouragement to achieve personal autonomy

T: Good. That's very good for you. And you've worked so hard to get to this point, haven't you?

P: I didn't think so.

T: You didn't think you'd have to work so hard, or you didn't think you'd make it?

P: I didn't think I'd make it.

T: And instead you've been very good. Did you notice how your boyfriend has responded to all this? Now he's got the pleasure of having an entirely female girlfriend.

P *smiles.*

T: . . . and not a half female. Right? I'm very happy with you. So, from now on the main question is "How would I behave if there had never been anything wrong with me?". OK? In all areas. Let's start enjoying life, as they say. OK?

P: So I close now and forget everything that's been.

T: Well, you know you can't make yourself forget. You will, though. Ask yourself . . .

P: Sometimes I even feel nostalgic!

T: Yes, but now ask yourself "How would I behave if there had never been anything wrong", all right? Listen, at this point I'd like to see you again in three months, all right? If there's any problem, the door's always open. If you have any doubts, call me. No problem.

P: It's just that my parents are mad at me for exercising. I told them . . .

T: Did you tell them I said so?

P: Yes, but they told me . . .

T: And look, you're relaxed, you're calm, so tell them to be quiet!

P: They say they don't need to call you, because they want to trust me.

T: Good.

P: Then they saw that I'd bought some exercise equipment and got annoyed with me.

T: Well, you know, if everything proceeds normally, as it has, they won't be annoyed with you any more. OK? If this kind of situation continues, call me and I'll have you all come and see me together, OK?

P: (*smiles*)

T: And we'll have a good talk with the whole family, but without asking them to come in as a punishment, all right? But I don't think so; since you've returned to the world from a physical standpoint and everything's going well, it only does you good to exercise.

P: And I don't do it the way I used to.

T: The important thing is to avoid reducing your food intake again. Everything is going well, OK? Please give them my warmest regards. I won't give you an appointment now, because in three months, obviously . . . you'll call me and we'll set an appointment, all right?

P: But do you guarantee that I've succeeded?

T: I really think so. The important thing now is to act as if nothing had ever happened. All right? Congratulations! There are so many beautiful things to do in life. You've discovered some, right! There are so many of them.

P: (*in tears*) Thank you.

T: Goodbye.

CHAPTER FIVE

Bulimia: formation, persistence, change

> "If you allow yourself something, you can decide to do without it; if you deny yourself that thing, it will become irresistible"

The formation and persistence of bulimia

In the course of our research–intervention we found that, like anorexia, bulimia,[29] is characterized by distinctive, redundant modes of persistence and by a specific system of perception and reaction.

Like anorexics, persons suffering from bulimia tend to be very frail from the emotional point of view. However, while anorexics tend to be extremely sensitive, intellectually sophisticated, and self-controlled, bulimic women are usually less complex and have great difficulties in controlling their own reactions. Their basic system of perception and reaction is characterized by a tendency to binge eat, and to feel an immense enjoyment when doing so. As a consequence, they live in constant fear of losing control. Their prevalent attempted solution is not abstinence, but an effort to resist their food cravings. Paradoxically, the harder they try to control themselves, the stronger their cravings become.

Initially, the bulimic's compulsion to binge originates from the simple fact that eating is a very enjoyable experience; however, she gradually discovers that food can become a refuge from difficulties in other areas of life—particularly from her fear of being unable to control her own reactions. Binge eating then becomes a kind of functional adaptation to a reality that is perceived by her as unmanageable. Fat comes to represent a protection, especially in the context of interpersonal relations. Metaphorically speaking, most bulimic women fit the description of an artichoke, whose good, tender heart is protected by its coarse outer leaves. Similarly, the bulimic person uses her fat as a protective shell between herself and other people, as well as between herself and her own intemperance.

In the course of our experimental work, we have identified two main categories of bulimic subjects. We jokingly named them *Boterians* and *Yo-yos.*

The Boterian bulimic

This type of patient looks as if she has just stepped out of a painting by Botero. She weighs at least eighty or ninety kilos; her character is usually placid, calm, and seraphic. She is completely unable to stay on a diet. Subjects in this group are often diagnosed as suffering from chronic obesity and are treated with drug therapy or different types of surgery.

Most Boterians are aware of being "artichokes"—aware, in other words, that they have constructed a protective system for themselves after being scared by some experience—real or imagined—of losing control over their own impulses. They recognize that their relationship with food is a form of protection, and are conscious of their desire for uninhibited behaviour in other areas of life.

More rarely, we encounter Boterians who are unaware of the protective aspect of their disorder, and perceive food as a kind of "demon" by which they are possessed. They do not see any connection between their compulsion to eat and their inability to control themselves in other areas. Their rigid self-image is often based on a strong sense of morality that makes them feel guilty about their excesses and leads them to deny themselves pleasurable experiences in many other contexts.

Some authors of the dynamic school of therapy believe that the bulimic's denial of her own impulses can be linked to a denial of sexuality, as a consequence of traumatic childhood experiences (principally sexual abuse). Our research shows a different picture: according to our patients themselves, most did not experience any sexual abuse during childhood. They did, however, have normal erotic experiences (games involving bodily exploration between girls and boys). A form of moralistic bigotry has led them to consider such experiences very sinful. They have deep guilt feelings associated with their bodies. This rare type of bulimic is completely unaware of her own defence mechanisms; in addition to her eating problems, she has significant difficulties in all her relationships, especially with the opposite sex.

A third category of Boterians is formed by persons for whom the bulimic symptom has come to represent an irreplaceable form of pleasure. These persons tend to be seriously overweight. They are mostly women over the age of forty-five or fifty, who develop bulimic symptoms when their children move away from home, depriving them of their motherly role, into which they had invested much of their energy and sense of identity. Their relationships with their husband are also problematic: usually, the husband has a life outside the family, while the wife had invested everything into her relationship with the children and now finds herself alone in an empty nest. She often also shows signs of depression. Binge eating is for her a form of compensation—a way to fill time and spice up her life with surrogate pleasure.

As we shall see, we have found it necessary to construct an *ad hoc* intervention for this last category of Boterians in order to break the particular mode of persistence of these patients' system of perception and reaction.

Yo-Yos

Persons suffering from this most frequent type of eating disorder rarely see a psychotherapist. Their first solution is usually to consult a doctor of medicine or a dietician. The designation "yo-yo" refers to a category of bulimic women who tend to stay on a diet for a certain amount of time and subsequently lose control, continuously oscillating between their ideal weight and five or six kilos too many. Yo-yo bulimics lose weight every time they've gained some and gain weight every time they've lost some, in constant alternation between having and losing control. Perennially battling with diets, they never gain an excessive amount of weight, but manage to stay just a few kilos overweight.

In dealing with this type of eating disorder, we discovered that it is essential to intervene on the patient's dysfunctional attempts to control food intake as well as her attempts to control her lack of restraint. Like Boterian bulimics, most yo-yo bulimics are "artichokes" who become afraid as soon as they have lost some weight and start feeling the "dangerous" effects of desirability. They start eating again in order to reacquire a protective layer of fat between themselves and the rest of the world. Only a small percentage of yo-yo bulimics are unable to control themselves in both the realm of food and that of interpersonal relationships. As it is usually unnecessary to work on interpersonal problems, our interventions tend to focus exclusively on the subject's relationship with food.

Because of their particular system of perception and reaction, yo-yo bulimics are the most resistant to treatment. They have usually tried numerous other solutions before seeing a psychotherapist, and if they do not see any quick results, they immediately get discouraged and abandon the therapy before its completion.

Treatment of bulimia

For several reasons, we consider bulimia to be the easiest to treat of all the eating disorders. First of all, bulimic women are more cooperative and much less complicated than women suffering from anorexia and vomiting. Second, as we shall see, the main intervention that we have devised for this type of case has the power to unblock bulimic symptoms almost immediately. This intervention is usually applied at the beginning of the second stage of treatment. Third, the therapist can establish a very different type of relationship with bulimic patients than with anorexic or vomiting patients. With bulimic patients we can be much more directive, sometimes even harsh and seemingly merciless, and our therapeutic sessions are very short.

The treatment for bulimia can be either individual or mixed. Our interventions on Boterian bulimics generally include both individual and family sessions; our sessions with yo-yo bulimics are usually individual. The choice of treatment (individual *versus* mixed) always depends on whether the patient's family is attempting solutions that complicate the problem; for example, by trying to prevent her from eating, hiding food away, or buying only diet foods.

Treatment protocol for bulimia[30]

First stage (first/second session)

In the first session, the therapist needs to form a precise and concrete definition of the problem and the dysfunctional interactive system that maintains it. The therapist must also "capture" the patient by learning to speak her language and tuning into her logic and system of representation, a necessary condition for creating a climate of positive suggestion that will give us therapeutic power and enable us to overcome the patient's resistance to change. For example, the therapist might start the first session, by saying something seemingly offensive, like: "My, you really are a disgusting ball of fat! What in the world goes through your head when you look in a mirror, or when you walk around and feel all that fat bouncing up and down?"

Surprisingly, none of our bulimic patients has ever shown any anger or offence at this seemingly brutal remark. On the contrary, they feel that they have finally found someone who understands them—someone who sees things from their perspective, who sees them exactly as they see themselves, and has the courage to say so.

The therapist repeats this manoeuvre over and over throughout the first session and then reframes the situation as follows:

> You know, your urge to devour all that food is like an overflowing river. It can't be contained. So, if it can't be contained, we've got to let it flow out slowly. From now until the next session, please eat as much as you want. Let's see how much more weight you need to put on in order to start losing some. It's impossible to contain the flood; it's useless to try to stop it. It's as if you were possessed by a demon. All your efforts are useless. We can't stop a river from

overflowing. All we can do is let the water pass. Let's see how much more weight you need to gain before you can start losing some of it."

After this provocative intervention, at the end of the session, the therapist performs the first therapeutic manoeuvres. These are generally the same for all types of bulimia:

1. *The miracle fantasy;*
2. *The useful function of the problem;*
3. *Prescriptions to the family* (if it is a mixed intervention).

The miracle fantasy. We usually prescribe this fantasy to bulimics as well as to anorexics and vomiters. As we noted earlier, this manoeuvre is important both as a positive influence towards change and as an aid to the diagnostic examination, because it reveals the problem's secondary advantages.

Useful function of the problem. The following prescription is specific for bulimia:

> As I'm sure you already know, if something exists and persists over time within complex systems in nature, it must necessarily be playing an important role within that system—a positive role, or function. Otherwise, it would tend to disappear. Since we are natural beings, and it's becoming clear that our mind is a complex ecological system, everything that arises and persists within our minds must be performing some independent function, or have some positive use. Otherwise, it would have become extinct by now. Well, I wonder, what positive role or function might your disorder have within the natural, complex system that is your organism, beyond the suffering that it is causing? I want you to think once a day about what positive functions this problem might have for you—there must be some, because if it had no function, the problem would be extinct by now. Think about that once a day, for a few minutes, and bring me all your positive answers.

This manoeuvre (a version of the technique of *positive connotation of the symptom*) encourages the patient to find the positive uses of her problem, and essentially produces two effects: first, it tells the therapist what aspects need to be worked on in order to eliminate the *secondary advantages* that maintain the disorder. Second, as soon as the person starts to realize the positive and protective aspects of her problem, she will start fighting less against it, thus allowing it to decrease spontaneously in accordance with the ancient Chinese stratagem of "muddying the water in order to catch the fish".

Prescriptions to the family: When the patient's family is significantly involved in maintaining the disorder, and we can count on the participation of at least one family member (usually the mother), we usually prefer a mixed intervention. We often find that the patient's family is making numerous attempts to control the situation by hiding food, locking it away, buying only what is strictly necessary, etc. In many cases, it is the patient herself who asks them to do this. All such attempts only help increase the bulimic person's desire and compulsion for food.

In order to stop this retroactive, vicious circle that feeds the problem, we use a series of paradoxical prescriptions similar to those described earlier in our treatment for anorexics. The therapist asks the family to openly boycott all the young woman's attempts to start a diet by insisting that she eat, asking her if she has eaten enough, neglecting to hide the food, etc. This use of paradoxical logic interrupts the dysfunctional solutions attempted by the family, and completely reverses their usual attitude and behaviour towards the disorder.

Finally, if we wish to learn more about the patient's eating habits, we might ask her to keep a *food diary*, writing down everything she eats for at least a week. This intervention helps us find out how much and when she eats, and what her favourite foods are, enabling us to construct our successive manoeuvres without overly upsetting her eating habits and preferences. The food diary also has a therapeutic effect in itself. When associated with the other manoeuvres described here, it often contributes to a decrease in the person's habitual calorie intake.

In most cases, we observe a significant decrease in food intake already between the first and the second session.

Second stage (from the second/third session to the fifth session)

Our main intervention for bulimia is a paradoxical one, based on the logic of the Chinese stratagem of "putting the fire out by adding firewood". As we mentioned previously, the basic attempted solution that maintains the problem lies in trying to control the compulsion to eat, by enacting a series of restrictions that range from dieting to locking food away, and to avoiding any context that might present some temptation. These limitations have the effect of reinforcing the person's compulsion to devour food, making this compulsion more and more uncontrollable.

To reverse this attempted solution, the therapist uses the following paradoxical prescription, usually at the end of the second or third session.

> Of course I won't prescribe a diet, because you know a great deal more about diets than I do, and we both know that if I gave you a diet, you wouldn't be able to follow it. So please choose any eating programme you like. My only condition is that it mustn't be too restrictive. Eat what you want at meal times—just make sure you do what I ask you. From now until our next session, if you eat anything outside your diet, you must eat it five times. For example, if you eat one piece of chocolate, you must eat five pieces of chocolate. If you eat one piece of cake, you must eat five pieces of cake. So if you eat one, you eat exactly five, not one more nor one less. You may choose not to eat anything outside your diet, but if you do, you must eat five. So you either avoid eating that piece of food, or eat five.

This prescription usually has two possible effects: (a) the person never strays from her chosen diet, thus immediately acquiring an ability to manage and control that she never had before; (b) after "eating for five" a few times, she stops, because when binge eating is prescribed by the therapist, it is not as enjoyable as before. Only a few very resistant bulimic patients report that they "ate for five" all the time. Whatever the result, in the following sessions we multiply the amount of food eaten outside the diet by seven, nine, eleven, or fifteen, until this saturation process finally breaks down the symptom.

In some cases, we may not wish to leave the choice of a diet completely to the patient, and prefer to establish an eating programme together with her. In such cases, we usually suggest an eating programme that is not too strict, complicated, or restricted. We explain that in the first half of the day it is better to eat carbohydrates, because they are easily and quickly digestible and produce readily available energy. Protein, which requires more time to be digested, should preferably be eaten at night. We agree on a plan that includes a breakfast of milk or yogurt, fruit and carbohydrates (bread, biscuits, or croissants), a lunch consisting of any amount of vegetables and 100 grams of pasta or 80 grams of rice seasoned with olive oil, butter, tomato sauce, or vegetables; a fruit snack in the afternoon, and dinner consisting of any amount of vegetables, meat, fish, eggs, or low-fat cheese, and a slice of bread. If the patient eats anything outside the diet, we keep the rule that "if you eat one, you must eat five (or seven, nine, etc.)".

This paradoxical prescription is extremely effective. In approximately ninety per cent of our cases it has completely stopped the bulimic symptoms within a few sessions, This must surely be the swiftest, simplest, and most effective intervention in the field of eating disorders.

With those bulimic patients who express a strict sense of morality, our first manoeuvre employs some very provocative techniques based on analogies between food and sex. The therapist reframes the problem by presenting food as an erotic surrogate. Our aim is to play the bulimic symptom against the person's value system and moral convictions. The therapist spends the entire session gradually leading the patient to "discover" the analogy between food and sex.

> I want you to start thinking that when you eat without being able to stop, it's actually as if you were doing something else . . . doing something in the most transgressive, most perverse manner possible . . . Try to imagine that when you eat, you're actually doing something else—but I won't tell you what it is. I'll let you figure it out by yourself . . .

Once the patient realizes (often with a sense of surprise and shock) what the therapist has been hinting at, the therapist reframes the situation with the *fantasy of the gate.*

> From now until we meet again, I want you to avoid making any efforts to not eat. You'd keep on eating anyway . . . But every time you do it, think about it as if you woke up in the morning possessed by a irrepressible sexual urge, walked out on the street, and grabbed the first man you saw. It doesn't matter whether he's handsome or ugly: all you're interested in is sex. So you grab him and push him through a gate. Behind that gate, you have the most

> perverse, most transgressive, but also most pleasurable sexual experience imaginable, until you reach the highest point of pleasure. As soon as it's over, you walk away feeling guilty and dirty. For the rest of the day, you feel terrible—but the next morning, you wake up with the same uncontrollable compulsion. You go out and grab the first man you see, handsome or ugly, and do the same thing all over again, until you reach the highest pleasure. Then you walk away, feeling guilty.

This use of the reframing technique usually has a shattering effect. The mere thought of doing something of that sort completely blocks the patient's compulsion to binge eat. With this type of bulimic patient, it is thus essential to use provocative manoeuvres that pitch her sense of morality against her symptom, so that that "*ubi major, minor cessat*". If the symptoms do not disappear completely after this manoeuvre, we proceed with the paradoxical prescription "*if you eat one, you eat five*".

We also ask the patient's family to continue boycotting the patient's efforts to control her food intake throughout the second stage.

A different approach is required in treating the last category of Boterians. These are bulimic women over the age of forty-five or fifty, for whom eating has become an indispensable pleasure due to their family situation. The paradoxical prescription "*if you eat one, you eat five*" is often unsuccessful with this group, either because the patient is prepared to eat the quantity of food consumed outside the diet multiplied by fifteen, even twenty, or because she chooses not to follow the prescription at all, or to try to outmanoeuvre it somehow. Our research–intervention showed that these persons' system of perceptions and reactions is characterized by a sense of conflict between duty and pleasure, where any imposition of duty opens the door to some enjoyable transgression.

In most cases, these bulimic patients try to control themselves by eating only "good" (diet) foods and avoiding "bad" (calorie-rich) foods. However, this leads them to give in to temptation, and they end up binge-eating the "bad" foods as well as the "good" ones. If we suggest even minimal restrictions (as, for example, with the paradoxical prescription *if you eat one you eat five*), they generally respond with even greater transgressions. We must therefore lead them to abolish all eating patterns based on the distinction between "good" and "bad" foods, or on any sense of restriction and, above all, lead them to allow themselves a relationship with food conceived as pure pleasure, eating only what they really want. After eliminating all prescriptions that might suggest some kind of restriction, we encourage these patients to seek pleasure in food, and to enjoy it as much as possible, in a manoeuvre that we have called *the granting of pleasure*:

> From now until the next time we meet, I want you to avoid setting any restrictions on what you eat. On the contrary, try to eat anything you want, purely for your own enjoyment. You know, if I can allow myself to eat whatever I want, and especially if I try only to eat what I like the most, I'll no longer feel tempted. I won't feel like making transgressions, because I'm allowed to eat. On the contrary, if I set restrictions for myself, I'll want to overstep them. *If I give myself permission, I can do without it; if I deny myself permission, it becomes irresistible.* So, from now on, you need to do away with all prohibitions and allow yourself to eat only what you really like. Try to enjoy your food to the maximum. Avoid eating things you don't like just because they're "good", i.e., low in calories. Eat only for enjoyment. So this week you'll be doing something you've never done before: allow yourself to eat whatever you like and, I would add, *only what you like.* That's the best way to reach a balance.

It is essential to teach this type of bulimic to feel pleasure from eating, to allow herself to enjoy the food, in order for her to learn to control and manage it. Unless the therapist leads the patient to enjoy food even more thoroughly than before, there will be no change. When a disorder is based on an irresistible pleasure, change is possible only in favour of an even greater pleasure: "The limits of very pleasure lie in some greater pleasure". Therefore, we need to help the bulimic not only to allow herself pleasure, but to actively seek and progressively refine it, so that she can have a *corrective emotional experience* of concentrated pleasure.

This prescription usually has the effect of reducing the quantity of binges by seeking a higher quality of enjoyment. Again, according to the Chinese saying, we "sail the seas unbeknown to the sky". The benevolent concession that the bulimic makes to herself at the therapist's suggestion is a way to rebalance her relationship with food, so that her interaction with it may become one of pleasure, not duty. Usually, after a few weeks, these persons start eating with gusto, but in smaller quantities, and begin to lose weight.

By transforming a dysfunctional attempted solution (eating for pleasure) into a functional solution, the *granting of pleasure* responds to a real need in this type of bulimic patient. Thus, our intervention is not based on blocking and replacing attempted solutions, but on changing the direction of the existing attempted solution. In most cases, this very effective manoeuvre leads to a complete disappearance of the bulimic symptoms.[31]

The manoeuvres applied at the second stage usually unblock bulimic symptoms in a very short time. In ninety per cent of our cases, we achieve this result with the paradox *if you eat one, you eat five;*[32] in the remaining ten per cent it is achieved by our provocative use of the reframing technique with the *fantasy of the gate*, or by the *granting of pleasure*. Of course, this only represents the first step towards a complete solution of the problem.

Third stage (from the fifth/sixth session onwards)

At the third stage, the therapy proceeds in two directions: we work directly on the patient's relationship with food (a necessary step with all types of bulimics), and intervene on problems with interpersonal relationships (indispensable for "artichokes").

1. As far as the relationship with food is concerned, we must help the bulimic person to follow a balanced eating programme, proving to her that she can maintain her ideal weight by following a very varied and flexible diet that (very importantly) includes transgression. As described in the chapter on anorexics, we teach the patient about *the small disorder that maintains order* and prescribe *one small food transgression per day*: "A healthy balance is always based on some small disorder that keeps order: we need a small transgression in order not to lose control. If you succeed in allowing yourself a small transgression every day, this will enable you to stay in control over the rest."

It is very important to make the patient understand that eating a piece of chocolate or an ice cream does not jeopardize the results achieved, and that giving in to a small temptation is not equivalent to losing control. Therefore, the therapy does not end when the bulimic patient has acquired the ability to stay on a diet and lose weight, but when she is able to transgress without losing control. Only when she has learned to maintain an order that includes transgression can we say that the therapy is complete.

In this phase of the treatment of "artichokes", it is also essential to work on the patient's interpersonal relationships. For this category of bulimics, the final part of the treatment involves the reconstruction of relationships between the self and others, and between the self and the world, and particularly the patient's relationships with the opposite sex. To that end, the therapist uses reframing techniques and prescriptions aimed at solving her relational difficulties, encouraging her to allow herself some small pleasures and to experience relationships with the opposite sex without losing control. For example, the therapist might introduce the *artichoke metaphor*: "Think that until now you've been a splendid artichoke, protected by your fat. When you see an artichoke growing in a field, can you imagine that there's such a good heart inside that horrendous thing? No. You need to peel the artichoke in order to discover its heart. You've been protecting yourself just like that artichoke. We're peeling you now, drawing out your good heart. But you need to learn not to be scared in order to be able to manage it. Armours protect, but they eventually become a kind of prison, so you must now learn to live without your armour."

The therapist may also use the *as if* prescription, adapting it according to the patient's needs: "Every morning while you wash, get dressed, get ready for the day . . . I want you to ask yourself: 'How would I behave differently than usual *if* I felt secure in my relationships?' Choose the smallest, the tiniest of all the things you might do, and put it into practice. Every day, do one small but concrete thing *as if* you felt secure. Choose a different thing every day." Thus, the therapist gradually teaches the patient to allow herself some small forms of pleasure in interpersonal relationships as well as with food, without the fear of losing control.

It is important to emphasize that our intervention on the interpersonal sphere must normally come after unblocking the symptoms, which is our aim in the second stage of treatment. While the first change is occurring, the therapist must concentrate exclusively on that, without touching upon the secondary advantages or use of the disorder. Only after eliminating acute symptoms can we intervene on other aspects, otherwise we run the risk of a recrudescence of the symptoms.

There is one exception to this rule: in those rare cases (usually *artichokes*) where the bulimic symptoms are not decreased by the paradox *if you eat one you eat five*, it is necessary to work on relational problems first, by introducing the *artichoke metaphor* in the second stage and postponing any direct work on the patient's relationship with food to a later stage in the therapy.

Fourth stage (last session)

In the last session, we do the same as with anorexic patients: we redefine the new balance achieved, and end the therapy with incentives towards personal autonomy.

Clinical case example (bulimia)

Session one

Defining the problem

T: What is your problem?

P: It's obvious, isn't it?

T: Oh. "What you see is what you get?"

P: Yes. I'm on a diet, and my nutritional therapist has suggested that I get some psychotherapy. Otherwise, I might end up "playing the accordion" as usual.

T: As usual?

P: Yes. This isn't the first diet I'm on.

T: How did you find out about me?

P: From a friend of mine who came to see you for a different reason. She said "Go to him. He's good." So maybe you can help me. I'll give it a try and see.

T: We'll see, we'll see! So you've tried to lose weight several times before?

P: Yes. I even tried taking a kind of pill that reduces hunger, but hunger isn't the problem. The problem is wanting to eat, which is . . . which is different. Even if I'm not hungry, I still want to eat. I did lose some weight as a result of taking the pills, because I was eating less of course. But I was only eating the things I like, so my eating habits became completely unbalanced . . .

T: What do you like to eat most?

P: It goes in phases, but I especially like pizza, pasta, sweets . . . The less calorie-rich foods, as you can see!

T: The less calorie-rich!

P: Yes, "quote, unquote".

Investigating the patient's attempted solutions

T: Well, well, well. And how have you been trying to control yourself, until now? You've been taking pills, and what else?

P: When I feel good, I have no problem following the diet, but any kind of disappointment or frustration, or simply boredom . . . having emotions I don't want to have . . . is enough to throw me off track.

T: So those kinds of things make you start eating again every time.

P: Yes, that's usually what happens, because it's the only thing that gives me immediate satisfaction.

T: Oh. What kind of life do you lead?

P: A sedentary life.

T: OK, sedentary, but what kind of job do you do? Do you work, or not work, or study?

P: I work. I'm a clerk, so I sit at my desk, doing accounts. And since I work in a pastry shop . . .

T: That's fantastic!

P: My temptations are right there.

T: But do you work in the shop itself?

P: No, I'm in the office, but I'm surrounded: on one side there's the bar and the pastry shop, and on the other side there's the pastry kitchen.

T: Fantastic. You're really caught between two fires. I don't know which of the two is more tempting!

P: Yes. So . . .

Enquiring about the patient's family and social relationships.

T: Do you live by yourself or with your family . . .?

P: I live by myself. I've been separated for a year, and was in psychoanalysis for six months.

T: Was that because of your weight problems, or problems with your marriage?

P: It was because when I separated from my husband, I separated because of an identity problem. I didn't know who I was any more.

T: Hmm . . . Fun!

P: I didn't trust myself any more. I didn't know what I wanted, whether my behaviour was a kind of reaction, or whether it was really what I wanted. So I decided to go into analysis, After six months I found myself again, and stopped, against the analyst's advice.

T: Why didn't you go back to her instead of coming to me?

P: Because when I stopped, I lost faith.

T: Why?

P: I don't know. Maybe it's a kind of defence on my part. In any case, it happened at a stage when I was dealing with separations. I was beginning to understand what it meant to be separated from my family, and ended up separating from him, too. I made a bundle of everything! No, it was also that he went to England for a month, and when he came back I didn't want to be with him any more. We had two sessions where I convinced him, I mean informed him, that I didn't want to continue . . .

T: Do you like yourself the way you are?

P: No, obviously not. Otherwise . . .

T: And you're living alone now?

P: (*nods*)

T: Do you still have a relationship with your family, and with your ex-husband?

P: Yes.

T: Did you have the same problem when you were living with your ex-husband?

P: Yes. It increased . . . After I met him, my problem became enormous!

T: Really!

P: Yes. In the beginning, after two years of being with him, I put on twenty kilos in six months, because I had three jobs: I worked in a rotisserie-delicatessen. There too . . . for a whole year, I couldn't accept having a sexual relationship. It wasn't that I couldn't do it, because I did. I just couldn't accept it psychologically. I didn't feel OK towards my mother, because I had a very strict education. I wanted to be a virgin when I married, but there was no way. I felt very guilty, and it took a long time before . . .

T: How do you experience that part of your life now? Or are you not experiencing it?

P: No, I am!

T: I thought maybe you weren't.

P: That might be partly true, because actually I'm unable to let go, so it's not a complete experience.

T: Are you in a relationship now?

P: Almost, half a relationship. It's not well-defined. I mean, there might be a relationship but there's always something that comes in between.

T: What does that mean?

P: Technical problems, for example. I went to Egypt and got a big crush on a . . .

T: Oh. A dashing Egyptian?

P: Yes. I decided to have that relationship. I absolutely wanted it. Usually, it's the opposite with me. I play the rabbit and hide. Just as things were getting good, I found that I didn't have a condom. I'd left it in my suitcase. And the other night, I went out with this man, and it was about to happen, but I didn't have a condom again. I had left it at home. Then last night, I discovered one in my wallet. Do you think I didn't know it? I must have known it, surely! There's always something getting in the way!

Reframing the patient's fat as a protection against relationships

T: So it's not enough having the fat in the way!

P: That's right!

T: Is it a good safeguard?

P: Yes, there's a lot of skimming going on.

T: Oh . . . of course . . . I . . .

P: Yes. If somebody wants me, he has to want me a lot.

Artichoke metaphor

T: I usually call people like you "artichokes".

P: Why?

T: Because, like artichokes, you protect your beautiful, sweet, good heart with those spiky protective leaves. Fat is useful . . .

P: No, but it's a great . . .

T: It's a great armour, because the person who wants you has to love you for what you are and not because of your looks, right?

P: Right. But the problem is that even when they accept me, I don't accept myself.

Capturing the patient: using her logic and language

T: Of course, because you feel like a disgusting ball of fat.

P: Bravo! That's exactly it!

T: Well, you are a disgusting ball of fat. You're not so crazy to think so.

P: That's true. Otherwise I wouldn't be here.

T: Well, well, well. And now you're on a diet again?

P: Yes.

T: But are you able to resist diets?

P: What do you mean? Do you mean am I able to follow or to not follow them? Resist, how?

T: Are you resisting when you don't follow them, or when you do?

P: I resist . . .

T: Let me explain.

P: It's a difficult question to answer.

T: You've started a new diet now. How long do your diets usually last?

P: Oh, maybe even a year!

T: And do you usually lose weight?

P: Yes.

T: And then you put it all back on.

P: Yes, that's how it's been so far.

T: Every time. Have you ever managed to reach your ideal weight?

P: Yes, but never for more than a year.

T: How much weight would you like to lose?

P: Well . . . fifty-five kilos is my ideal weight.

T: And you weigh . . .?

P: A hundred and fourteen.

Use of irony

T: Oh. Congratulations.

P: Thank you.

T: So you would need to lose sixty kilos?

P: I'd like to get down to seventy-five.

T: Seventy-five?

P: Yes, because that's how I like myself.

T: You're pretty stubborn.

P: No, that's not true. It's not because I like myself physically at seventy-five. It's because when I reach sixty kilos, my face gets too thin and I have a complex about my chin.

T: Oh, OK.

P: So that would be the next problem.

More use of irony

T: From being a disgusting ball of fat to having a big chin.

P: Yes. (*She laughs*)

T: OK.

P: Seventy-five kilos is a good compromise. Do you think . . .

T: I think I understand enough about your problem to be able to say that I can help you, to get a change under way—in a short time, even. Obviously we can't lose weight that quickly, because there's a technical time frame.

P: Yes.

Agreement on the modalities of the treatment. Therapeutic double bind

T: But we can quickly start a change. However, I don't know how far you'll be able to follow me.

P: Why? Is it very complicated?

T: I don't know if the person who sent you here told you that I have some very peculiar methods. I don't make people talk a lot. I don't talk a lot. I give people things to do, and usually the things I ask them to do and think aren't very ordinary. They may seem illogical, banal, stupid, funny, or strange. There's nothing scary or menacing about them, but they must be carried out to the letter even if they seem strange. OK? And without asking any questions, because I always give my explanations afterwards. Moreover, I only give myself ten sessions to see if we get any results. If we get to the tenth session and see no results, I stop the treatment. I continue only if I see some results. If everything goes as usual, the problems will be solved by the tenth session, but I don't know whether that will be true in your case.

P: Is this a challenge?

First prescription: think about the artichoke metaphor

T: We'll see, we'll see. It was just a remark. I have two tasks for you, OK? One is simply this: I want you to think that you are a splendid artichoke, protecting yourself with fat. But you're also a ball of fat, rolling around . . . Think about that, at least once a day.

P: That's not difficult!

T: It's easy for you, isn't it? The next reasoning is a little bit more complex. As I understand it, you've had this problem for quite some time.

P: I think I've always had it.

Second prescription: usefulness of the problem

T: Well, as you know, every phenomenon that occurs in the natural world and persists for a long time must be fulfilling some function, some role, some use. Otherwise, it would disappear spontaneously, right? We are natural beings. Our mind is a complex ecological system, but it is still a natural system. Everything that appears and persists fulfils some function, some useful or positive role, otherwise it would disappear. Now, I ask myself, and you too: what might be the positive function of this problem for you? What advantages does it give you? Because, if we don't discover what this problem's role or positive function is, we won't be able to solve it.

P: But I know . . .

T: Think about it every day. Don't tell me now. Think about it every day, and bring me a list of all possible answers. All right?

P: All right.

T: The other thing I would suggest is a bit . . .

P: Oh, so there are three things then?

T: Well, the first was really . . . ball of fat, artichoke, well . . .

P: OK.

Third prescription: miracle fantasy

T: The third is a little bit more imaginative. From now until I see you again next week, I'd like you to make up a fantasy every morning while you wake up, get dressed, and put on your make-up. A magical fantasy . . . Every morning, I want you to imagine that, when you walk out of here, as you will today, and close the door behind you, as soon as the door has closed: "Puff!" By magic, your problem disappears, leaving no trace behind it. What would immediately change in your life? What other problems would you have to deal with right after this one? Think carefully. Every morning, imagine that you walk out of here, and as the door closes . . . "Puff!" Your problem magically disappears. What problems would follow? What would change in your life?

P: That would be a nice mess!!!

Session two

Redefining the effects of the prescriptions

T: How are things going?

P: Well, the first thing you told me to do was to tell myself that I'm an artichoke and a ball of fat. After three days, I called myself "a splendid ball of fat", and now I have to make an effort to say the other things. And I wrote the list . . . do you want to hear it all?

T: Yes.

P: I wrote . . . Let's see . . . First, the useful function of my behaviour, and by that I mean both eating and being fat . . .

T: What's the positive use of eating and being fat?

P: The positive use of eating is that is decreases my emotions.

Restructuring the protective role of fat through the "armour" metaphor

T: Oh, I like that. But who's wearing the armour? You're essentially anaesthetizing your emotions.

P: Yes, but not the positive emotions.

T: The negative ones?

P: Of course!

T: And what are the negative ones?

P: The negative ones are: anxiety, anger, anguish, tension before any kind of test, dissatisfaction, impatience, as well as fear of rejection, failure, and suffering.

T: Oh. And then?

P: And that's the way it is . . . also because, if I don't control them that way, one emotion leads to all the others, see? As for the fat . . . partly . . . though I don't usually have any problems talking to people any more, even men, even in a normal way, I still start from the premise that I won't be liked, so I feel neither free, nor in competition, nor . . .

T: You tell yourself "I can't afford anything".

P: Yes. That way, they won't misunderstand my intentions.

T: That's right. They take you for what you are.

P: Yes. They don't consider me at all, so I can play and do whatever I want.

T: Right, bravo! So again, it protects you.

P: Yes, and it also helps me deal with myself, in the sense that I use it to pull the brakes.

T: Against what?

P: I feel very vulnerable because, like everyone else, I like to be liked. I like to seduce and be seduced. I like skirmishing, sexual and otherwise. So I'm afraid that if I let go, I won't be able to control . . .

T: Who knows what would happen!

P: Yes, so what do I do? I put all this stuff in between!

T: I see.

P: What good does that do? If, on the other hand, I walked out of your office . . .

T: How did you feel after making such lucid reflections on the positive aspects of eating and staying fat?

P: I thought most of it was about avoiding pain . . . Then I realized that most of it functions at the level of sexuality.

More use of irony

T: Oh . . . You little pig!

P: Yes, more so than I thought. It's a big part—actually, the main part of it, especially if I think about "what if I didn't have this problem?"

T: I see. And if, "puff", by magic . . .?

P: Well, first of all I'd have to find a different way to relieve my tensions. Now that I'm on a diet, I need to find a different way, but we're assuming I've already found it, otherwise I couldn't just say "puff!" And I'd be able to feel some emotions . . .

T: Oh . . .

P: Any emotion, because I anaesthetize even positive ones.

T: So?

P: Very often now, I feel the urge to eat, and know there's something wrong, but I don't know which emotion is involved deep down. At that magic moment, I'd know exactly what the problem was, and that would be positive. I mean, I'd know what to do about it! Then I could go out whichever way I want. I'd have freedom of movement. I wouldn't seem clumsy. I could move, run, play, let people hug me without fearing that they'd feel all that disgusting fat. And I'd be desired, admired, courted by the men I like. But I would have to change my behaviour. Right now, I have no problem talking to anyone, but in that case, I'd . . .

T: Of course.

P: And that bothers me, because I like being free as I am now.

T: I see.

P: And I wouldn't have all that fat to protect me any more, and that's a big problem. Protecting me from myself, I mean. From myself. Because I know that what I'm saying makes no sense at the rational level . . .

T: That's true in terms of common sense, but at a more complex logical level, what you're saying makes a lot of sense.

P: Really?

T: (*nods*)

P: Well, in any case, I think that if, for example, I could get complete satisfaction from sex . . . what if I become addicted to sex?

T: Oh, dear.

P: Then I'd always need to have someone near me. And if I liked it a lot, which I assume I would, I'd become an amoral person. I mean, I'd be worse than a prostitute, and . . . this is what doesn't make sense . . . I can excuse a prostitute because she's doing it as a job, but not myself, because I'd be doing it for fun! See? The problem is that, even being fat, that kind of thing is increasing!

T: Oh, dear! Even while you're fat! So the fat doesn't really provide you with a lot of protection?

P: No.

T: It just forces you to choose unattractive men?

P: No, not just unattractive ones, because I am lucky. I always find attractive ones.

T: Oh!

P: The problem is that, afterwards, I don't let myself go, not even when I'd like to, so in the end it becomes an obstacle to the things I do want. And there's also the problem that, once you become attractive, you don't know whether they want you for yourself or for you appearance.

T: That's right.

P: And there's another thing. If I get rejected while I'm fat, I can always blame . . .

T: The fat! But otherwise, you can't!

P: Right.

T: What nice thoughts.

P: But the positive aspect would be that I'd feel more sure of myself and be less afraid of rejection.

T: Well, then, give me all your sheets of paper. I see that we're working well, so I want two things from you. The first one is a bit peculiar, but first I want to know how you behaved with food this week. Have you been eating more or less?

P: It was disgusting.

T: You ate even more than usual? You've been protecting yourself even more, right?

P: Yes.

T: Who knows where we'll get to before you start losing weight. Maybe we'll have to gain some more kilos before you'll want to lose weight.

P: No, don't say that!

First prescription: "If you eat one, you eat five"

T: It's possible. Now . . . between now and next week, I want you to choose one of your diets. Any diet, as long as it's not too restrictive, OK? So certainly no less than 1,000, 1,200, 1,400 calories . . . not less than that. OK? In any case, you know a lot more than I do about diets.

P: Sure.

T: I want you to prepare yourself as if you were to follow this diet. Any time you eat something that's outside the diet, if you eat one, you eat five. You could decide not to eat that piece of food . . . but if you do, you have to eat five of them. If you eat a sandwich that's not in the diet, you have to eat five sandwiches. If you eat one piece of chocolate, you have to eat five pieces of chocolate. If you eat a piece of cake, you have to eat five pieces of cake. Every time you break the eating arrangements you've made for yourself, you have to multiply what you eat by five. All right?

P: And you'll want to know what it was, right?

T: Yes. You'll tell me next time.

P: That doesn't seem like such a difficult task!

Second prescription: nightly letter writing

T: This one isn't. But here's the next one. Every night, before you go to sleep, the last thing I want you to do as you're resting on your pillow, is . . . get letter stationery, if you don't already have some . . . and write me a letter. Every night. It should start with "Dear Doctor". After that, you can write anything you like. Tell me about everything that's going on. When you've finished, sign, seal the envelope, and bring me all your letters next time.

P: OK.

Session three

Report on the past week. Redefining the effects of "If you eat one, you eat five"

T: How did things go this week?

P: They went well.

T: What does "well" mean?

P: I lost some weight.

T: Lost weight? Really? Should I get scared?

P: No.

T: How much weight did you lose?

P: Two kilos.

T: Two kilos in one week?

P: Yes, but I had gained one kilo the week before, so I really just lost one kilo.

T: Hum. Well, well. I was naïve when I suggested eating five times for each one. So, did you change your mind afterwards?

P: Yes. As soon as I walked out of here!

T: (*laughs.*) Really? Why?

P: Because you've ruined it for me!

T: I've ruined it for you? How did I do that?

P: Yes. . . because . . . there's usually a pleasant rhythm to it, which I enjoy immensely . . .

T: I can imagine!

P: . . . And now you've ruined it for me.

T: How?

P: Because every time I wanted to eat something, I had to imagine eating five of the same thing! In the end, the pleasure didn't match the price I had to pay . . .

T: Oh.

P: Because if I gain one kilo from one portion of *mascarpone* that I really want, it's worth it, but if I have to gain three kilos from eating three extra portions that I don't want, then no, it's not worth it!

T: Fine. How many times did you have to eat multiplied by five? Did it ever happen?

P: Once.

T: Only once?

P: Yes.

T: The first time?

P: Yes, because I figured it all out on my way home, so I had it all figured out. I was really mad at you because you'd ruined it for me.

T: Oh. Mad at me? Did you curse me?

P: No.

T: Why not? Curses prolong life.

P: It was a forlorn kind of anger. I mean, I can't let you ruin the only thing I enjoy! I was mad at you in that sense.

T: When you had to multiply your intake by five, what food did you eat?

P: In the morning, I was talking to the pastry chef. He was using some almonds. Without thinking, I took five almonds and started eating . . .

T: Five almonds . . .

P: Yes, five. Which was what I wanted at that moment. But then, as I put the first almond in my mouth, I remembered the number five . . . I felt like strangling you.

T: So did you eat five?

P: No, I ate five times five: twenty-five.

T: Excellent!

P: Don't think I hadn't devised a loophole . . .

T: I can believe that. But I had warned you, remember? Twenty-five!

P: Twenty-five. But it was so . . .

T: So . . .?

P: I mean, having to eat something you don't want isn't pleasant at all. It's a big constraint. And since then, I felt persecuted by this rule. I mean, every time I wanted to eat something, I immediately imagined five of them and thought " I don't want to eat those things". But I still wanted that one portion. And I didn't feel like eating any more. The first two days, I felt incredibly deprived . . .

T: And then?

P: Then . . . I didn't even feel like eating anything . . .

T: Really?

P: Yes. In fact, in the letters I wrote you, I wrote: "Is it possible that I've already started associating desire to frustration, so I'm not even allowing myself to have any desires at all?"

T: We'll see.

P: That would be too easy. And there's another thing. Last night, I didn't feel like having dinner, because I had to go to a class and would have had to eat beforehand, and I wasn't hungry, and didn't feel like eating the same thing they were eating. I felt like having some biscuits with café au lait. But the biscuits weren't in my diet. It was one of the prohibited foods, and I didn't feel like eating twenty-five of the same kind of biscuits. In a few seconds, I changed my mind. I thought five biscuits with milk could very well replace dinner, and it wouldn't mean breaking my diet, so I ate them.

T: You gave yourself permission . . .

P: Yes.

T: Good.

P: And when I told my nutritional therapist, she said I did the right thing.

T: Very good.

P: Because when I told her about your prescription, she was afraid I might feel very frustrated, which she said would only make things worse. She said "There's a risk of ruining everything with that *eat for five* rule!"

Redefining the role of the dietician; avoid speaking about the therapy with the dietician

T: Yes, but the nutritional therapist should stick to her own job.

P: No, but then she said I had the right reaction . . .

T: Very well, but she needs to stick to her own job!

P: But she's happy with you.

T: I want you to avoid speaking with her about the things I make you do.

P: All right.

T: Because people who aren't really familiar with my work . . .

P: I had to tell her, because if I gained weight . . .

T: For those who aren't really familiar with my work, it may seem very bizarre and illogical . . .

P: Yes, but she's heard of you.

T: All right, but even a passing comment might . . . Do you understand?

P: Oh . . . I understand. All right.

T: So tell her that I'm happy to collaborate with her, but my job is my job, and you need to avoid speaking about it. We'll observe the results.

I should tell you that many people who only know me through my books interpret them in their own way.

P: OK, I'll stay mute on this subject.

T: Fine. So there's been what we might call a small magical effect.

P: Yes, I've been able to control my urges.

T: You've lost two kilos . . .

P: I also had many dreams. I wrote them all down for you.

T: What did you do concretely, aside from dreaming, in your emotional–romantic–erotic life?

P: (*laughs*) Well . . . that's something I didn't write about.

T: You didn't?

P: I've fallen in love—at first sight.

T: Wow! But have you made a conquest?

P: No, I just fell in love at first sight, because I didn't think . . . I mean, I felt a bit lost, honestly, because I saw this person where I work, and just stood there, watching him. He noticed . . . I could neither bring myself to say something, nor move away from there . . . I mean . . .

T: (*laughs*) You stood in his way . . . "You'll have to leave over my dead body!"

P: No! I was behind the counter, so . . . I mean . . . I could stand there as much as I wanted, but you can't keep staring at a person . . . and with that expression on my face . . . I can imagine . . . and without saying a word. I could see there was a questioning look on his face: "What do you want? Tell me!" But I wasn't telling, until he broke the ice and said "Hello!" and I said "Good morning", although it was evening. I was happy, because I felt the same thing in Egypt last January, for that person I had a sort of love story with . . .

T: The handsome African!

P: Yes.

T: Good. And now what are you going to do? Are you going to pursue this fellow?

P: No.

T: Good.

P: I don't know . . . it depends how I'll behave when I see him . . . If I feel paralysed, then I won't. I mean, it's useless for me to pursue him.

"Go slow" technique

T: Stop! Slow down! Let's not go too fast! What do you think I'm going to ask you to do now?

P: I can almost guess. Please, tell me!

First prescription: continue writing letters at night

T: I want you to continue writing me letters about everything, including dreams, fantasies, and the things you do . . .

P: About anything?

Second prescription: "If you eat one, you eat seven"

T: Anything. You may even curse me if you wish . . . write anything. You can even pretend that I'm naïve, but you must write. As for food, if you eat one you eat seven: no more, no less. You could choose not to eat that item, but if you eat it, you have to eat seven.

P: Things I don't want to eat!?

T: That's right. I mean, not things you don't want . . .

P: But of the things I'm not supposed to eat.

Reframing with "small disorder that maintains the order"

T: Right. You set up your own eating system. You can include one small disorder now and then, like you did last week, as long as it's a disorder that maintains the order, just as five cookies with milk replaced your dinner the other night. That was perfect! Now, a diet doesn't have to be torture. A good eating system must include pleasure, otherwise it's not a good eating system, especially for a little hog like you. You can't take it if there's no pleasure in it. Aside from that, you know a lot more about diets than I do. But if you eat anything outside the diet, you have to eat seven times as much. You can choose not to eat it, but if you eat one you eat seven. All right?

P: Easy!

T: You said that last week too!

P: Well, five or seven sounds pretty much the same to me.

T: Good.

At the following session, the patient reported that she had never multiplied her eating "by seven" and that she was steadily losing weight.

Binge eating

The binge eating disorder requires a different approach. Binge eating is another example of specialization in the field of eating disorders, because it does not fit into the other categories. We consider binge eating as a separate disorder that has evolved from bulimia. It is much less common than other types of eating disorders: in our research–intervention, we only encountered ten cases (five per cent).

Binge eaters alternate long periods of abstinence and hyper-controlled diets with more or less extended periods of intensive transgression, when they abandon themselves to the pleasure of bingeing. The bingeing (which may or may not be followed by vomiting) is generally concentrated within a limited amount of time, followed by another long period of "punishment" and fasting. Then the cycle starts again.

The perceptive–reactive system of persons suffering from this disorder is, thus, based on continuous switches back and forth between fasting and bingeing, controlling and losing control. These persons' ability to maintain control is, indeed, so successful that it cannot be kept up for more than a certain amount of time, after which they lose control. This prolonged abstinence from food and continuous effort to exert self-control always leads to a subsequent loss of control. This is yet another example of an attempted solution that complicates the problem.

To unblock these symptoms, we have devised a reframing manoeuvre similar to that of the *fear of help*, previously applied to phobic disorders (Nardone, 1993). In other words, we reframe the *fear of fasting*:[33] "When a person considers herself fat, she often thinks fasting is the best way to lose weight. '*The more I fast, the more weight I'll lose*', she thinks. But this common-sense logic does not take into account some rather strange effects that happen to all of us—for example when we abstain from food for a whole week and then lose control and start bingeing. Although fasting and abstaining from food may *seem* to be the best solution, it actually turns out to be the best way to construct a huge binge. What tends to happen is that a person makes an incredible effort not to eat and then spoils it all in a single moment. Not only does she spoil it all; she ends up eating extra calories and getting even fatter. What I want you to think about is that you need to be *afraid of fasting*, because every one of your fasts opens the door to yet another binge. When you abstain from eating, you're doing nothing but preparing the next binge. If you fast for a period of time and then start bingeing again, you absorb much more of the food you eat, so you don't lose any weight that way. I agree that you need to get thinner, but I want to find a way for you to do that *and* learn to maintain your ideal weight. The best way to avoid bingeing would be to avoid fasting while keeping your eating levels slightly lower than necessary. That would enable you to lose weight gradually, until you reach your ideal weight. So you must start thinking that *fasting is dangerous*. It's something to be avoided, because whenever you fast you end up bingeing, which makes you gain weight instead of losing it. The solution you've adopted doesn't work; in fact, it makes things worse. I know you can do this. Just consider that every time you feel like starting a fast, you're actually preparing your next binge, and that the best way to avoid bingeing is to avoid fasting."

This manoeuvre reframes fasting (which these patients consider to be a great feat) as the very thing that brings on their dreaded binges. The patient's perception of the problem is, thus, completely reversed: the attempted solution (fasting) is redefined as dysfunctional, ominous, and dangerous. This manoeuvre is extremely effective for this type of pathology, because it retraces the patient's tendency to control, but redirects that tendency *against* the symptom. In other words, the *fear of fasting* uses the patient's controlling tendencies against the dysfunctional control. The same thing that used to make the patient adopt a pathological behaviour (bingeing) is now restructured as something that will lead her to a more healthy kind of behaviour, i.e., allowing herself to eat in order to avoid bingeing.

Following this reframing manoeuvre, most patients start eating regularly again without being directly requested to do so, because they now see allowing themselves to eat as something that will enable them to control what they dread the most—bingeing.

Clinical case example (binge eating)

Session one

In the following exchanges P is the patient, T is the therapist, M is the patient's mother, F the patient's father, S is the patient's sister, and CoT is the co-therapist.

Defining the problem

T: Please sit down! I'm pleased to meet you. I'm Dr Nardone. So, what brings you here?

M: My daughter has problems with anorexia and bulimia. We haven't been able to help her, so we've come to you.

T: Could you please give me a detailed description of her problems? Afterwards, we'll decide whether it's better that you stay or wait outside.

M: About a month ago, I noticed that she was losing weight very fast. A friend of mine kept telling me that her own daughter was losing weight and vomiting . . . She told me "Be careful, because it could be the beginning of anorexia." I paid attention, noticed that the bathroom was full of stains, and started to understand the problems. It's been a crescendo.

T: Since one month?

F: No, more than a month. A couple of months.

M: Then she missed her period.

F: We've also noticed that she's sad. She's noticeably depressed.

T: Has she lost many kilos in a short time? How many kilos has she lost?

M: Seven kilos, right? (*Turns to her daughter*)

F: More. Eight or nine kilos.

Investigating the family's attempted solutions

T: (*To the patient*) You've been good! (*To the parents*) How did you react? What did you do to try to help her when you found out?

M: First of all, I took the bathroom keys away.

T: Oh. She could have vomited somewhere else!

M: I know. Of course, she could have vomited in a plastic bag.

T: Outdoors.

M: Then we talked about it with her. I prayed to God, because these kinds of things are serious.

T: And what transpired from your talks with your daughter?

M: She partly admitted that she was doing this.

F: Because it doesn't depend on her, doctor. It's a conditioned response, really. She told me: "Dad, it just happens to me."

M: She recently wrote me a letter asking me for help. I wanted her to see someone who could help from the very beginning. I would have brought her to you immediately, but logically she has to want to get well . . .

T: OK. Your daughter has told you it doesn't depend on her. What did she tell you?

F: Practically, Doctor, it's beyond her control . . . sort of . . . against herself.

T: A kind of rapture that takes over, something irresistible that you have to do . . .

P: As if I had two different personalities.

M: I've brought you a letter she wrote me. If you think it might be useful—if you want it . . .

T: That letter was addressed to you. Let's avoid . . .

M: No, not to me specifically. She was asking me for help.

T: What did you do?

M: I bought some books to try to understand more, and those books perfectly described the state she was in. I tried to tell her that she needed some external help. And . . . sometimes, she eats and eats and eats, without really tasting the food.

T: How often does that happen? Every day? Several times a day?

M: No, no, no. She's afraid of getting fat, basically, and since she has a strong character, she manages . . . but when she starts, it's the end. She starts eating and gets very sick.

T: (*To the patient*) What's your name?

P: C.

Investigating the functioning of the symptom

T: So, C, if I understand this correctly, if you manage to stay away from food, that's fine, but if you lose control you have to vomit. Right?

P: (*nods.*) And apart from that, I just can't stop eating. Like two plates of pasta, and everything I can find—milk, biscuits . . .

T: Until you've cleaned out everything?

P: Until there's nothing left to eat.

T: OK, but does this happen every time you eat, or only when you lose control?

P: Well, when, like, my mother says "Eat this, too!", then I say "OK, if I eat this, I'll eat it all." I can't control myself. I can't tell whether I'm full or not.

T: Does this always happen or are there some things that you're able to eat without vomiting?

P: No, I can't.

T: You can't?

M: No, but she can. She can, now.

T: What are you able to eat without having to vomit?

P: Well . . . meat, vegetables, milk . . .

T: And exactly what foods make you vomit? Sweets, pasta, carbohydrates?

P: Pasta.

T: What about pastries and sweets?

P: Well, chocolate too.

T: But if you eat only meat and vegetables, you don't vomit?

P: No.

T: But in order to lose eight kilos in two months, you must have eaten very little?

P: Yes.

T: That means very little meat and vegetables.

M: She has an iron deficiency.

P: No, it's that sometimes, when I was sick, I mean, I only had breakfast and that was it. I didn't eat anything else, not even at night.

F: In any case, we need to mention that you've only recently discovered meat and vegetables.

M: Yes, only very recently.

P: I'm talking about now. I used not to eat them..

M: Since we had some tests done, and it turned out that her iron blood-count was very, very low.

P: I used to vomit all the time. Whenever I had meat, I used to vomit it!

T: OK, but since when have you been eating meat without vomiting? Since recently?

P: Yes. I've gained one or two kilos, but that's because I've been eating meat . . . fruit in the mornings, and . . . milk.

Investigating the dominating system of perception and reaction

T: What's danger number one for you now? Is it gaining weight, or this uncontrollable eating and vomiting that happens to you?

P: Both.

T: OK.

P: Not vomiting any more, because I've learnt that I mustn't vomit, but I feel really sick, as if my stomach were swelling . . .

T: In the past week, how many times have you binged and vomited?

P: Three times, but without vomiting.

T: Three times in one week you've binged but not vomited. Three times . . . But what do you do after bingeing? Do you fast for a long time?

P: Well . . . I do eat less.

Reframing the attempted solution of fasting as the thing that sets off bingeing

T: So you tend to fast, or to slow down a lot, so that the urge to eat will increase, right? And you end up bingeing again. If you vomit, the urge to eat immediately increases. If you fast, it lasts for one, two, or three days, and then you binge again. So actually, your temporary solutions for solving the problem are actually the very things that maintain the problem.

P: Hmm.

T: But both fasting and vomiting inevitably lead you back to bingeing. So those would be the first things we need to try to change. Otherwise you'll stay a victim of the bingeing and vomiting, or maybe just the bingeing, and then you have the problem of gaining weight. Do you have an ideal weight in mind?

P: Well, yes.

T: What is it?

P: Forty, forty-one kilos.

T: How many kilos would you still like to lose?

P: No, but . . . I mean, I had reached that weight, but they told me I was too thin.

T: Who told you that?

P: Oh, a lot of people. They told me I was too thin, so . . . but . . . I mean . . . sometimes . . . I think that's what *they* think.

T: But if you look at yourself in a mirror, C, do you see yourself as being fat?

P: Well, I don't think I'm as thin as people say. Not at all.

T: But does the fact that you don't see yourself the way others see you make you think they're mistaken, or that there's something wrong with you? What's your judgment?

P: I don't know, because . . .

T: But what's your immediate reaction?

P: That they're telling me that because . . . Who knows? I don't know why they do it!

T: But you think "I'm right, they're wrong!" OK. Fine. Now (*to the parents*), what are you trying to do about food?

M: (*shaking her head*) I'd like her to . . .

Investigating the family's attempted solutions

T: Do you insist that she eat?

M: Well, I insist on the right things. I'd like her to eat a good-sized piece of meat, some fruit, everything that . . .

T: You keep after her a lot, right? (*To the patient*) How do you feel about your mother keeping after you so much?

M: It annoys her.

T: (*to the patient*) Does it annoy you?

P: (*nods*)

F: That's why I avoid forcing her, because that makes her go too far.

P: Also because, as soon as they take me out to lunch, I lose control and eat loads of food.

T: Oh, because you do like food after all, we know that.

P: I keep eating the whole afternoon, but . . . without enjoying it. I mean, I can't tell when I'm full.

T: Of course, of course. We understand how it works. Good. So you try to insist that she eat.

M: Like any mother would.

T: Aha.

F: I avoid it . . . but my wife takes care of that.

T: (*to the father*) What she does is sufficient. What about you? How do you intervene?

F: I try to be available to her, and she knows it. I'm very close to her, and try to . . . "C, you've got thinner and thinner for the past year. Look at this part of your body." Without exaggerating, because I don't like to exaggerate. Her mother's different.

Investigating the family system

T: I understand. Now, do you make up the whole family, or are there any other members?

M: We have three daughters. One is married, with three kids, and one that we're on bad terms with.

T: Oh! How so?

M: She's twenty-five years old. About six months ago, she had a minor argument with her father, and hasn't been living with us since.

F: She speaks with her father through her mother . . .

T: (*to the patient*) Is she also in conflict with you directly, or only with them?

M: Oh yes.

P: She hates me.

T: She hates you? And do you hate her?

P: No. I mean . . .

M: (*to her daughter*) Maybe it's more anger on her part. Right?

P: I never hated her. Now I've said "enough"!

T: Have you done anything to try to mend your relationship with your other daughter?

M: Yes!

T: But it hasn't worked?

F: No. Our relationship . . .

M: With you . . . (*to her husband*). With me, at first she was . . . At first she had a conflict with her father for several months. She had a better relationship with me, but now . . .

F: But I think we should tell the professor that this conflict started because of her jealousy towards her sister, and it's . . . it's terrible. She (*looking towards his daughter*) was born eight years after her sister. She came, and the other one was the big girl. Like an only child . . .

M: An only child . . . And the second one came after a still-born girl, so all our attention was focused on her.

F: You see, this child has suffered a lot because of it. Last summer, her sister discovered that some money was missing. She said "With all these friends of C's coming into our room... taking this and that." That's what sparked off our . . . our argument. Much later, we discovered that a dear friend of C's had been stealing things. I had defended

C so strongly that I put myself against the others. It's unbelievable. I don't know whether it was that friend who took the money . . . All I know is that some of C's things were missing . . .

P: I discovered that some of my things were missing. I saw her [take them] with my own eyes, but I didn't see her taking my sister's money.

F: Of course, we can't be sure of it!

P: G always keeps her wallet on her, so . . .

F: When our other daughter found out, it got worse: "See, I was right!" So, at age twenty-five, she said "Dad, I'm twenty-five and want to live my own life. I want an apartment." We're dividing part of our home to make her a small apartment. So she's out of the house, but it's as if she were still in there.

T: Not really out.

M: In the same building.

F: I should mention that she's a very serious student. Neurotic, of course, considering the times we live in . . . So that's what happened between the sisters. Of course, she's suffered from it . . .

T: Right, of course. And it's as if it were her fault (*looks at the patient*).

F: Yes, and she feels like it's her fault, when it isn't.

T: Now, what do you do in life?

M: I stay home.

T: You're at home. And what about you?

F: I used to work, but now . . .

T: So you're both very focused on your children?

M: He still does a lot of administration . . .

T: But at the moment you're even more focused on them than usual. (*To the patient*) Do you feel that you have a good relationship with your parents, or that they keep you under observation a bit too much?

P: Sometimes there's a bit too much observation, but maybe my family is the only place where I feel safe.

Inquiring about the patient's life outside the family

T: What's your life like outside the family?

P: Well, I used to like going out with my friends, but now I've lost all my energy.

F: She's lost her gaiety.

M: And she's always been such a joyful person.

P: I mean, I remember that I used to argue with them because I wanted to go out . . . Now things have changed, and I don't want to go out any more. I don't want to do anything.

T: On the contrary, other people are always telling you to go out.

P: Yes, my friends are always saying "come out with us", but I don't want to go out.

CoT: Since when?

P: A month and a half, two months.

T: Well, well, well. Now . . .

P: Another strange thing is that my school grades have changed. I used to get Ds and Fs; now I have all Bs.

T: Of course, because you're at home all the time!

M: She doesn't study.

P: Not at all.

T: But you pay a lot more attention!

M: That's true. She studies in the classroom.

T: Good.

P: When I get home I eat. In the afternoon I go for walks, because walking helps me relax. Then I go to the gym. In the evening I fall asleep at 8:30 and don't accept any phone calls.

T: What do you do at the gym? Aerobics, I suppose?

P: Aerobics, gymnastics, exercises.

T: OK. How many hours a day?

P: One hour, but I don't go every day.

M: She'd like to go every day. Right? (*To her daughter*)

T: And when you don't go to the gym, you walk?

P: Sometimes I stay home, because I fall asleep.

Agreeing about the modes of treatment. Therapeutic double bind

T. Fine. We've found out enough to be able to tell whether we can do anything to help you. I think this case is within our competence. I think we can help you—relatively fast, even. But I don't know to what extent you'll be able to follow us. I'll explain why . . .

M: It all depends on her, not us.

T: A fundamental aspect of my work are the things I ask people to do in between sessions. The things I ask may seem strange, sometimes banal or illogical. But they must be carried out faithfully. I always give explanations, but later. OK? Another rule is that I only give myself ten sessions, not one more. If I don't see any results by the tenth session, I stop, because if my methods aren't working, at least I want to avoid becoming an accomplice in maintaining the problem. If we see that things have changed and improved by the tenth session, but that we haven't finished, then obviously we continue. If everything goes as usual, the situation will have improved or be completely solved by the tenth session. But, I repeat, I don't know whether that will be true for you. One question: what made you decide to come to me?

M: Well . . . I asked around, everywhere. I asked a friend of mine in Rome, at the Istituto Sacro Cuore, if there was anyone there. I heard Professor . . . speak on television about different treatment centres. There's a centre in P too, but I wanted something reliable. I spoke to a cousin of mine, a friend of . . ., and she looked for information, and that's how we ended up here.

First prescription to the family: "conspiracy of silence" and "observe without intervening

T: Good. Then we'll start today, by giving you some things to do between now and next time we meet, OK? As I've already warned you, these things may seem strange, against common sense. But, you know, as we work on pathological problems that may seem irrational, but actually have a rationality of their own, a different logic than usual, we need to make use of that logic, or we won't be able to solve the problems. So what I'm about to ask will seem strange, but please trust in what we've said so far. You must carry them out faithfully. I need two things from you parents, and from the sisters, if they come to the house. The first thing is that we need to form a conspiracy of silence around C's problem—that's the opposite of what you've been doing up to this point You must avoid speaking about it. In fact, you must think that every time you talk about it, it's like pouring a special fertilizer over a plant. It makes it grow. It makes it important. So you need to *be afraid* of speaking about it. All right?

M: All right.

T: The other thing is that you must avoid making any suggestions regarding food. No "eat this" or "eat that". On the contrary, you must completely avoid nagging her, telling her what and how much to eat, because doing that just adds another element that can make the problem persist, instead of leading to an improvement. I know it's very difficult for a mother to watch her daughter sit at the table and not eat . . . or when she doesn't even come to the table . . . without trying to intervene. I know it's the most difficult thing I could ever ask you to do. But you've made a long trip to come here, and I can see that you've already worked very hard. You can do this too. In other words, first thing, we need to bring her back to the table. If you take on all responsibility, she won't come out of it. We may see some improvements or changes, but we won't see a complete remission.

The mother starts to cry.

T: I understand that it's legitimate to cry, also because I've asked you to do something very difficult, but I think you can do it. OK? So now I'm going to say something even harsher: if you feel like this sometimes, you have to avoid crying in front of C.

The father starts to cry. The therapist offers them both a tissue.

T: Otherwise, this can become yet another way of maintaining the problem instead of solving it. Because the more you feel guilty of her suffering, the more fragile you'll be, and the less able to resist certain temptations in one direction or another. The first thing to do is to establish a measure of serenity in dealing with the problem, OK? Please keep in mind that that is the first and most important step towards helping her . . .

M: Please tell me something that can me better too, because with all these problems and those with my other daughter, I think my nerves have . . .

T: Reached the limit.

M: I think I'm pretty strong . . .

The father cries again.

T: Well, you're going through a critical period, with one daughter refusing to be part of the group because she senses some injustice, another daughter with acute symptoms, the father in a crisis, you in a crisis. So the first step is to get everyone back on their feet again, OK? There's another thing we have to ask you. Would it be possible for you to bring your other daughter next time?

M: Yes, that might be possible, if you believe in miracles.

Adopting the sister's language to persuade her to attend one session

T: I'd like the whole family to be here next week. Tell her I asked for it, and that it's something I require only once, because in order to change the family's rules, it's useful for me to see the whole family. I'm sure she'll accept if you tell her to come because after observing you, I've decided that I need to see you all together, because in my opinion the problem lies in the existing patterns of communication patterns between family members. It's like telling her she's right, for once, even if it isn't so, to make her come here. I think it's important for your other daughter, too.

F: Do we all have to come, or [. . .]?

Second prescription to the family: broadened version of the "anthropologist's task"

T: I need to see the whole family first. If she needs any explanations, please call me and I'll talk to her. All right? In the meantime, I want all of you to do the following homework. Each of you should get a pocket-sized notebook and amuse yourselves by observing the others' behaviour and attitudes, as if you were my colleagues in a way, observing what the others are doing. So I'd like you to write down your observations on your daughter and your husband, and you on your daughter and your wife, and you on your parents. All right? Obviously, write down the things that seem strangest to you. And bring all your observations to me. Good. When can I see you again? I usually give appointments once a week until I start seeing some improvements; then we decrease the frequency. How about in a week?

F: The same day?

T: No, we always change.

M: It's a bit of a problem with her school.

T: When would be good?

P: How about the eighth?

T: Would 3 p.m. on the ninth work for you? Then I'll expect your notebooks with your observations. And please do what I've asked you, though it won't be easy. And you should do whatever you feel like. Avoid restricting yourself in any way, or pushing yourself in any direction. We want to see what happens spontaneously, OK? Otherwise, we won't know how to intervene. OK? Also because you've tried restricting yourself, and the more you restrict yourself, the more you want to do it.

Session two

Redefining the effects of the prescriptions

CoT: How have things been going?

P: Not so well. Mostly the same. Some days I fasted, some days I ate more than usual, I had some attacks without stopping myself. I don't know how to say stop.

CoT: And did you observe your parents and write . . .

P: Yes, I've been writing.

CoT: Did you bring your notes?

T: Is the whole family here? Your sister too?

P: Yes, but I'd prefer to speak with you alone, because my mother gets upset, and I feel uncomfortable talking because she feels really bad about all this, worse than me.

T: Oh, oh. Did your mother go away when she felt like crying this week, as I prescribed, or did she do it in front of you?

P: No, she didn't do it in front of me, but . . .

T: Did she or didn't she?

P: No, no, not at all, but my parents are always unhappy, and even if they don't do it in front of me, I still notice.

T: OK.

P: And my mother was nagging me every minute, always asking me what I was doing, "you have to eat this, you have to eat that . . ."

T: In that case, they didn't follow my prescription to avoid trying to make you eat!

P: No!

T: OK.

P: And I feel uncomfortable eating in their presence, because it distresses me, so I eat everything. I do it to make them happy, but then I feel sick. And the same thing repeats itself again and again.

CoT: So you do it because otherwise they'll be unhappy.

P: Yes.

T: Did you let things happen, or not? If you remember, I said "Eat if you want to eat, fast if you want to fast."

P: No, because, the more I said "Mum, I don't want to eat" the more they wanted to force me to.

T: Did your sister accept to come, or did she protest?

P: I asked my father how he made her come. He said that at first she asked "Do I have to come?", but in the end she came. I don't know. We're not speaking to each other.

T: You didn't exchange one word for the whole, long trip?

P: (*shakes her head*)

T: Never?

P: (*nods*)

T: Fine.

P: My father told me I had to say hello to her. I said hello. But it bothers me that they expect me to do everything, say hello, say something . . . What about her? My conscience is clear. I did what I could before. I don't care any more.

T: OK, fine. Did you eat more or less than usual this week?

P: This week?

T: Yes.

P: Actually, some days I ate very little. I felt good about myself. Then some days I ate too much, too much, and felt terrible.

CoT: What did you do then? Did you vomit?

P: No, I didn't.

T: Did you fast?

P: *(nods)*

CoT: Because last time you told us that you can keep down some foods, like meat and vegetables, while you vomit sweets and carbohydrates.

P: I mean things that make you fat. For example, I can have vegetables and fruit, that kind of thing, but . . .

T: So this week you didn't eat any meat at all?

P: No, I had some meat, but my mother kept insisting "Eat your meat." I eat fish too, and eggs. I prefer to cook for myself and eat by myself without anyone saying anything. It bothers me that they look at my plate, or that they look at each other and tell me to eat this and eat that. It bothers me.

CoT: So when they don't talk, they look at each other, and when they talk they make comments about what you're eating?

P: I'd rather eat without them. Eating with them makes me nervous.

T: Stop, stop. It doesn't seem so crucial to me. What seems crucial is that you said you felt good the past week because you ate very little. What do you mean by very little?

P: I didn't exactly eat very little, because the first few days I ate little, meaning meat and fruit at lunch, but I had a lot of fruit.

T: But you ate regularly at every meal?

P: Yes.

T: And then you binged?

P: Yes.

T: During the binge, did you eat sweets, carbohydrates, meat, or everything?

P: Well, the first time I had two plates of pasta with one sauce and two more plates with another sauce; two baskets of bread; lots of breadsticks, ham, cured meat, mozzarella, biscuits. Then, when I got home Saturday night I ate again—I mean, after finishing my dinner. I kept eating . . . all kinds of things.

T: So did you binge once or twice?

P: Twice.

T: And after bingeing, you started to fast?

P: After bingeing, I started to fast.

T: For how many days?

P: No, wait, I binged the day before yesterday. Yesterday I didn't eat, but today I ate normally, almost. I had pizza, meat and potatoes. Today I feel as if I've eaten . . .

Reframing: the "fear of fasting"

T: Now C, what we'd like you to understand is a kind of reasoning that I think you'll be able to follow, since you are intelligent. Keeping in mind your wish to lose weight, I think what you fear most is bingeing. So the main thing to check are your binges. Now, along that reasoning, what I think is most important for you to understand is that you end up bingeing every time you've restricted your food intake for a few days—you even started to fast. Every eating restriction prepares a binge . . .

P: Mmm.

T: . . .Which is then followed by a new fast, which prepares a new binge.

P: Yes. I'd like to find the right balance.

T: It's an endless game. Calm down, that's what we're here for. Wait. But what makes the problem persist—this is what I want to tell you—is not the fact that you have to control your bingeing, because you'll never be able to do that. You have to control your fasting, in the sense that if you fast, if you restrict yourself daily, you'll end up bingeing.

First prescription: avoid fasting because it leads to bingeing

T: If you want to avoid bingeing, you have to stick to a rule that will seem harsh at the beginning: you must have meals, as restricted as you wish, but *regular* meals. But wait, here's the most difficult thing: if you binge, you have to eat regularly the following day, otherwise you'll fast the next day and then you'll feel like bingeing again. So we want you to keep in mind that what you should fear most are not the binges, but the fasts, the restrictions, because they are what causes you to binge. If you just try to resist your bingeing, you'll end up doing it more. And you've tried it: the more you try to restrain yourself, the more you do it. Instead, if you want to fight your tendency to binge, you must avoid prolonged fasting or restrictions. We're not telling you to do anything extreme, but only to have a series of regular meals.

Second prescription: to allow herself one small transgression per day

T: But wait, there's more. If you want to be really good, we're also going to ask you to introduce a tiny percentage of the things you eat during your binges: sweet treats, candy . . . because if you try to avoid them, your craving for them will become too strong.

So now you should try to start thinking that every time you fast or restrict your food intake, you're not only maintaining the problem but making it worse and increasing your bingeing. When you avoid some food because you fear it, you make it more desirable, because you're denying yourself that food. The more you deny yourself that food, the more desirable it becomes. You need to eat a small quantity of it every day, to immunize yourself from the sweet food—as if it were poison. You have to immunize yourself. So we'd like you to think about that, and, as a consequence, eat regular meals—reduced, but regular. And we want you to allow yourself one small transgression, one tiny little sweet every day. Do you think you can do that, or are we asking too much?

P: I don't know. I think I can, but . . .

T: But think mostly about the fact that if you fast or reduce your food intake, you're preparing another binge. All right?

P: Also because every time I binge, I tell myself "I'll eat a lot now; later, I won't eat."

T: But it's an endless game. You'll never be able to stop that way, do you understand that? Instead, whenever you binge, you have to tell yourself "I'm eating now, and in six hours I'll eat again anyway. In fact, I'll binge this afternoon and have dinner this evening." That's how you'll succeed in controlling yourself.

P: By the way, while we're on the subject of bingeing, I sometimes weigh myself. I've gained three kilos.

T: And now you have to fast. But that's what we're all like, you know.

P: But not for three kilos.

T: That's right. After two days, you're not there any more. But this is important: what you need to think about now is that each time you fast or restrict your food intake, you're setting up your next binge. If you want to keep your binges in check, you have to keep your fasting in check. All right?

P: (*nods*) But how can I not think . . .

"Fear of fasting" again

T: And if you deny yourself some food, you mustn't think about it at all, but think that you need to *be afraid* of fasting and denying yourself food.

P: Sometimes I can't sleep. I keep thinking about what I'm going to eat in the morning.

T: But do you know why?

P: Always . . .

T: Because you deny yourself that food. If you allow yourself that food, you can do without it. If you don't allow it, it becomes irresistible. OK? Now we'll see your parents without you. Next time we'll see you again without them, and then we'll see them. We'll work with your sister today only.

(*Her parents and sister come in*)

T: Now, we let C come in first . . .

S: Are we being videotaped?

T: Everything that happens in here gets videotaped, because if we have any doubts we go back and look at the videotapes. We have transcriptions too. That way, we don't lose our concentration or our memory. And because there's a new law about this now, everyone has to sign an authorization for the videotaping. We asked C to come in by herself because we thought it would be interesting to verify some things together with her, and it has been useful. We've given her some instructions that concern her personally, on how to fight those fasts, above all. It's the fasting that prepares the binges. And she's accepted those instructions—at least that's my impression. Then we asked her about what's been happening so far, and we found that you've been good at not crying in your daughter's presence, and that's already a big step. But according to your daughter, you haven't been as good at not insisting on making her eat.

M: I really was. I said . . . I reproached her about how much she eats in the morning.

T: Oh.

M: That's true. In fact, I hid all the food, because then she feels sick and gets bad stomach cramps . . .

T: That's exactly what you're supposed to avoid. Do you remember that last week I asked you to observe without intervening?

M: You mean I shouldn't hide the food away?

T: Absolutely not.

M: She didn't see me hiding it.

Again, prescription to "observe without intervening", augmented by fear of complicity with the symptom

T: That way, you become her accomplice, because you make the food seem even more desirable, because there's even more transgression involved in searching for it, finding and eating it. Last time, we talked about how difficult it is for parents to observe without intervening, but the more you get pulled into the game, the more you try to help her, the more you end up producing the opposite effect. You must keep that in mind. You need to be *afraid* of helping her. The more you help her, the more you damage her. Now, if you keep on hiding the food, you make this duel of searching for the food and eating it seem even more fantastic.

M: But she doesn't know.

T: But she finds out. Do you really think your daughter is that naïve? Your daughter is very alert and astute, more than you imagine.

F: That's obvious.

T: And now we've succeeded in bringing you here too (*to the sister*). We asked you to come here because we wanted to see the whole family together, and also because there's this conflict among little sisters who don't talk to each other, and such drastic positions on both sides.

S: Excuse me if I interrupt, but I'm the one who's taken a drastic position, since I expected her apologies a few months ago.

T: But your sister says "I've nothing to apologize for. I'm in the right." Did you expect that? Did you ever imagine that she might adopt that position?

S: She's always adopted that position, that's the whole problem.

The therapist reframes the sister's conflicting position by redefining it as a form of unconscious complicity: by perpetuating the conflict, she is granting her sister that importance and power which she would like to deny her.

T: OK, but listen. We're fifty per cent on your side. We agree with you when you get angry at them. OK? We disagree with you fifty per cent when you assume a position that's a bit like your mother's position when she hid the food these past few days . It's just another way to encourage your sister's behaviour. As far as you're concerned, you're trying to apply a corrective measure, but instead of being a corrective measure, it makes you an accomplice of the situation, because this way you've given her even more power than she had before, without realizing it.

S: That's true. (*She nods*)

T: This way, you've increased the functional aspect—the secondary advantages of having the disorder. In fact, the more you maintain your position, the more she will maintain hers, because that gives her yet another advantage: she's put you away in a corner. But it wasn't she who put you there. You did it yourself. That's wonderful.

M: But she suffers badly from her sister's absence, because she was . . . She misses her.

Reframing the secondary advantages that the patient obtains through her problem

T: Yes, but see . . . I don't want to sound cynical, but when we're dealing with this sort of problem, the first thing we need to do is avoid overestimating expressed and declared affection or emotion, and pay more attention to the dynamics that maintain the problem. In this case, whenever your older daughter expresses opposition, she takes a drastic position against her and you. That becomes an advantage for C, because this way she keeps everyone even more under control, and her pathological disorder makes her the most important person in the whole world. She's at the centre of the universe. As long as this game continues, she'll have no motivation—I don't mean conscious motivation, but no emotional motivation—to get rid of the problem. As long as having the problem places her in the most advantageous position possible, she will unconsciously wish to keep the problem. We invited you to come here simply to ask you: "Do you still want to be your sister's accomplice?"

S: No, not at all.

T: We were sure of that, if nothing else because of your anger. You don't like the thought of helping her, right? So if you want to avoid helping her stay in her position, you need to reverse your position completely.

S: (*nods*)

A prescription to the sister to help her overturn her attempted solution towards the patient

T: And while we told your parents to observe without intervening, and to be detached, in your case you need to assume an almost exaggerated attitude of understanding. "How well I understand you"; "How can I not have understood you before"; "I understand that you're really unhappy"; "Your problem is a difficult one to solve"; "You do all you can, but you just can't make it"; "But you know, we all have to accept our destiny, that's the most awful thing." On the one hand, you should make her feel that you understand her; on the other, you need to gently disqualify her, saying "You know, everyone has to accept their own destiny. Some people are intelligent; some are born too high up, so to speak, others too low, and there's nothing to be done about it, is there?" Do you think you can do that?

S: I don't know (*she laughs*).

T: That would be a great help to us all. But more importantly, it would save you from being an accomplice like you are now. Because by trying to stay out of the game, as you're doing now, you're maintaining the game—in the exact same way that your mother does when she tries to make your sister eat less because otherwise she'll be sick afterwards, so she hides the food away. She's playing that game too. Have I made myself sufficiently clear? What do you think will be the most difficult thing for you?

S: No, I . . . I mean, I don't know. They live in P, I live in V, so we don't see much of each other in any case, and I don't know how much she eats, whether she does or doesn't eat, how she eats . . .

The parents are again told to "observe without intervening"

T: Yes, of course, but when you do see each other, you can do something, since you know that if you don't—like today, when you didn't speak to each other for the whole trip—you're doing her a favour and playing her game. I mean, until now, you thought you were the only member of the family who wasn't playing her game. Instead, you're just her alter ego—the two attracting opposites. So think about it. So . . . (*to the parents*) as far as you're concerned, we need to take one step further, and that step further is to observe without intervening, OK? We've given you daughter some suggestions that she can put into practice, and she seems even more willing to collaborate than we expected. All right?

S: Yes, but one aspect of her character is that she's a big liar. She's always bowing her head, but then she does exactly what she wants.

T: Yes. That's typical—not of her character, but of the kind of disorder she's suffering from. You're underestimating this. All persons who suffer from eating disorders are liars, are false . . . but not because of their character. It's an effect of the pathological disorder, not of her character. All right? But do you want to be her accomplice? Think about it.

S: No.

T: (*to the mother*) Do you want to be her accomplice?

M: (*shakes her head*)

T: Good. If you think you should do something, call me here before doing it, OK?

M: I took the notes you asked for.

T: Yes . . . please give them to us. I'll see you in fifteen days. (*To the sister*) At this point, it's unnecessary for you to come here again. If you want to come, fine.

S: No, I'm not coming.

T: OK.

M: C can't sleep at night. Did she tell you?

T: Because she thinks about what she's going to eat the next day.

M: Should I give her some camomile tea, or . . .

T: What would that be? It would be an intervention. So observe without intervening, all right? Good.

F: Doctor, is it all right if my wife comes without me?

T: Yes, certainly. I only need one of you, and your daughter. We've already done what we needed to do with the whole family. All right?

M: Thank you.

Session three

T: Are your parents here?

P: No, I came with my sister.

T: Good! Your sister brought you here. I received a call from your mother yesterday. She called to update me on the situation. So, what do you have to tell us?

P: On what subject?

T: How have things been going?

P: Not very well, because I still have the usual problems. I don't think about anything except food . . . I can't, there's no way. I've tried eating really small amounts of food at lunch and dinner, but I can't. Sometimes I ate a lot at dinner, and the next day I didn't eat anything until the next evening. I mean . . . I didn't do many days of fasting.

T: Oh, really? Good.

P: But for example, I might only eat at night, and while I was eating I kept thinking "I shouldn't be eating this." And I can never tell whether I'm hungry or not, or whether I'm full, because I tell myself "I'll eat later". Nothing changes for me whether I'm eating or not. I mean, it's weird.

T: But how did you feel about avoiding fasting? How did you manage to do it?

Redefining the effects of the "fear of fasting"

P: To avoid fasting? I ate in the evening, but not a lot, like I used to eat a lot and binge. I ate enough, but a bit less than before. And then I told myself "No, OK, I'll eat tonight, and then I won't eat for two days" but then I ate again the next evening. I sat at the table and ate . . .

CoT: C, did you think about the fact that every fast prepares . . .

P: Yes, yes. That's why . . . that's what scared me, because then I'd say "I'll just eat a little . . ."

T: But I'll eat something!

P: Yes.

T: Good. Did you ever fast for a whole day?

P: Yes.

The therapist uses the patient's experience of the past week to reiterate the reframing

T: Did you notice that you tried to binge afterwards?

P: Yes.

T: So you've had proof. How many times did that happen?

P: For two days. For example, one day I fasted, but the next day, in the evening, I was hungry and ate a lot.

T: Did you eat a lot of carbohydrates, bread, pasta?

P: Yes, I did. And maybe because I was hungry for sweets, I had sweet snacks, a lot of fruit . . . bananas, that type of thing. I used to avoid fruit, maybe I'd have just one strawberry because strawberries are low in calories. This time I had fruit, and meat . . . For example, I went to a restaurant and had meat and a salad, and nothing else. And tonight, for example, I'd like to eat pasta, but I'm having fish instead because I'm afraid of gaining weight.

T: Now, your mother, who's always so anxious, told me you've lost weight. Is that true?

P: That I've lost weight?

T: Yes.

P: No, I'm exactly the same as before.

T: OK.

P: Compared to three weeks ago . . . one week I stayed on a diet. I didn't fast, but had a small piece of meat at lunch and a leaf of lettuce at dinner. So maybe . . . but I realize . . . for example, when I started out, I said "I want to reach forty-five kilos", and I did. "I want to weigh forty". Now I weigh thirty-nine kilos and think "I'd like to weigh thirty-five kilos, so I can eat anything I want." I mean, that's my reasoning. Maybe it's wrong . . . I mean, I'm sure it's wrong.

T: Don't you think you've gone down so much because you're deceiving yourself by following that reasoning, so that after you've gone from forty-five to forty, you'll keep losing weight to below thirty-five kilos until you've completely lost control?

P: Yes. I'd like to stay at the same weight, but then I'm afraid of getting fat. I don't know . . . I mean [. . .] finding a rule.

Again, "fear of fasting"

T: The rule is the one we suggested and which you are trying out: avoid fasting, because otherwise you'll end up bingeing. Apart from that, every time you binge after fasting, your body assimilates a lot more. If you eat regularly and avoid fasting, your body will assimilate only what it's supposed to assimilate.

CoT: Because when you fast, your system slows down and you assimilate more calories.

T: So not only does every fast prepare a binge, but the binge will weigh much more than eating regularly. You know, despite your excellent intentions, you've constructed the worst possible situation, because it takes a lot of effort to deny yourself pleasure, and the effect of doing so is exactly the opposite of what you want. Instead, you could be enjoying food a bit and eat what you like, avoid fasting, and maintain your weight.

P: But, for example, I always feel like having something sweet, but I'm afraid that if I have just a little, I'll want more.

T: Do you remember that we suggested a small transgression every day?

P: Yes, but I'm scared of losing control . . .

T: But did you do it?

P: Yes, I did eat.

T: But did you have your little transgression, something small and sweet?

P: No, not sweets . . .

T: Why? What do you consider a transgression?

P: One part of me says "OK, I can avoid it . . ." and another part of me . . .

Reframing: "if you allow it, you can do without it; if you don't allow it, it will seem indispensable" and suggestion that the patient allow herself one small food transgression each day

T: But if you avoid it, later you'll want it very much. If you allow it, you can decide to do without it, but if you don't allow it, it will become irresistible. If you allow yourself one small, sweet transgression a day, it will help you avoid bingeing on it. You can control your desire, just like if you allow yourself to eat regularly, avoiding fasts, you can avoid bingeing.

P: Right.

T: On the other hand, if you try to abstain, the urge will increase and lead you to another binge. You've had proof of that these past few weeks.

P: (*nods*) Also because if, for example, I gain two kilos from bingeing, I say "OK, I'll diet for a week."

T: As long as you keep doing that, you'll keep oscillating . . . Instead, if you eat the way we told you, being afraid of fasts . . .

CoT: And allow yourself a small transgression every day . . . because if you don't, you'll start thinking about it at night too, and then you'll start bingeing.

T: On one of those things you've been denying yourself.

CoT: Instead, if you allow yourself to eat it, you'll get rid of those thoughts.

T: The best way to learn to control something is to allow it while managing it. If I deny myself something, I lose control over it. But isn't it strange that you came with your sister today?

P: Pardon?

T: It's very odd that you came alone with your sister.

P: That's because my father told my sister that he had a lot of work to do, and asked her if she could take me, and she did.

T: But it's interesting that she accepted to do it, and that you spent the whole trip together.

P: No, well . . . but we were fine, I mean, we weren't unhappy about it.

The therapist investigates the effects of the reframing performed with the patient's sister during the previous session

T: Really?

P: No. I'm not saying that because I'm here with her. There's another thing . . . For example, when some friend of mine's having a birthday party, or if I'm going on a trip, I tell myself "I'm going on a trip, so I'll have to eat." So I stop eating until the day comes, and on that day I eat.

T: That's right, but then you eat much more.

P: Yes!

T: Instead, you should say: "I'll eat, and eat again, and that day I'll be able to manage my eating." But I'd like to get back to your relationship with your sister. Has anything changed?

P: We don't fight any more.

T: You're no longer enemies?

P: No.

T: That means that the talk we had last time was useful. Good. So she hasn't taken any hostile positions towards you.

P: No!

T: That's great! Are you happy about that? You've got your dear sister back again.

P: Yes.

T: What about your parents? Have they been following my suggestions, or not?

P: Except for two days ago—no, yesterday—when they received the test results . . .

T: That's why they called me.

P: The tests said I'm very low in iron.

T: Your potassium is low too.

P: Yes. Low potassium, and all those kinds of things.

T: But that was to be expected, wasn't it? How many kilos do you think you weigh below what you should be? According to other people's criteria, not your own.

P: I don't know. I don't see myself as being thin at all. On the contrary, I think I'm . . .

T: You think you're fat.

P: Not fat exactly, but I could be thinner.

T: Well, well. So, your parents got scared when they saw the test results, right?

P: (*nods*)

T: And they started nagging again after that?

P: Yes. For example, last night my mother started saying: "Come to the table, C, eat. Eat this, eat that."

The therapist again presents the reframing of the "fear of fasting" and prescribes a small daily transgression

T: I've asked your mother to call me tonight after our meeting. I'll tell her again that the rule stands as I told her last time. She must observe without intervening. OK?

P: [. . .]

T: And we want you to think about what we've told you: if you avoid fasting, you can learn to manage; if you fast, you'll lose control.

P: Right.

T: And if you allow yourself that small transgression, you won't have the fantasy of that little treat, and you won't end up eating a lot of them. So we want you to eat one small treat a day, between meals, OK? And we're very happy to hear that you've mended your relationship with your sister. OK?

The therapist invites the patient's sister to come in and congratulates her for making peace.

Session four

T: I see you've already got a tan. Is it already very warm where you live?

P: It's sunny.

T: Is the water still pretty cold?

P: No, not very cold.

Redefining the effects of the prescriptions

T: I see. Well, what's new?

P: I tried to do what you said, and I've got to say the first few days everything went very well, apart from the fact that I'm still fixated on weighing myself every two . . . I mean, I weigh myself all the time. The first few days went well. I had lunch and dinner, not eating too much, but normally, but later . . . One day I ate a lot, the whole day, lots and lots of food. At the end of the day, I thought "No, I mustn't eat tomorrow", but instead I ate a lot again.

T: As you see, when you say "I mustn't" you end up doing it.

P: I mean, I was able to control myself the first few days, but not the others. In fact, I've gained two kilos this week.

T: Those first few days, did you allow yourself a treat a day in between meals?

P: Yes, yes, yes. I used to not eat bread, for example, but this time I had some. I ate things that I like. It's just that I wasn't supposed to think about it. I mean, once I start eating, I keep thinking about that food the whole day, all the time, I don't know what to do, but I keep thinking about eating, not eating, eating not eating . . .

T: Now, you said you gained two kilos last week. What was your reaction to that? Did you get scared?

P: Yes.

The therapist uses the patient's narration to reiterate the "fear of fasting" and the importance of the small daily transgression

T: And how did it happen? Did you binge?

P: (*nods*)

T: While you wanted to restrict yourself, right?

P: (*nods*)

T: Does that make you think more about my suggestion?

P: (*nods*)

T: . . . About the fact that every time you fast, you're actually preparing the next binge, and that if you really want to find a balance you have to allow yourself what's necessary, and also a tiny transgression. If you don't allow yourself that, you'll end up doing it more and more and more, like you did last week.

P: For example, after I ate normally, I was afraid of gaining weight. I hadn't gained weight yet, so I told myself "I won't eat tomorrow" and I didn't have any breakfast or lunch, and at dinner I just had very little salad. Then, around ten o'clock at night, I felt that urge . . . and started eating a lot more. That's because I hadn't eaten earlier, I think.

CoT: And you assimilated even more food, because you hadn't eaten anything during the day.

P: Yes.

T: As I keep emphasizing, whenever you binge after a fast, apart from the effect of the bingeing itself, your body is like a thirsty plant. It takes in everything, and absorbs everything. On the other hand, if you eat at regular intervals without leaving your stomach empty for too long, there's less assimilation and all the nutrients you don't need are eliminated. But that will only happen if you give yourself—your body—permission. Now, you see, the most important thing you have to work on isn't the physiological aspect, but the psychological one. Every time your deny yourself, or intend to deny yourself something, you start resisting and resisting until you finally give in, and then . . .

P: But the other day I thought . . . I went to a bar with a schoolmate before school and had a small pizza. I just started eating it, and then at recess I had two braided pastries, small croissants with chocolate, and potato chips, because . . .

Reframing by using a metaphorical image and humoristic narration

T: Simply because you're like an overflowing river that's already been dammed, and you try to dam it, but it floods, and when the river banks break, there's a flood at first, but if you let it flow, it will reach the right level again. I mean, the first dam breaks, the flood comes, you make another dam and that one breaks too, you make another one and that one breaks too. It's an everlasting game. Do you know the joke about the person who gets up one morning and sees a hole in his garden, and can't stand the idea of having that big hole there? So what does he do? He goes out with his shovel, digs another hole, takes the earth from it and fills the first hole, and goes back into the house, happy that the hole is filled. The next morning he wakes up and sees another hole. So what does he do? He goes out with his shovel, makes another hole, takes the earth from it and fills the first hole, and goes home happy, but the next morning he sees another hole in the garden. You're doing the same thing. If there's a hole, first of all we need to accept it and then fill it up some other way—not by moving the earth and making other holes. That's what you're doing. And it's interesting that you told us that when you do as we told you, the first few days, the binge doesn't occur.

P: No, absolutely, it was . . . I ate right, I always ate at mealtimes, I didn't eat too much, but ate normally: meat, bread with mozzarella and salad. And at dinner maybe some pasta, some fruit . . . but after that . . .

I don't know . . . I thought . . . because maybe I had a craving for things like ice cream, I had a little, and then I saw that I liked them . . . maybe I thought, "well, tomorrow I won't eat, so I can have more ice cream the day after."

T: But if you allow yourself a small treat every day, you don't need to do that. You see, when you think "I'll fast, so I can binge", you're already planning it. "Tomorrow I won't eat, so the next day I can have a lot of ice cream." You're shortchanging yourself that way.

P: Uhm.

T: Are things still going well with your sister? Have you revived your relationship?

P: Yes.

T: Doesn't it seem strange to you that it took so little to save such a difficult relationship?

P: Uh-huh.

Positive suggestion towards change

T: (*laughs*) It's the same thing with your problem. You only need to do a little, but do it well.

P: I'd like to be normal, like before, when I didn't think about it.

T: If you follow our suggestions, you will be. So, remember: fear fasting, because every fast prepares a binge, like when you thought "Oh, I can eat a lot if I anticipate it . . . by fasting." There are two mechanisms at work here: either I want to eat, so I stop myself and end up bingeing, or I feel that I like something, like ice cream, and think "yes, I like it, but it's bad for me". So what do I do? I fast one day, and eat a lot the next. That's cheating yourself too. The first thing we want you to do now is to get used to enjoying the taste of the things you like most, within the small daily transgression. OK?

P: Hmm.

T: And include some foods that you like in your regular meals, not just things you think are good for you, avoiding the things you think are bad for you.

P: Because I may eat something because it won't make me fat, but then I end up eating the other thing as well.

Prescription to avoid fasting and introduce the patient's favorite foods in her regular diet

T: Exactly. If you eat both, you've lost the game. Instead, you really have to set this rule for yourself: "I'll only eat what I like. If I know that it's calorie-rich, I'll eat less of it." But you must only eat what you like. If you can allow it, you can do without it, but if you can't allow it, you can't decide to do without it. So right now we have to work on making your relationship with food an enjoyable one, as it should be, and it will be manageable because it is enjoyable. If you make it into an exercise in control, you'll lose control over it. So keep in mind that if you allow it, you can decide to do without it, and if you don't allow it, it will become irresistible.

The therapist invites the patient's father to come in, and informs him that the therapy is proceeding well, and that the family should continue to follow the suggestions received at the previous sessions.

Session five

The patient reports that she has gained around one kilogram. She feels a bit worried about that, but has none the less been following a regular, albeit reduced, diet and (most important of all) has avoided fasting. She also says she has rediscovered the pleasure of eating in company, especially with her friends.

The therapist reiterates the importance of seeing her relationship with food in terms of "enjoyment", not as a struggle or an attempt to keep control. He reemphasizes that it's the attempt to control that determines a loss of control, which leads to bingeing. He also encourages the patient to seek other sources of enjoyment, such as spending time with friends and combining the pleasures of eating and having company.

T: Well, we're very happy, but remember, just as we've been telling you to avoid fasting, now you should also avoid filling up on fruit to aid your bowel movements, because that's the same kind of thing, OK? Enjoy your new relationship with food. It's nice that you enjoy it more when you're enjoying other things, like your relationship with your friends, OK? You know, transforming a torment into a pleasure and being able to manage that pleasure is the best kind of change one can make, don't you think? OK, let's reassure your mother now, all right? Goodbye, my dear, and I'll see you soon.

P: Thank you.

The therapist invites the mother to come in, and repeats that she must stop controlling her daughter's eating habits and make an effort to give her daughter all responsibility for her relationship with food.

T: I know that you are very good and obedient, but also very anxious and anxiety-provoking.

M: Yes, yes, it's true.

T: Your daughter's as fit as a fiddle. Now she just needs to get used to managing her own affairs without any accomplices to her problem. I mean, if you keep in mind that this is the fifth time we've seen your daughter . . . we met a young girl in a super-blocked situation, bingeing and fasting, and now she's not fasting any more. On the contrary, she eats regularly—in fact she tends to eat more, to eat well, and . . .

M: I wouldn't want her to become (*she holds her arms out wide*)

T: Fine, I agree. To avoid her becoming that way, we need to give her back the whole responsibility for managing her relationship with food. If you try to help her, you'll damage her.

M: I understand.

T: You see, we need you, we need your help . . .

M: Fine.

T: . . . which means that we need you to avoid helping your daughter.

M: Very well.

T: Give all the responsibility back to C. She's going camping with her friends. Good. Let her fend for herself. Absolutely avoid saying "I'll speak to your friends". If we make her feel like a target, we'll certainly see some symptomatic behaviour again.

M: (*nods*)

T: Give her back all the responsibility. We're very pleased with C, Mrs ____. When we first met her, the mere thought of gaining half a kilo would have given her a fit. Now, she told us once that she gained two kilos, and another time a kilo and a half. So including liquids, that's two and a half kilos, but she hasn't made any scenes. So be happy.

M: All right.

Session six

The patient is back from a vacation with her friends, during which she has eaten a great deal and gained another four and a half kilos. She says that she is not particularly worried by the weight gain, because she no longer feels an urge to eat as much, and follows a regular diet that includes some small transgressions. Since she is following a balanced diet, she is no longer afraid of getting fat or losing control over her relationship with food.

T: Well, well, well. Can we say that you are not having any problems with food at the moment, or are there some problems?

P: I don't know. I can't tell. I mean, I hope not.

T: What we'd like to know is, do you still have the idea that you have to control, have to lose weight, or not?

P: Yes, sometimes . . .

CoT: Less than before?

P: Less than before, but . . .

T: How often do you get it? Is it something that torments you every day, like before?

P: Yes, it torments me, but not the whole day, because I have other thoughts.

T: Oh really? What kind of thoughts?

P: Oh . . . thoughts. I'm about to leave now. I'm going to London. The fact that I'm going away . . . a lot of things to think about. Basically my mind can't concentrate on that all the time. But I still think about it, though less than before.

CoT: And you also have other thoughts?

P: Yes.

T: Good. We're very pleased with you, very pleased. The important thing now is: if everyone else tells you that you look much better this way, do you think they're saying it just to please you or does it mean that you still have deforming lenses in front of your eyes?

P: No, maybe it's true. I don't doubt it, but . . .

T: But?

P: I don't know. When I look at myself, I think "I ought to slim down my legs, I need to get slimmer here." I mean, I'm always thinking that.

T: But you don't do it.

P: No.

T: Good.

CoT: It's the thought that remains.

P: And sometimes I tell myself I need to get more exercise, also because . . . I'm the kind of person who doesn't want to do anything.

T: Lazy.

P: Yes, for example, at the pool, I never swim. I've been making an effort to get some exercise, to move, to swim, always moderately because I get tired immediately. And I'm always trying to keep busy.

CoT: Is that partly to keep yourself from thinking about food?

P: Yes.

T: Good. So listen, we're very pleased with you and want to do an experiment. We'll give you another appointment in one month. Keep in mind what we've said before: if you want order, try to have a small disorder that allows you to maintain control. And as we've said—and we are pleased—avoid fasting, because the fast brings on the binge. The flood has passed. We think you've become able to establish the right water level—in other words, your hunger—under the risk level, OK? So we'll see you in a month's time. We're very pleased with you, OK? We'll tell your father that too.

The therapist congratulates the patient's father for the results obtained.

The patient returned after one month reporting stabilization of her eating pattern and body weight. Those results were maintained in follow up appointments after three months and one year.

CHAPTER SIX

Vomiting: formation, persistence, change

"While it cannot happen without lacerations, it is a matter of escaping the contagion of nothingness. It is the comfort of vertigo"

E. Cioran, *La Tentazione di Esistere* (1984)

As we have mentioned, eating disorders are rapidly evolving towards a kind of "technological" specialization. Young women with bulimic or anorexic tendencies eventually discover that vomiting enables them to control their weight without giving up the pleasure of eating. Also, by staying just a few kilos above or below their ideal weight, they avoid alarming their families and being pressured to eat normally. Thus, in recent years, we have observed a considerable increase in cases of vomiting compared to the more "traditional" disorders of anorexia and bulimia. For example, out of 196 cases of eating disorders treated in our research study, 123 turned out to be cases of vomiting disorder.

Although the literature of our field (APA, 1994) still classifies vomiting disorder as a variant of anorexia and bulimia nervosa our empirical research has shown that the vomiting disorder is based on a completely different structure and model of perception of reality. Although bulimia (bingeing and gaining weight) or anorexia (abstaining from food in order to lose weight) form the basic matrix of vomiting disorder, the latter, once established, loses all connections with the disorder that initially produced it. In that sense, vomiting disorder is an example of an emerging quality, just as water is an example of an emerging quality with respect to hydrogen and oxygen. Although hydrogen and oxygen are the elements that constitute water, they lose their individual characteristics, as water is something different and more than their sum.

Vomiting should be considered a food-based perversion rather than an eating disorder. Although subjects with vomiting disorder and subjects with bulimia both have food compulsions, only a few vomiters tend to gain weight (a characteristic of bulimia). In most cases, vomiters tend towards anorexia, in the sense that they manage to stay a few kilos below their ideal weight, thus avoiding an excessively feminine appearance while continuing to enjoy the pleasures of food. In our experience, moreover, vomiters who tend towards bulimia are usually easier to cure, because they do not strive to control their emotions as anorectics typically do.

Undoubtedly, when these persons initially start to binge and vomit, the vomiting represents an attempted solution, a way to lose weight, or avoid gaining weight, while continuing to eat. In other words, it is a way for the person to keep eating without feeling the harmful effects of her relationship with food. Initially, this is an attempted solution that works; but when the cycle of eating and vomiting is continuously repeated, it becomes an increasingly enjoyable ritual; after a few months, it will have become the young woman's greatest pleasure, and one that she can no longer do without.

This process is reflected precisely in the studies of Henri Laborit (1982), the Nobel prize winner for biology, on the synaptic organization of the human brain. Laborit's studies have proved that any type of behaviour, if repeated a certain number of times, may gradually become associated with intense feelings of pleasure. By this process, the ritual of eating and vomiting becomes what we have metaphorically described as the "secret lover", a sort of demon that possesses the person, from which she becomes unable to free herself even if she wants to.

Therefore, once the vomiting syndrome has become established, the problem is no longer one of weight control, but one of controlling the compulsion towards pleasure. Eating and vomiting, which started out as an attempted solution with respect to anorexia and bulimia, becomes the problem, and the reason it persists lies in the pleasure that it provides. One of the findings of our research–intervention is that the obsessive search for pleasure and strong sensations is, in fact, a prevalent characteristic of these subjects' system of perception and reaction. From that aspect, vomiters present many analogies with those groups that Zuckerman (1987) has called *sensation seekers*, i.e. people who specialize in the search for intense situations. This category includes all "substance abusers" such as heroin addicts, cocaine addicts, etc.

In time, the symptoms of the vomiting syndrome become so invasive that they lead to an inhibition of sexual pleasure. All the 123 cases in our research study (which included two men), showed a complete inability to enjoy a satisfying sexual life as long as the symptoms persisted. In no case were the vomiting syndrome and a complete erotic satisfaction present at the same time. By stating this, we certainly do not intend to express any sort of Freudian "pansexualism" by implying that the vomiting syndrome is caused by a hypothetical sexual disorder. On the contrary, we believe that this compulsion, which is based on pleasure, gradually takes up so much space in the subject's life that it replaces all other pleasures. Thus, the inhibition of sexual pleasure does not configure itself as the cause, but rather as the effect of the eating disorder. Unlike bulimics, vomiters seek sexual pleasure in a transgressive manner, but they are unable to feel that pleasure, because their ritual of eating and vomiting already provides them with the most intense and exclusive form of pleasure.

Not only does this ritual provide the highest of pleasures, but also the easiest to obtain. It can be performed without any need for another person, and without facing the risks associated with having a relationship. Food is always available, and the ritual always works. Moreover, the eating and vomiting sequence is isomorphic with the sequence of sexual activity. We may recognize within it a phase of tantalizing fantasy, when the young woman anticipates the food-binge; a phase of consumption, as she eats; and a phase of discharge or liberation as she vomits. In many subjects' description of their relationship with the ritual, the importance of both the "erotic" food fantasy and the moment of discharge often stand out as the elements of a successful erotic act. This makes the symptoms even more appropriate as a surrogate of sexual activity.

As the vomiting symptoms decrease, the sexual dimension spontaneously reappears, and the subject regains the ability to feel sensual and erotic pleasure. On the other hand, once she starts to feel that kind of pleasure again, the symptoms tend to decrease until we observe a sort of "coincidence" between the recuperation of the ability to have an orgasm and the disappearance of the symptoms.

Clearly, then, although the vomiting syndrome is a product that has evolved from anorexia and bulimia, it cannot be considered simply as an eating disorder, but should rather be considered a perversion based on food. The vomiter's problem is no longer connected to a wish to avoid gaining weight, or a wish to lose weight, but to the fact that eating and vomiting is an extremely pleasurable perversion that she is unable to stop, even though she might wish to. From that point of view, we might say that the clinical disorder closest to vomiting is obsessive compulsion, but with the important difference that obsessive–compulsive tendencies are based on phobia, while vomiting is structured as a compulsion based on pleasure. It is precisely because this symptom is based on pleasure rather than suffering, that it is so very difficult to eliminate.

Our experimental work has lead us to distinguish vomiting subjects by three types, which we have somewhat ironically named (1) unconscious transgressive; (2) conscious but repenting transgressive; (3) conscious and complacent transgressive.

Unconscious transgressive vomiters are inexperienced subjects who have not reached the realization, from the cognitive point of view, that eating and vomiting is a perversion. They are a relatively small category (about twenty per cent of our cases), usually girls between the ages of fourteen and nineteen who have never had a complete sexual experience or a true sentimental relationship. They are very inhibited, and often blocked by a strong sense of morality.

Conscious but repentant transgressives (about fifty per cent of our cases) have realized that their symptoms are a perversion based on pleasure. They have reached the point of no longer being able to stand the situation; they no longer want to be "carried away by the demon". These vomiters would like to stop but cannot do it on their own, so they are generally willing to collaborate.

Conscious and complacent transgressives (about thirty per cent of our cases) are fully aware of the character of pure pleasure associated with their symptom, and they easily recognize the analogy between the bingeing–vomiting sequence and sex. They are the most lustful in their relationship with the ritual, and have no intention of giving up their "secret lover", their demon, i.e., their relationship with eating and vomiting. These cases are, therefore, the most difficult to treat, and the most resistant.

The patients in this third category take a seductive and provocative stance; they are very good at manipulating others, very transgressive, and very good at controlling and managing things. With a male therapist, their provocation is usually erotic and sexual; with a female therapist, their seductiveness is based on being "good", making the therapist feel that she's their best friend, their best mother, their best role-model in the world. They are also the most transgressive in their relationship with the ritual. If no one buys them the food they want, they might steal it, or steal the money to buy it, and this increases the thrill of the transgression. In most cases, their family brings them to therapy, often against their will, and usually after having tried several other types of treatment, including hospital stays, forced feeding, and violent control to keep them from vomiting. At times, their hospital stay may have led to some improvement, since they were sedated by drugs, but this improvement only lasted until the moment they checked out from the hospital. This should not surprise us, if we consider that such a strong, pleasure-based compulsion cannot be solved through hospital treatments, because it is strongly connected with the young woman's everyday life, and her relationship with herself, others, and the world, and therefore the problem tends to reappear as soon as she returns home.

Finally, a small percentage of women in this category find it amusing to "devour" their therapists, initiating therapy of their own free will. These persons are an example of the "barracuda patient" (Bergman, 1985) who feigns collaboration but generally suspends the therapy as soon as the first results begin to appear, and resumes the therapy only when the problem has returned to its starting point.

Treatment of vomiting

As we described earlier, although vomiting is a product that has evolved from anorexia and bulimia, once it becomes established it must be considered an autonomous disorder, with its own modes of persistence. A different therapeutic intervention than with the other two types of food disorders is therefore required. The types of interventions we use to treat this syndrome vary largely according to which variant we are treating. However, we always prefer a mixed treatment (individual and family sessions), because, as for all eating disorders, we generally find a great number of attempted solutions practised by the family, all of which reinforce the persistence of the problem.[34]

Treatment protocol[35]

First stage (first/second session)

At this stage, "capturing" the patient is our main objective, because vomiters, like anorexics, very often do not collaborate, or may even completely reject the therapy. From the beginning of the first session, the therapist must therefore start mirroring the girl's language and vision of reality, anticipating her feelings, and presenting the eating and vomiting sequence as a metaphorical meeting with her "secret lover": "Bingeing is the greatest of all pleasures for you, isn't it? It's something extremely difficult to do without, because it's so intensely pleasurable . . . like having a secret lover. Every time you eat and vomit, it's as if you were meeting a secret lover, very discreet and always available." We carry on along the same lines for the rest of the session. In most cases, as soon as the therapist succeeds in tuning in on the patient's language, the patient will start describing, very clearly and without shame, how her ritual is, indeed, the most enjoyable thing in her existence. Patients sometimes say they feel as if they were possessed by a "charming demon".

On the other hand, if the young woman is an *unconscious transgressive*, and refuses to accept the idea of the ritual as secret lover, the therapist may use this aspect as a lever for change at the next stage of therapy.

If the parents are present, the therapist must try to make them see the situation from the same perspective, and explain that this disorder is based on pleasure, not suffering. The therapist must enable all the persons involved to collaborate in the therapy after explaining what these kinds of symptoms are based on.

Towards the end of the session, after exploring the nature of the problem and ascertaining what dysfunctional attempted solutions are maintaining it, the therapist gives the first prescriptions. These are the same for all three types of vomiting disorder:

1. *The miracle fantasy*;
2. The *conspiracy of silence*, which is prescribed to the family;
3. *The food list*, which is prescribed to the patient's mother.

The miracle fantasy. This prescription has proved to be a very effective aid to performing the diagnostic examination. It also gives an important positive suggestion towards change for vomiters, as well as for anorexics. The miracle fantasy is described in detail in the section on treatment protocol for anorexics.

The conspiracy of silence. At this stage of the therapy, it is essential that the therapist intervenes directly on the family's system of communication, by using prescriptions that have the power to block the usual dysfunctional solutions attempted by the family. The family receives the following prescription:

> I need you to understand—although, granted, it may be difficult—that what your daughter is doing is playing a little game of pure pleasure. Although it may seem absurd to eat and vomit purely for enjoyment, start putting that fact into your heads. Moreover, the more you try to restrict her behaviour, the more you prompt it. From now on, we must maintain a conspiracy of silence concerning your daughter's problem. We won't talk about it at all any more. You'll have to get really good at avoiding any mention of it. Think that every time you mention it, you're actually encouraging the disorder. I don't know whether you'll be able to do this, but please think about it, and keep in mind that every time you speak about it, or try to intervene, you'll be feeding the disorder. Think that every time you try to persuade her to desist, or try to help her in your own way, or speak about it in any way, you'll be feeding the disorder.

The food list. In our treatment of the vomiting disorder, we have developed a specific paradoxical prescription, the food list, which we give either to the patient's mother[36] or to the family member who tends to intervene the most with attempts to help the young woman.

> I'm about to give you a task to be carried out from now until the next time we meet. This task is a bit peculiar. Every morning, I want you to wake your daughter up, and ask her: "What would you like to eat and vomit today?" Make her give you the menu. Then go out and buy everything that's on the list, everything she asked for. This should all be separate from your family's daily menu. Place the food well in sight on your living room table, with a note: "Things to eat and vomit for . . . [the patient's name]". No one else is allowed to touch that food. Only the person who eats and vomits can have it. If your daughter refuses to list the menu, then either buy the foods that were on the previous day's list, or you may choose what to get, because you know what her preferences are. If there are leftovers from the previous day, leave them out on the table. Whatever doesn't get eaten should stay there, together with the food you buy on the following days. All right?

By displaying the food and the note in public, we completely reverse the family's previous attempted solution, which consisted of hiding the food, preventing the young woman from eating too much and from vomiting, pretending not to see. We also deprive the ritual of its special characteristic, i.e., its transgressive value. As soon as the vomiter is free to binge, her perception of the ritual changes completely. By prescribing the transgressive action, we deprive it of its transgressive connotation. When confronted with this prescription, the vomiter usually gets angry, throws the food away, or eats it a few times and then stops. This is because the emotional experience of eating and vomiting is no longer as enjoyable as before. Moreover, the fact that the food is displayed for all to see, with the note that says *"Things to eat and vomit for [name]"* , is usually a strong inhibiting factor.

Second stage (from the second/third session to the fifth)

During this stage, the intervention takes widely different forms depending on what type of vomiting is being treated.

Unconscious transgressives. With this category of vomiters, who are generally rather moralistic and inhibited, we use a provocative intervention, similar to the one we developed for some types of bulimics. The objective is to play their sense of morality against their symptomatology. Often, the mere suggestion that they think about the fact that their behaviour is actually a form of sexual perversion is sufficient to make them stop eating and vomiting, because they start to see their symptom as being in contrast with their moral values.

To that end, we start by asking the subject about the positive uses of her problem. ("What do you think is the useful function of this problem? What is it protecting you from? What are you gaining from it?"). We gradually lead her to reflect upon her disorder until she recognizes that the sequence of eating and vomiting presents some analogies with sexual intercourse. "When you get this compulsion, this irresistible need to binge and purge, what do you feel exactly? You have a fantasy, you see images of food, you feel an almost physical desire, a physical activation that makes you feel you *have* to eat, right? And then you eat until you're full, completely full, and in the end you have to vomit. After you vomit, you feel good, you feel liberated, you feel relaxed . . . But listen, what does this cycle remind you of? What's another activity where human beings have this kind of sequence: fantasy, activation, consummation, discharge . . . what is the vital activity of human beings and animals, which starts with activation, a kind of irresistible impulse, which is then followed by a phase of consummation, a phase of discharge and relaxation?"

After succeeding in making the patient recognize the analogies between bingeing/purging and sexuality, we introduce the fantasy of the irresistible sexual urge. This manoeuvre is described in detail in the treatment protocol for bulimics.

With unconscious transgressives too, this reframing technique immediately blocks the symptomatic compulsion, because the mere thought of doing something so perverse makes the cycle, which seemed enjoyable until that moment, seem disgusting and shameful (this follows the ancient Chinese stratagem "beating the grass to make the snakes run away").

Conscious but repentant transgressives. As we mentioned, although these patients are aware of the pleasure-based character of their rite, they are tired of being "possessed by the demon". Therefore, they tend to be collaborative, ready to follow the therapist's suggestions.

The most common dysfunctional solutions for these cases involve attempting to reduce or control the bingeing and consequent vomiting. This only results in increasing the frequency of the ritual. Since any intervention in the direction of control or repression would only exacerbate the desire to binge and purge, with this type of patient we use a tactic based not on controlling the symptom, but on altering the perception of pleasure that makes the compulsion to binge and purge so irresistible. (*The Interval Technique.*)

> So, are you truly prepared to do everything you can to free yourself from this demon? Well, then, from now until next time we meet, I'm certainly not going to ask you to try not to binge and purge, because you wouldn't be able to do that. Do it whenever you wish, but you must do it as I tell you. From now until the next session, every time you eat and vomit, you will eat and eat and eat like you love to do. When you have finished eating and get to the moment when you usually need to go and vomit, you will stop, get an alarm clock, and set it to sound half an hour later. Then you wait for half an hour without doing anything—without putting anything else into your mouth, solid or liquid. When the timer sounds, you run and vomit, but not a minute before or a minute later.

If we succeed in making them follow this prescription, the temporal sequence of the ritual is interrupted. This alters the ritual's aspect of irresistible pleasure. In fact, this intervention interferes with the pleasurable sequence proceeds from an exciting fantasy to consummation and discharge. Since the pleasure lies in eating compulsively and vomiting immediately after, our insertion of a time interval between the bingeing and the purging deprives the ritual of its intrinsic enjoyment. Thus, we take control of the symptom through a therapeutic manoeuvre that follows its structure but inverts its direction, leading it to self-destruct. In other words we "make our enemy go into the attic and take the ladder away".

If the person accepts this prescription, at the following sessions we increase the interval to about an hour, an hour and a half, two hours, until we reach an interval of three hours or three and a half hours. At that point, usually the subject either stops vomiting or gradually decreases the frequency of the ritual until it stops completely. By altering the spontaneity of the cycle, the *interval technique* takes away her enjoyment of the liberating act of vomiting, which is usually accompanied by a feeling of almost orgasmic urgency, and by increasing the time interval we make the vomiting more and more difficult and unpleasant. Thus, we transform a rite based on pleasure into an act of self-torture. Moreover, when these women stop vomiting, their relationship with food also becomes normalized: since they are afraid to gain too much weight, they stop consuming enormous quantities of food. As the symptom decreases, the person's social and interpersonal life starts taking up more space, especially for what concerns her enjoyment of relationships with the opposite sex.

Conscious and complacent transgressives are the least collaborative group. They have no intention of stopping the bingeing and purging, and therefore tend to sabotage the therapy. If we prescribe something that interferes with their enjoyment of the ritual, for example by introducing a time interval between eating and vomiting, they immediately refuse to do it, or do it once and then stop.

With this type of vomiter, therefore, we have to use indirect strategies to reduce their enjoyment of the symptoms. Since we cannot intervene on the symptoms, we use a different key: the patient's own narration, but in an exaggerated form (Nardone, 1997) . For the duration of the first session, the therapist uses and mirrors the patient's language, complying with her logic of pleasure. "You are *so right*. Pleasure is the most important thing. It's all you have . . . and it's the most beautiful thing . . ." This encourages the patient to describe the details of her perversion. She will usually do this with great pleasure. The therapist continues: "I really want to hear . . . I'd really like to know *how* you feel this pleasure, what the most delicious foods are, how you like to do it. Do you prefer it by day or by night, by yourself or with someone watching? Do you like to eat quickly, or more slowly? What do you enjoy most, the fullness in your mouth or in your stomach?"

The therapist then applies the following manoeuvre.

> Yes, you really do love to eat. But I think you're just pretending to be a true transgressive. You don't really know how to do it right.

> I'll say more: I don't think you're getting enough pleasure out of it. If you want to, I can teach you to do it even better. Right now you're just eating randomly, whatever you can find. Don't you think that, just like in an erotic "performance", quality is more important than quantity? So why would you need to eat and vomit three, or five, times a day? I believe that there can be only a few truly satisfying moments. Why don't we, together, choose the best way to do it, the tastiest food items, how you like it most, where you like to do it, when you like to do it. Have you ever tried choosing? I propose doing it just once a day, but doing it *really* well. So, from now until next week, think about the foods you like the most, in what order, where . . . Actually, let's do an experiment. I propose that this week, after midnight, which is the hour of the Witches' Sabbath, when your family is in bed, you go barefoot into the kitchen, having previously lined up all the different kinds of foods, and do it in the tastiest, most transgressive manner possible, and then go back to bed.

Thus, the therapist gradually leads the patient to concentrate on her quest for pleasure, by helping her construct the "perfect binge", stimulating her transgressiveness even further. By teaching her to concentrate and choose her pleasure, the therapist achieves the important result of progressively reducing the frequency of her ritual. The spontaneous reduction symptoms that results from improving the quality of the patient's bingeing follows the teaching of the Chinese stratagem "to sail the seas unknown to the sky".

At the following sessions, as we perfect the ritual binge, its frequency decreases from five or six times to only once a day. The next step is to decrease the frequency even more until, after a few months, the patient performs one eating and vomiting ritual per week. Meanwhile, we work on her interpersonal relationships, encouraging the complacent transgressive patient to start exploring other types of pleasure. "You, who are such a master at distilling pleasure . . . do you really think that the only enjoyable thing in the world is eating and vomiting? Try to find something else that gives you pleasure." As we work on the patient's relationships, we encourage her to seek out other enjoyable feelings and transgressions, until she eventually recovers the ability to find pleasure in her interpersonal relationship. As a consequence; her symptoms decrease even further. Indeed, every pleasure ends where a greater one starts.

TO ______________________________

TIME ______________ DATE ______________

While You Were

M ______________________________

OF ______________________________

PHONE NO. ______________________________

☐ Telephoned ☐ Please call back

☐ Returned your call ☐ Will call again

☐ Left the following message:

____

____

____

____

____

____

SIGNATURE

Third stage (from the fifth/sixth session on)

After unblocking the symptoms, it is important to teach the vomiting patient about the *small disorders that maintain the order*, and prescribe a *small eating transgression* per day, just as we do with anorexics and bulimics. As far as the vomiter's fear of relationships is concerned, once she has freed herself from her compulsion, she is usually able to resume a normal social life without any particular difficulties. The therapist needs only lead her to gradually introduce other small pleasures into her life, pleasures other than eating and vomiting, and healthier transgressions.

Conscious and complacent transgressives are a case apart. As we discussed earlier, this group of patients is the most difficult to treat, and the one that requires the longest therapy, because they need to be followed step by step, in a style and language that complies with their logic and their constructions of reality.

At this stage, it is very important that the therapist insists that the young woman continues with one planned ritual binge once a week, telling her: " If let yourself do it, you'll be able to do without it. Prohibiting it will make it irresistible." This continues until the patient herself decides to stop, because she no longer has any desire for it. Usually, as they begin to enjoy different pleasures (especially those connected with the opposite sex), these young women start forgetting to perform their weekly binge. As the ability to feel pleasure increases in one direction, it decreases in the other direction. However, the scheduled binge should be maintained until the patient decides that she no longer needs it.

It is important to note that this method of choosing the tastiest form of binge has only achieved a complete elimination of the symptoms in 30–40% of our cases. The method is successful when our concurrent work on the social and interpersonal context is successful, i.e., the person starts developing relationships and discovers that some things can be more enjoyable than bingeing and vomiting. A relatively high proportion (more than fifty per cent) of our cases of *conscious and complacent transgressives* managed to significantly reduce the quantity of their binges by trying to make them as enjoyable as possible, but without being able to eliminate them completely. These cases find it enormously difficult to completely give up their symptom. They generally keep bingeing and vomiting once or twice per week, and their therapy tends to be very prolonged.

At that point, we may proceed with a specific prescription. If the vomiter is still performing two ritual binges per week, we can start by asking her to perform them on two particular days (which we mutually agree upon) for example once on Tuesday and once on Friday. At the following session, we ask her to continue with the Tuesday binge, but to move the Friday binge to the following day, Saturday. At the next sessions, we keep moving the second binge a day at a time, first to Sunday, then to Monday, etc. At some point, we reach a week when two ritual binges are prescribed for the same day (in this example, on Tuesday). Faced with such a request, vomiters will usually only binge and vomit once, even if they are free to do it twice. The result of just one binge per week is thus achieved without asking for it directly.

Having achieved that, the therapist continues to prescribe two binges for the same day, but moves that day forward by one day from week to week, i.e. on Wednesday one week, Thursday the next week, and so on, keeping up the illusion that we are adding one day at a time. We never ask the patient to decrease her binges from two to one, but always leave her the freedom of doing it twice in the same day, even if it won't happen. (In most cases, it never happens.)

By decreasing the number of binges and increasing the time between them, we then gradually eliminate the single remaining weekly binge without requesting it openly. By this extremely simple strategy, we are able to reduce the frequency to once every two weeks. At that point, the vomiting patients are usually able voluntarily to give up the remaining binge. By continually moving the binge by one day, we are also giving the patient more space to gradually bring new experiences into her life—again, without ever directly asking her to do it. Therefore, this prescription is particularly suitable for those vomiting patients who need to have total control over the situation and find it difficult to accept the therapist's direct prescriptions. This prescription allows them to maintain the illusion of being able to control what is happening.

Alternatively, or in addition to the above prescription, we can use the *interval technique* as a final manoeuvre. As we described earlier, this prescription introduces a time interval between the binge and the purge. Although this manoeuvre may already have been tried and refused, or proved ineffective, it may be re-presented at this stage of the therapy. Something that the patient refused to do at the third session may well be accepted by the tenth or fifteenth session if we have established a good therapeutic relationship, and the vomiter has reached the point of really wanting to get rid of the symptom. The same manoeuvre may have different effects when used at different times, and be successful even though it may have failed previously.

Our observations so far suggest that vomiting is a rather complex disorder that requires the continuous introduction of new variants within the specific protocols of treatment. The latter need to be rewritten into composite protocols that can be adapted and made to fit the numerous, variable ways of persistence assumed by this disorder. All the treatment manoeuvres described so far[37] may therefore be interpolated and juxtaposed in diverse sequences within the same therapy. Again this shows how eating disorders are rapidly evolving, increasingly often presenting mixed types of persistence that require original adaptations of the treatment protocols.

Fourth stage (last session)

In the last session, we do exactly what we described in the previous sections on anorexia and bulimia: we put the final frame around our finished work.

Composite cases

Very often, the therapist may encounter composite cases where the patient's symptomatology does not indicate just one circumscribed eating disorder. For example, there are situations in which the patient alternates between anorexia and bulimia. In that case, we need to evaluate which is the person's dominant, redundant system of perception and reaction towards reality. In other words, we need to determine which are the dominant attempted solutions—to lose weight (anorectic base) or to binge (bulimic base)—and, on the other hand, which symptoms are effects, although causality becomes circular in these cases. After recognizing the basic structure of the disorder, we follow the protocol for the dominant disorder—naturally, with some variables that take into account the complications introduced by the accessory disorder.

In any case, the most frequent situation is one of anorexia that evolves into vomiting disorder (about fifty per cent, according to the APA). In this case, the therapist first intervenes on the vomiting syndrome. Once the latter has been solved, the therapist often has to work on the anorectic structure, thus producing two distinct therapies.

Clinical case example (vomiting 1)

Session one

In the following exchanges, P designates the patient, T the therapist.

Defining the problem

T: What brings you to me?

P: I'm bulimic.

T: Oh.

P: I've been bulimic for several years. I had a period of treatment in a centre in P. One of the psychologists there was Doctor C. I got well, so to speak, but only relatively so, because I didn't . . . have time to follow up on that type of therapy.

T: When you say that you got well, what do you mean?

P: I didn't binge and vomit any more

T: Oh.

P: I was living in P at the time, but then I moved, so we had to shorten and accelerate the whole thing. I moved home, near my parents, and after seven or eight months I started again. That was in 1996.

T: OK.

P: That's when I started again.

T: Oh. Since 1996, then?

P: Yes. End of '95, beginning of '96.

T: Well . . . and now?

P: Now it's . . . it's continuous.

T: How often do you eat and vomit?

P: Sometimes even four, five, six times. Once it starts, I sometimes find it difficult to stop, until I'm exhausted and fall into bed.

T: What made you come to me this time, instead of going back to the people who treated you successfully once before?

P: Well, I was looking for . . . I was trying to go back to P and start working there again, or in that area, so I was . . .

T: Where did you live?

P: Right now I live in C, but with very little enthusiasm, so to speak.

T: Hmm. What do you do?

P: I'm a doctor.

T: Ah. So you'd like to go back and work in P.

P: Yes, and I feel torn on that subject too, because one part of me wants to go, but the other part is scared of everything, my family, my fear of starting something new . . . I can't find the strength to actually make this decision.

T: Hmm.

P: I was there a few days ago, to see this new place where I might work, and one of my friends—they are very worried, because clearly I'm ruining my life with this obsessive behaviour—asked a friend of hers who's about to get her degree in psychology. She told my friend, "Send her there, because he's the only one who can make her well." Because, it's true, I could go back to the same doctor, but . . . I don't know. I've also been reading a lot on the subject, but, after all, I know what . . . but . . . I can't get out of it. I mean, I know what makes it start, I know I should be eating every three hours, but the fact is, I'd like to lose weight. I hate food, but I love it too.

T: Uh-huh.

P: That's how it works. And in any case, if I start eating normally . . . I mean, *I* think if I start eating normally I'll get fat, while I want to get thin.

T: Hm.

P: So, in the end . . .

T: Right now, you're a few kilos overweight?

P: Yes.

T: OK, and for you that's unacceptable?

P: Yes.

T: Uh-huh. And when you eat, what do you eat mostly? Salty or sweet foods, or both?

P: It depends. I . . . there are times when I prefer sweets, or both. I mean, the absurd thing is . . . I go shopping for my binges.

T: It's not that absurd. All specialists do.

P: Also because, I think . . .

T: Specialists.

P: I've really become specialized in this sector.

T: Specialists in vomiting do that.

P: Yes. I go shopping for food. I organize my binges . . .

T: How to do you organize them?

P: I organize them . . . first I disconnect my cellular phone. I don't answer the doorbell if it rings. I go out and buy the food, then I isolate myself.

T: OK.

P: And when I do all that . . . it's as if . . . It's absurd, but it almost seems as if I take pleasure in . . .

T: Look, it's not absurd.

P: No, it's . . . how can it be?

Reframing the vomiting syndrome as a secret lover

T: Your appointment with eating and vomiting is like an appointment with a secret lover.

P: Exactly. We've come to that.

T: It's the greatest pleasure a person can obtain. So you get organized as if you were preparing for a magnificent, delectable encounter with a . . .

P: With a great lover.

T: A great lover. Obviously, a very transgressive, very perverse affair.

P: That, too.

T: Because otherwise, there wouldn't be any thrill to it.

P: Yes. I also feel there's a transgressive side to it, because it can't be anything else. I mean, it's impossible to stop this frenzy, and I can't stop it. I mean, when I get into it, I can't . . .

T: They say that once you've tried it, the pleasure is too great to be resisted.

P: Oh, God, don't say that, because I don't . . . (*embarrassed*). I want to get out of it, also because . . .

T: Now, how many times . . .

P: Pleasure . . .

T: . . . do you organize this every day?

P: I can even do it every day.

T: Not "I can". What I'd like to know is, what's the average?

P: Well, basically, I do my job, which doesn't require me to give very much, because I work in a place where no great effort is expected on my part. The place is small, very peripheral, and I work out in the country. I go to these villages where I might see a few patients, so . . .

T: Do you work for the public health service?

P: Yes, at the local health unit.

T: Good.

P: Yes, I work for the local health unit. I mean, I used to work at a great hospital, so . . .

T: OK.

P: And at the hospital, I found myself . . . And I did it for love.

T: For love, what does that mean?

P: For a man.

T: Oh.

P: Then the man wasn't there any more, and everything became a gigantic problem. I did it for him, so now I need to punish myself, because, in any case, I've done everything I could do.

T: Or, "now I have to find a secret lover, because I don't have a real one any more."

P: Oh, well, yes. I hadn't thought about that, but . . .

T: When you were together with him, did you eat and vomit, or not?

P: No (*seems unsure*).

T: When you were falling in love, did you eat and vomit, or not?

P: Well . . . I should mention that this was a long-distance relationship. Yes, I did.

T: When you didn't see each other. And what about when you were together?

P: When we were together, there was so little time, right? I didn't have time to . . .

Investigating the patient's family and social relationships

T: And now you don't have a relationship any more?

P: No.

T: How long has it been since you had a man?

P: (*Sighs*) Practically not since it ended with him. Two and a half years. After him, I had a few flings, not a real relationship. A few transgressive flings. To my way of thinking, well, occasional flings that might last a short time, but . . .

T: Do you live with your family?

P: No, I live alone, but I go home often, every Saturday.

T: Do you live near your parents?

P: About 100 km. away.

T: OK. You live alone, so you can organize things whichever way you prefer. Good. From what you've been saying, it sounds like you have a lot of friends.

P: No, not where I live. I'm very lonely. My friends are almost all in P, or in that area. I occasionally see a group of people in my parents' town, but . . . they're people I'm fond of, but we don't have a lot in common.

Examining attempted solutions

T: When you were in therapy some years ago, what method did they use? What did they propose that you do?

P: It worked on two fronts, because there was a specialist in dietary medicine who taught me how to eat; I used food diaries. I had to write everything down, that kind of thing.

T: Of course, OK.

P: And then there was a psychologist. But I don't have any great memories of those meetings, because they didn't deeply influence . . .

T: So . . .

P: It was less influential

T: Was it mostly a behavioural kind of treatment, a readjustment?

P: Yes, to food. How to eat.

T: Good. Now what are you doing to try to get out of this, if you're trying anything?

P: I'm not doing anything.

T: OK.

P: All I know is I have no reason to get out of it because, in any case . . .

T: "If I deny myself even this pleasure, what will I have left?"

P: Exactly. The place where I live makes me sick, and the job I do makes me sick. I have no . . . I get no pleasure out of relationships, because I can't find any, and the ones do I find mean nothing to me.

T: Hm.

P: I've got no reason to want to get better, and no reason to want to be beautiful.

T: OK.

P: I mean, when I reach a low point because I really can't stand it any more after two days of continuous vomiting, then I might decide "I'm not going to work tomorrow." And even if I don't go, it makes no difference, because my presence is not so important. Then I can dedicate myself completely to my self-punishment, and so . . .

T: Don't call it a punishment.

P: Pleasure, it's a great pleasure, but . . . well . . .

T: Stop calling it a punishment.

P: Oh . . . that comes later, when I look in the mirror and see . . .

T: You see . . .

P: What I don't what to see.

Provocative reframing of eating and vomiting as a transgressive erotic act

T: Your condition is like that of a very bigoted person . . . a very moralistic woman who, at the same time, has strong sexual impulses. But she represses those impulses. She considers that sort of thing extremely immoral. One morning, she wakes up with a formidable sexual urge, walks out on the street, and grabs the first man she sees . . . it makes no difference whether he's handsome or ugly, because sex is all she's interested in. She takes him, pushes him inside a gate, and has sexual intercourse with him, in the most transgressive, perverse, pleasurable manner. Ah . . . When all is done, she walks away and feels guilty for the rest of the day. She feels guilty and unhappy. But then, the next morning, she wakes up with the same irresistible urge, walks out, and grabs the first man she meets, handsome or ugly, doesn't matter. She takes him behind the gate, and . . .

P: (*laughs*)

T: Again, she has the most lustful, perverse sexual encounter, until she reaches the point of highest pleasure. Aahh . . . discharge . . . Again, she walks away feeling guilty and so on.

P: And then maybe she goes to church.

T: And she goes to church, too.

P: Because I feel this double nature in myself—this need for a spiritual quest. I try, I mean . . . I try, but I can't.

T: Then you should begin to think that if you let yourself do it, you can give it up, but if you don't allow it, it will become irresistible, impossible to give up.

P: But I can't allow myself . . . I mean, I can't allow myself . . . For me, maybe because of my education . . . it's acceptable to have a relationship with a person, thinking that maybe I'll build a future with that person, so sex will be part of it too, but . . .

T: But it's not as pleasurable.

P: I don't think I'm . . . I mean, at least, I don't know, I never thought of myself as someone who has those kinds of needs . . . (*laughs, embarrassed*).

T: Start thinking about that. (*Pause*) Considering the things you're doing . . .

P: Well . . . gosh . . . Could it be related to that? I don't know . . .

T: Start thinking about it.

P: I've always thought that my problem might be . . .

T: Start thinking about it.

P: Well, but that doesn't mean I have to go with every man I find . . . I mean . . .

T: I didn't say that. But you can do it with food precisely because you're not doing it with men, or because food is not men.

P: Oh.

T: You're not losing dignity.

P: No, I lose it that way too. Maybe not in front of other people, but . . .

T: That's right.

P: But with myself.

T: Well, then, with yourself, tell yourself clearly (*pause*) that what you're doing is nothing but a series of extremely perverse sexual acts, as perverse as can be.

P: But are you sure of what you're saying? (*Embarrassed laugh*) Excuse me, but it seems . . . I am truly shocked now.

T: I can imagine!

P: Because I had no . . . one small part of me . . . I've written about this . . .

T: Yes . . .

P: Pleasure . . . I've always defined my binges as food "orgies", but it was more of a formal . . .

Agreeing on the treatment modes. Therapeutic double bind

T: No, no. Tell yourself very clearly, an orgy is what it is. Well, well, well. Now, since I've thrown this rock in the water, and I see that it's making a lot of little waves, I think I know what I need in order to tell whether your case is within my competence or not. I think I can help you, and I think I can do it rather quickly, but I don't know whether you'll be able to follow me.

P: What do you mean?

T: Well, I've got some very peculiar methods. Perhaps you've realized that already. These methods are based on the fact that I talk, and let you talk, and make you talk, and most importantly, I give homework to be done between sessions. Things to do or to think, and the funny thing is that these things that I ask people to do seem strange, more often than not. Sometimes they may even seem illogical or bizarre, ridiculous or banal. They need to be carried out to the letter. I always give explanations, but afterwards. I won't ask you to do anything immoral, uneconomical, or dangerous. Small things, but you have to do them. All right? The other rule is that I give myself only ten sessions, and not one more. If I don't see any results, then I end the therapy at the tenth session. I continue only if we see that we've obtained some good results and need to finish our work. If everything goes as usual, however, the problems are completely, or almost completely solved within that time frame. But I don't know whether this will be true in your case.

P: What do you mean?

T: Every case is a new game of chess. I don't know who's going to win this one. We'll see. I don't know how much you'll be able to follow me, in doing what I ask.

P: (*fearful*) Do my efforts count?

T: In other words, I think I've got some good methods that have been applied on many, many cases, but I don't know whether you'll be able to follow them. We'll see. This doesn't . . .

P: (*agitated*) But is my case too serious? Because . . .

T: No, no.

P: . . . I can't do it?

T: It's simply because I don't know whether you will follow me. We shall see. We shall see by doing. We understand problems through the process of solving them, not *a priori*. We get to know people as they do things, not *a priori*. I have two tasks for you. I've already told you the first. I want you to continue to eat and vomit the way you want to, whenever you want to. It's your secret lover, the most beautiful thing possible, the only beautiful thing you have in your life, so why do without it? So . . .

P: You mean . . .

First prescription: think about the fantasy of eating and vomiting as a transgressive erotic act

T: But I want you to think about what I said: that when you eat and vomit, you're actually behaving just like that lady who wakes up in the morning with an irresistible, formidable sexual urge, walks out on the street, and takes the first man she sees (it doesn't matter whether he's handsome or ugly). She pulls him inside the gate. Sex is all she's interested in, so she has the most transgressive, perverse sexual encounter, with all the most creative variants of intercourse, with the utmost pleasure. Ah! She gets to the end, then she walks out of that gate feeling guilty, but the next morning she starts again. I want you to think about that. But do it anyway, because it's the only pleasure you have, so you have to do it. You don't want to deny yourself that, do you?

Second prescription: nightly letters

Second, every night before you go to bed, as the last thing you do on the pillow . . . I want you to get some nice stationery—do you have any?—buy some that looks nice . . . The last thing to do, on the pillow, is to take an envelope, a sheet of paper, and write me a letter. There's just one prerequisite: the letter must start with "Dear Doctor" and that's it. After that, you may even write that I'm an imbecile, a disagreeable person, whatever you want. Write anything that goes through your head—past, present, future. Everything that's going around in your head at that moment.

P: About my life?

T: Whatever you want. Any fantasy, reality, memories, inventions, whatever you want. Write the letter, sign it, seal the envelope, and next time bring me the seven envelopes with the seven letters. That'll help me get to know you better than many, many talks. All right? I'll see you next week, OK?

Session two

The young woman comes in, having lost a few kilos and looking prettier.

Report on the past week

T: So, how did everything go this week?

P: Well, I have to say things are better in that I've drastically reduced my binges without any particular effort.

T: Really?

P: Now, I don't think . . . I want to consider this a chance occurrence . . .

T: Oh, I agree, we mustn't have any illusions . . .

P: (*nods*)

T: But what did you mean when you said they had been reduced drastically?

P: Well, let's see . . . Since the day I came here . . . in practice, I must have vomited once a day on the average . . . I counted the days I didn't do it and the days when maybe I did it twice, so . . . It's around that average. I used to have a much higher average.

T: So were there some days without any episodes at all?

P: Yes.

T: Really? How many days?

P: Yesterday, the day I came to see you (but I vomited the next day), and I didn't the next day, and I did on Saturday, and Sunday, and Monday, but not on Tuesday, and . . .

T: Hm, good, good. So what per cent decrease have we got?

P: Seventy?

T: You mean seventy per cent less?

P: Yes, well . . . I used to spend whole days doing it.

T: And what made you stop?

P: Well, first of all, something serious happened to me emotionally. I had colitis, I mean a stomach ache that doesn't go away with any kind of therapy, and it's been a week, and considering what I felt, it was like awakening from an emotional inertia that lasted years, considering the emotions I felt.

Redefining the effects of the first prescription (Fantasy of irrepressible sexuality)

T: And what happened that caused this awakening of the Sleeping Beauty?

P: Well, I don't know. Maybe looking at the problem from the perspective you suggested . . . It was . . . like . . . realizing that there's some truth in that . . . I probably have this relationship with food that . . . I mean, it's not just that. It could be one aspect, and I thought a lot about it. It might be one aspect of my behaviour . . .

T: Yes, but what brought about this awakening?

P: . . . But it shocked me, in the sense that I walked out of here, went to the station, and I took the wrong train, arrived in Florence and . . . I thought it was one train, and it was another. So I came back to Arezzo, took another train. I travelled for two hours on the train. I was supposed to go to P. I spent last week in P, at my friends' house, and . . .

T: Are you telling me that I'm so shocking?

P: No, no, no, not at all. It's that thinking about what you told me . . . Well, I slept a bit and read a bit, because . . . I got distracted, and . . . That wasn't the only reason, but . . . I thought about it the past week, and I have to admit that there is a sexual aspect in my relationship with food. It's just . . .

T: I didn't say sexual. I said erotic.

P: Yes, erotic.

T: Sensual, not sexual. I don't like the term "sex" very much. It sounds cold, medical.

P: Well, erotic . . . seems too strong.

They both laugh.

T: Eroticism means a search for pleasure.

P: It seems a bit excessive, but . . .

They laugh again.

T: Shall we double the dose?

P: No. I don't know . . . If I stay shocked for another week, I'll never get rid of my stomach ache.

T: Let's double the dose. (*Becoming serious*) So what was the effect of seeing things from that perspective?

P: Well, I don't know . . . I started to think that maybe this charge . . . because I alternate . . . maybe I am a very vital person . . . I mean, a life-loving person, but then I have to limit that vitality in some ways, because there's an element of insecurity. I tell myself, "don't take this too seriously, because you might not succeed", so in anything I start, there's always something that holds back that part of me . . . that is capable of feeling great enthusiasm, and maybe I do the same at the sexual level too, I thought . . . You call it erotic. Maybe I use food to hold back that impulse. I don't know. I get satisfied . . . I mean, I don't know . . . I don't know, but there's some truth in it.

T: OK, good. And that's what started the crisis?

P: That shocked me, yes. It gave me rather a big shock.

Redefining the effects of the second prescription (nightly letter-writing)

T: Good. Did you bring the letters?

P: Yes.

T: Good. And was that terrible too?

P: No, no.

T: That was pleasant?

P: Yes . . .

T: What did you write in the letters that you'd have found it difficult to tell me in person?

P: Well, maybe . . . I wrote more or less . . . not what I just told you, because I wrote a lot more, but . . .

T: About this troubling feeling?

T: Yes. I mean, I wrote about that, too . . . feelings I've had this past week. I mean, maybe I'm getting rid of it, or maybe it's an external sign of the fact that I'm not feeling so well.

T: Who knows? We'll see. Now, please explain: what did you feel when you did it?

P: Oh, nothing in particular. First of all, the quantity of food I binged on wasn't the same as usual. It was a lot less than before. Certainly wanting to get rid of [the problem], because I'm getting fatter, and that makes me want to reach some goals. That's an important point for me, and so . . . and then, there's the boredom, coming home alone, to that house, made me want to have a pastime . . .

T: Aha. But did you experience the usual spasm of pleasure, or not?

P: No.

T: No?

P: No, it was a bit like this: "OK, let's spend some time doing this, then . . . OK, well, I've got the food, and there's nothing else I have to do afterwards. But I didn't experience that near loss of conscience, because when I . . .

T: Exactly what happened at the most intense erotic moments?

P: Yes (*embarrassed*), oh, well, usually . . . a normal person maybe, I know . . .

T: Well, well, hmm. So you didn't experience that almost total loss of control . . .

P: No.

T: That abandonment to the senses . . .

P: No, no. The first time . . . Let's see: on Thursday I was in P. I vomited because I had eaten foods that were too fat for me, so that was the reason, I knew that . . . I know what makes me start at those moments, because I eat excessive quantities of food more often than not . . . I might start out being good, eating what the others eat, or eating things I like, but then I start fearing that I've put in things that have too many calories, that will make me get fat, so I tell myself "OK, I'll throw it up."

Go slow technique, introduced through a metaphor

T: OK. So, technically, we might say, we've got the snowball rolling. It will gradually become bigger and bigger and bigger, until it becomes an avalanche, if we don't make the mistake of stopping it, because then it will break. But we mustn't push it either, because it would break either way. We're going to let the ball roll at its natural speed until it grows into an avalanche.

First prescription: keep thinking of eating and vomiting as a transgressive, pleasurable, erotic activity

T: To do that, I want you to think, again, that when you eat and vomit, you are like the lady in the story, who wakes up in the morning with an enormous sexual urge and pushes the first man she sees behind a gate, and has the most perverse and transgressive, but also most pleasurable and lustful sexual encounter, until, "aaah", she reaches the apex of pleasure, and then she walks away and feels guilty. But I want you to add that, aside from the transgression, there's an erotic aspect—a search for pleasure. OK? Well, well, well. That's the first task.

Second prescription: continue the nightly letter-writing

T: The second task is to keep on writing me letters at night.

Third prescription: one-hour interval between eating and vomiting

T: The third is the following. Since the feeling when you do it is not as overwhelming any more, are you prepared to do something to avoid it, or not?

P: Well, yes, I mean . . .

T: Good. From now until next time, every time you feel like doing it, I want you to avoid restricting yourself. Do it. But eat, and when you've finished eating and are ready to go and vomit, stop, take an alarm clock, set it to sound an hour later, and wait for an hour. One hour later, as soon as the alarm sounds, not one minute earlier or later, you run and vomit.

P: That's not the same thing?

T: I'm sure it's not. I'm asking: are you ready for it?

P: Yes.

T: Good. Let's see how you manage. And above all, let's think about the erotic question. (*Pauses*) And write the letters. All right? I'll see you on Wednesday.

Session three

The young woman comes in, looking noticeably thinner and much more well-groomed.

T: Here we are. Did someone accompany you today?

P: Yes.

T: Who?

P: Yes, my brother-in-law. He drove me, because . . . here are the letters.

T: Yes, travelling by train is a disaster, isn't it? Yes, we talked about it being impossible.

P: Yes, impossible. This week I was sick physically too, so . . .

T: How so?

P: Well, I had a sonogram, because I'm not feeling well. I had a high fever. The gynaecologist told me that it probably has something to do with ovulation . . . something rather abstract . . .

Redefining the effects of the prescription by using humour

T: A hormonal tempest . . . (*laughs*)

P: Yes, more or less. I don't know. In any case, I feel better now.

T: A hormonal tempest . . . Ah! These women! When they get agitated . . . Look what happens.

P: I don't know if it's because of that, but . . .

T: I was just kidding.

P: In any case, there was no reason, so . . .

T: Good.

P: I mean, I didn't have any other kinds of problems. My ovulation was a bit . . .

T: Excessive?

P: A gigantic egg! (*She laughs*)

T: Fantastic! What productivity! I told you, didn't I, that you're a big, sensual, erotic lady! (*He laughs*) You see, we've unleashed a hormonal tempest, an ovulation . . .

P: Gosh . . . I don't know . . . (*She laughs*).

T: You see, there's even a physiological referent . . .

P: Maybe, I don't know. In any case, I was sick. Now . . .

T: Good. And how did things work out?

Report on the past week

P: Let's see . . . well, I was here on Wednesday, so . . . the only day I did anything disgusting was Saturday . . .

T: Oh! Only one day? And how did you do it?

P: I tried . . . because you told me how to do it, so I wanted to experiment with that . . .

T: After an hour?

P: Yes, after an hour.

T: Oh, so you waited an hour ?

P: Yes, yes, but it's not . . .

T: What do you mean, it's not . . .

P: I mean, I used to organize my binges in such a way that I had to gobble down as much food as possible, and then I could throw it up immediately . . .

T: Aha. (*Nods*)

P: That's where the enjoyment was. Keeping all that quantity of food . . . clearly, I didn't know I'd be so sick, so . . . having to keep all that stuff in my stomach for an hour was like torture. It was really painful, physically. My stomach couldn't hold it all. I really felt bad, and . . . in any case, then . . . I was sick, too, so I don't know, I'm not saying that my problems are solved now, because they aren't. It was also a week when I didn't feel well, I had a high fever, a continuous pain here at my side, and so that may also have been a reason why I didn't have these "organized" days [for bingeing and vomiting].

T: Well, but you didn't have that last week either.

P: No, that's true.

Using humour again

T: Did you think about what I told you? Well, in any case, you see, you had a physical proof . . . (*laughs*)

P: Yes, I thought a lot about it . . . Well, what can I say? I don't know . . . Looking at bulimia from that point of view is certainly a disincentive . . .

T: Really?

P: I feel ridiculous, I mean . . . If I start thinking that preparing my binges is like preparing an evening . . .

T: Not an evening! It's going out in the morning with an incredible urge and attacking the first man you see . . .

P: Well, I feel a bit . . .

T: Pushing him behind a gate . . .

P: It just makes me laugh, and maybe that whole gloomy side of my bulimia has . . . gone away a bit. I don't know, the whole dramatic aspect . . . That's how I experienced it.

T: Good.

P: The whole thing feels lighter, somehow.

T: Well, well . . . so the whole idea feels lighter?

P: Yes . . . there's a humorous side . . . I mean, sometimes it makes me laugh. How can I . . .

T: Do one thing by doing another?

P: Yes, exactly. I mean, if my impulses tend towards one direction, I don't understand why they have to move in another direction.

Ironic provocation

T: But if a person is a little hog, so to speak, what can we do about it?

P: No, no, I don't think I am.

T: I was joking (*he smiles*). I'm having fun teasing you, since you're reacting so well.

P: I feel sick (*she laughs*), I feel sick . . .

T: Aha. You see, your organism is reacting with these torrential, tidal-wave ovulations. (*He laughs*)

P: I don't know, maybe.

Redefining the effects of the letter-writing

T: I'm having fun teasing you, but, you see, it works. Now, what did you write in your letters? Something new, or . . .?

P: Well, not much, because the days I was sick I didn't write much.

T: Now, what about the free or empty time that you have now that you're not organizing your ritual? How are you using it? How have you used it?

P: Well, in the past week, at home sleeping, because I wasn't feeling well.

T: Yes.

P: Next week, I don't know.

T: We'll see. Now, you told me that you played your little game on Sunday . . . no, on Saturday.

P: Yes.

T: Good. Did you organize that?

P: Yes, partly. On Saturdays I usually go to my parents' house, so I use part of the afternoon getting organized for it and going. The trip is about 120 km. When I get there I always fall into the pattern. I start opening all the kitchen closets, with my mum following close behind. In the evening, maybe I go out for a while. This time I didn't go home. I stayed in P. Between feeling sick and being bored, and being curious to see what it would be like to vomit after an hour, I ate and vomited, ate and vomited, and ate . . . more than once. I mean, it wasn't just once. I didn't go out, I didn't do anything, I didn't have any social events, I don't have a social life. I haven't had a social life for a lifetime, so I don't know how to use all this time that I have available.

T: Stop, stop, stop. We'll discover that soon, when you have this free time without the tempest blocking everything, the hurricane blocking everything, the hormonal hurricane that was blocking everything, the hormonal, vaginal, ovular hurricane. (*He laughs*)

P: Yes. We were saying that.

Redefining the effects of the interval technique

T: Good. Now, when you ate and then waited for an hour before vomiting, what did you feel while you were waiting?

P: Well, first of all I discovered . . . The first time, I couldn't wait. I kept looking at the clock, because I couldn't wait to go, to finally be able to go and get rid of this folly. But when I did it again, I noticed . . .

T: You did it several ways . . . several times that day, didn't you?

P: Yes, starting in the afternoon through the whole evening.

T: Good.

P: So, let's say, from 2:30 on. After the first time, I noticed that the push wasn't as strong. It's as if I started forgetting.

T: How?

P: As I told you before, you either do it immediately or you don't do it any more. That's the way it is. I mean, maybe because I was watching TV, or because I was reading . . . I forgot.

First prescription: keep up the fantasy

T: OK, OK. Well, well, well. OK. Now I want you to keep in mind, again, that when you eat and vomit, you're actually doing these transgressive, perverse little things, and your body has given us proof, OK? The tempest. Keep that in mind.

Second prescription: write letters only if she wants to

T: The letters are no longer mandatory, they're an opportunity. If you want to, you write them, and if you don't want to, you can choose not to write them.

Third prescription: two-hour interval between eating and vomiting

T: Instead, if you perform all the phases of your ritual, every time you reach the point of being really full, you wait two hours before vomiting. Set the alarm for two hours later. As soon as the alarm sounds, not one minute before or one minute later, you run and vomit. All right?

P: All right.

T: That's all. And I'm curious to see how you'll use all this time you have available. I don't know how you're going to use it . . . (*jokingly*).

P: Well, I don't know how I'll use it in the future, but . . .

T: Well, who knows? I don't know! See you next Wednesday at 4:30 p.m. Is that OK?

Session four

The patient comes back, saying that she has not had any more episodes of bingeing and vomiting.

Clinical case example (vomiting 2)

Session one

In the following exchanges P is the patient, T is the therapist, CoT is the co-therapist, and H is the patient's husband.

(*The patient comes in with her husband*)

Defining the problem

CoT: Good morning. What's the problem?

P: Well, I'm not sure how to define my problem. I was advised to come here because I've been having problems since I was sixteen years old. I began vomiting after eating. That's my problem.

CoT: Has it always stayed the same?

P: No. There are periods when I manage to keep it in check and other times when I vomit three or four times a day for two or three months at a time. But I've spent 6–8 months without doing it. It happens more often when I'm pre-menstrual; otherwise, there I've had some quiet periods.

CoT: Well . . . we tend to be more nervous in the days right before menstruation.

P: That's right. It doesn't happen every month, but almost. I've been through some periods when I made myself vomit up to six times a day, after just a drink . . .

CoT: Are you married?

P: Yes. We have a daughter. That's why I've decided . . .

CoT: . . . To conquer your problems, to face the problem . . .

P: Yes.

CoT: How long have you been married?

P: Three years.

CoT: Did getting married change anything in the evolution of your problem?

P: It stayed the same.

CoT: How about the birth of your daughter?

P: No, it didn't make any difference. A bit less, at first . . . As I said, it goes in periods. Now I do it when my daughter doesn't see me. I have to wait until she goes to sleep.

CoT: And during your pregnancy?

P: No. I vomited spontaneously.

Examining the solutions attempted by the patient

T: What have you done, so far, to try to solve this problem?

P: Nothing. I've always put it off.

H: We thought . . . She was doing it in secret and we knew little or nothing about it, and we . . .

T: Why "we"? Who else . . .

H: Her mother and father . . . we knew very little about it, so we decided to see . . .

T: Very well . . . So is this is the first time you've consulted a specialist, or have there been other doctors before?

P: When I was sixteen or seventeen years old, my parents found out and sent me to someone, but . . .

T: But?

P: Nothing happened. I kept on doing what I had to do.

T: Have you ever taken, or are you taking, any medicines?

P: When I was sixteen or seventeen, I took diuretics and laxatives.

T: So the vomiting doesn't occur every day now? Or does it occur every day?

P: Since October, it's been more or less under control, but from August to October I went through a bad period, vomiting three or four times a day, almost every time I'd eaten anything.

T: And now?

P: Not now. I've been trying to make an effort since October.

T: So you're making an effort?

P. Yes.

T: Are you making an effort not to do it?

P: Yes. For example, I go out after eating, instead of staying in the house.

T: Do you take walks?

P: Yes.

T: Do you walk a lot?

P: No. Sometimes I go downstairs to visit my mother; sometimes I walk to a friend's house.

T: Do you need to get rid of your tensions?

P: Yes. I need to get out. I can't vomit in other people's bathrooms, only in my own . . . So if I go out, I probably won't do it.

T: And if you stay home, you probably will do it. I understand. So your way to avoid doing it . . .

P: . . .Is to leave, yes.

T: Is that the only technique you use?

P: Yes, or I just don't eat.

H: She eats very little—almost nothing.

P: Well, no, he says that because he doesn't see me eat.

H: She eats various things, but not a good meal.

P: I'm very disorderly.

T: So you never eat a proper meal, right?

P: No.

T: You tend to eat things you don't consider dangerous, right?

P: No, no . . . chocolate, potato chips . . .

T: When you can vomit?

P: Yes. I already know before I eat that I'm going to vomit.

T: That's what I mean! When you know you can indulge yourself, you eat chocolate, potato chips and so on . . .

P: Ice cream . . . things that are easily expelled.

T: When you know you can't do it, you eat less dangerous things.

P: Or I don't eat at all.

T: OK. Very good . . .

P: Good?

Investigating the solutions attempted by the husband

T: Just to clarify . . . (*to the husband*) What do you do to help your wife?

H: Nothing. If anyone asks her to eat, she still does what she wants. I'm always at work. I only see her at night.

T: What do you do?

H: I'm a house painter.

T: (*to the patient*) Do you work, or do you stay at home?

P: Oh, no. I work in a hospital as the secretary of a department head.

T: I bet he's an expert in gastroenterology!

P: No, no. Emergency medicine.

(*They all laugh*)

T: Otherwise it would have been perfect! Who knows about this problem? Just your family, or other people?

P: No, no. My parents, my sister, and he (*turns towards her husband*).

T: So you were very good at keeping all this a secret for quite a few years?

P: Yes. I guess they never noticed.

T: How did you feel about it when they did notice? Did you feel that they had disturbed your balance, your secret?

P: I was embarrassed because I was ashamed . . .

T: Do you consider vomiting a strategy to avoid getting fat while enjoying the foods you like? Or is eating and vomiting, when you plan it, a kind of pleasurable rite?

P: I don't know. Sometimes I vomit because I've had too much to eat, and sometimes because I just feel like it. I know it in advance . . . it's like relieving oneself . . .

"Mind-reading" technique

T: So you have some moments of fantasy when you start thinking "Now I'm going to eat, and eat . . ."

P: Yes, I can't stop myself.

T: You get into a kind of rapture . . . You start eating, and eating, and stuff yourself until you feel as if you're about to explode, and then you run and vomit . . .

P: Yes.

T: What's more pleasant within that sequence, eating or vomiting? Or everything together?

P: The most pleasant moment is at the end, after purging myself.

T: At other times, you only do it as an emergency, to avoid gaining weight?

P: Yes.

T: Do you usually vomit after your regular meals, or do you sometimes plan the bingeing and vomiting?

P: Most of it happens outside regular hours.

T: Do you plan it . . . pursue it . . .?

P: Yes, also because since I work until two o'clock, I don't have lunch at noon. In the afternoon, I start with one thing, then another . . . Then I tell myself "I've had too much to eat, I've got to . . ."

T: Good. Who buys the food?

P: Well, I do the shopping.

T: You do the shopping . . . Do you live near your parents?

P: Upstairs from them.

Investigating the solutions attempted by the parents

T: Perfect. What are your parents doing to try to change this situation?

P: (*Turns to her husband*) What do they do?

H: They tell her to eat, to go and see a doctor . . . the usual things . . .

T: The usual things . . . Do they talk about it with you? (*to the husband*)

H: They tell me to check how much she eats. It's not very . . .

T: We all agree. So you buy the food that you eat and vomit?

P: Yes.

T: When do you usually do that? In the afternoon or the evening?

P: Either. More often in the afternoon.

T: When you're alone?

P: Yes.

T: Very well. I think we understand as much as we need now, in order to determine whether the problem is within our competence or not. I think it is. It's one of the problems that we've recently been dealing with most often. It's called *vomiting*—eating and vomiting. Who referred you to us?

P: I got your name from an acquaintance of Dr C's in M. I haven't met the doctor personally.

Agreement on the modes of treatment. Therapeutic double bind

T: Very well. I think we can help you solve this problem, maybe even in a short time, provided that you follow all our instructions to the letter. We never ask people to do anything threatening, frightening, too costly, immoral, or anti-economical. Only small things, but they must be carried out to the letter. We are going to need you (*to the husband*), and your mother, at least for some things. After that, we'll do most of the work with you alone (*to the patient*). We'll need your collaboration initially; we won't ask you to do anything difficult, but we will ask you to carry out some precise tasks.

The other rule is that although the things we'll ask you to do may seem a bit strange, illogical, banal, even comical . . . you must still carry them out to the letter. All right?

Finally, we give ourselves a very short time to see any results. We don't do long therapies here, only brief and focused ones. We give ourselves ten sessions. If we don't see any results after ten sessions, we usually stop. If we find that we haven't finished, obviously we continue. If everything works as usual, the problem will either have improved or been completely solved within ten sessions. But I don't know whether that's going to happen in your case. In other words, I believe we have some good methods, and we've experimented these methods on hundreds of cases, but every case is a new case. So I don't know how well you'll be able to follow us . . . Well. We have some homework for you already. (*To the husband*) The task for which we need you as a family (we'll give your wife some tasks privately, so we're going to ask you to leave the room) is the following: I'd like you to speak with your mother-in-law and tell her that she needs to carry out a task that we have assigned. The task is the following. (*To the patient*) What time do you leave for work in the morning?

First prescription: food list for the patient's mother

P: At eight o'clock.

T: Is your mother up by then?

P: Oh, yes.

T: Perfect. Every morning, when your mother comes to wake you up, or to pick up your daughter, she must ask you: "S, what would you like to eat and vomit today?"

P: Imagine my mother! (*smiling*)

T: You'll have to tell her the menu, OK? Your mother will buy you the things you order and put them on the table with a note that says "*Things to eat and vomit for S.*" No one, including your daughter, may touch that food, because it is only yours. All right? You're free to use it or not. Your mother must ask you that question every day. (*To the husband*) Please tell your mother-in-law that if S doesn't want anything, she should buy the same things she bought the day before. Now, we must ask you to leave.

(*The husband leaves the room*)

T. I believe you found this task amusing, but you're also not very happy about it.

P. That's right. I feel as if I'm being mocked. Nobody is allowed to speak to me in the morning, and now they're supposed to say "What would you like to eat and vomit today? (*She laughs*)

T: I warned you that the tasks we give are a bit funny and strange, didn't I? I was rather impressed by how clearly and precisely you described how enjoyable the whole sequence of eating and vomiting is for you.

P: But not always. Sometimes it's better, sometimes it's worse.

Reframing the eating and vomiting ritual as a secret lover

T: But when you set out to do it it's as if . . . we can say it, now that your husband is gone . . . it's as if you were visiting a secret lover. The fantasy . . . the rapture . . . the consummation . . . and the release.

I suppose that for you, if you'll pardon my provocation, this is the greatest pleasure in life . . .

P: Compared to many other things, yes.

T: Compared to anything else. Am I right?

P: Yes, yes, it's true.

T: That's why I'm saying it's your secret lover . . . because it's the most pleasurable thing in the world.

P: At that moment, yes.

T: Therefore, it's something very difficult to do without, because it's a pleasure, the most intense kind of pleasure . . .. I want you to do just one thing for us. First of all, reflect on the fact that your disorder, unlike other disorders, is not based on suffering, but merely on pleasure. So every time you eat and vomit, it's as if you were actually seeing your secret lover . . .

P: That would be better! (*smiling*)

T: You ought to find one that can give you as much pleasure as this thing does . . .

P: That's right!

T: I've been told it's not so easy these days. You must realize that you've actually chosen a very transgressive secret lover . . .

P: A discrete one, mainly . . .

T: . . . one that you can use whenever you want, who isn't invasive.

P: That's right!

T: . . . you control "him", "he" is always available, and that you can be sure he won't create any problems.

P: Yes.

Second prescription: miracle fantasy

T. Good. We suggest that you do something a bit strange. In the morning, when you leave your daughter and go to work, or as you wash, get dressed, and put on your make-up, try to imagine this fantasy: that you walk out of this office, as you will walk out today, and as soon as the door closes behind you, as it will close today, pouf! By magic, your problem disappears. What would immediately change in your life?

P: I can't imagine.

T: What would be the next thing you need to deal with, after this problem? What other problems would come after this one? Don't answer me now. Every morning, try to have this fantasy, project yourself beyond the problem (although we all know you like it a lot, so why are we calling it a problem?) . . . beyond your secret lover . . . Imagine that you leave from here, close the door and pouf! Your problem disappears by magic, your lover isn't there any more. What would change right away in your life? What other problems would come after this one? What difficulties would there be? What voids? What would you do differently? All right? Think about it. Have the fantasy, and bring us the answers. The tasks we give you are a secret among the three of us.

P: O.K.

T: We can see you in a week or in fifteen days, as you prefer.

P: Fifteen days is better.

T: Fifteen days it is. The important thing is that you follow the prescriptions to the letter.

P: It will be a bit difficult, knowing me.

Use of resistance

T: In any case, we need all your resistance. If you told me "I'll make an effort", I wouldn't believe you.

P: And you'd be right (*she smiles*).

T: I know very well that you're here, but you don't really want to be here.

P: That's true!

T: Because you want to keep your secret lover.

P: It's true!

Paradoxical provocation

T: In fact, why should you get rid of it? You're so happy with it!

P: Well, it's not true that I'm happy with it. I often feel bad about it, but it's not such a big problem for me as it is for my husband and my parents. I don't see it as being so serious.

T: For you, it's not a problem . . . It's a pleasure. It's their problem, right? I understand you perfectly. So feel free to say anything you want. If you told me anything different, I wouldn't believe you.

P: So?

T: It's all right, but do what I asked you.

P: OK, I'll try.

Session two

CoT: How did it go?

P: I did my little exercise every morning. It helped me think more about my problem.

T: Let's talk about it.

Redefining the effects of the miracle fantasy

P: Because before . . . even as I was leaving from here, I was thinking: "I never think about my problem." Apart from when I do it, I don't actually sit down and think about it. But now, every morning, as I repeated that sentence, I thought about my work, my daughter, my marriage, the usual things!

T: The sentence you are referring to is "If I walked out of here, and 'Poof!', by magic . . ."

P: Yes . . . what would I think about? What would I have to worry about . . .

T: What did you discover?

Redefining the effects of the miracle fantasy

P: First of all I thought about my problems with my daughter, whether she's well or not, whether she's eating, like all mothers do I suppose. Then my marriage, my work.

T: So many things?

P: Yes.

T: Were you able to go beyond the problem or not?

P: I don't understand.

T: Were you able to imagine the magic? Poof, the problem's gone?

P: No.

T: OK.

P: No, I never really thought about it. I said it, but I can't imagine . . .

T: You couldn't feel it?

P: No.

Redefining the effects of giving the food list to her mother

T: Well, well . . . Did your mum ask for the list?

P: Yes, poor mum.

T: Yes, poor mum! Let's talk about it.

P: All she needed was an idiot daughter like me! (*Laughs*)

T: How did you feel about your mother's asking for the list?

P: Every morning she asked me "What would you like to eat and vomit?"

T: And you'd give her the list . . .

P: It makes me laugh, also because she says it in a humorous way. She didn't make a tragedy out of it. I'd get home . . . the note would be there . . . except for two days . . .

T: What did you order? What was your menu? Did it vary?

P: Yes, it varied. I'd say anything that came to mind.

T: What did you usually order?

P: Something ordinary . . . a grilled sandwich, or some small sandwiches, without specifying the quantity of food. She'd decide.

T: You need to be more specific. In the menu, you also have to say how many you want . . .

P: I only did that twice: "Could you make me two eggs?"; another time, two sandwiches, which I didn't even eat.

T: What do you mean, you didn't eat them?

P: Because I felt nervous when I got home and couldn't even eat.

T: That bad?

P: It only happened twice.

T: You mean, twice you didn't eat and vomit?

P: No, no, I mean I just didn't eat. I ate later, in the evening. I just didn't feel like eating.

T: How come?

P: Because when I'm in a state of anxiety, or someone is rude to me, or something happens to me, my stomach locks up and I can't eat. I start to sweat . . .

T: Listen, C, did you set the menu for your ritual every day?

P: Yes, but I never vomited, except for one day.

T: How do you explain that?

P: It goes in periods: I might stay without doing it for several months, and then I might spend six months vomiting three times a day.

T: Right. But I thought there had been a different rhythm in recent weeks.

P: Yes, well . . . it happens right before my period, otherwise I'm pretty good at controlling it.

T: So in fifteen days there were two episodes?

P: One, on a Monday.

T: Did you eat and vomit everything you had ordered?

P: Yes.

T: What did you do on the other days? Did you eat and keep it in?

P: Yes, I kept it in.

T: Aren't you afraid of getting fat?

P: No, apart from one day when I'd had too much chocolate. But I didn't vomit, because I had been eating dry foods and it would have been too difficult. (*She laughs*) One has to eat things that are easily regurgitated, otherwise it's a useless effort. I already know that it would be for nothing . . .

T: Well, well, well. And were there no leftovers? You didn't leave anything for the Albanians?

P: Yes, I did leave something.

T: What did you do with the leftover food?

P: I gave it to the dog.

T: You have a dog?

P: Yes, my father who lives downstairs has one.

T: Did you think about the other things we told you about eating and vomiting?

P: I don't remember. What was it again?

Redefining eating and vomiting as a pleasure

T: We were saying that it's actually an important source of pleasure.

P: Yes. I didn't think about it much. I thought about it on my way home from here, the other day.

T: It didn't come back to mind?

P: In some moments . . . but just brief thoughts . . . I didn't . . .

CoT: Not even when you vomited? That Monday?

P: Well . . . to tell you the truth, I thought about it that whole day. But when I do those things, I don't really think about myself, my daughter, my husband, my mother . . .

CoT: Of course! Anyway, while you were vomiting, where you thinking about it as a source of pleasure for you?

P: No, it's not that when I vomit I think "How wonderful". Maybe it's a pleasure that I don't even realize is a pleasure . . .

T: Do you start by thinking "I'm going to eat now"? Do you have a fantasy about eating?

P: Yes, that happens too . . .

T: On that day, did you think about eating the whole day?

P: No, I didn't want to vomit that day. There were some things I felt like eating at lunch. It's like a rapture. Within ten minutes, I start thinking "Now I'll eat and then I'll go."

T: And did you?

P: Yes.

T: But not the other days?

P: No. Also because I was busy at work, lots of things . . . I wouldn't even have had the time . . .

T: Even if you had everything available?

P: No.

T: With the clear message "*Things to eat and vomit for C*", how did you feel when you saw that note?

P: Well . . . I felt sorry for my mother . . .

T: Poor her!

P: Yes, really.

T: Was she diligent, precise?

P: Yes. One day she forgot, and called me later at the office to ask . . .

T: Excellent. Apart from the episode that only presented itself once, how was your relationship with food? Did you hold back?

P: Yes, I held back.

T: Did you stay on a diet?

P: No, I don't restrict myself. I don't select certain foods. I can eat anything. But I eat few fatty or calorie-rich foods.

T: So you were very careful about what you ate?

P: No, just about how much I ate, because I had chocolate, desserts . . .

T: What limits do you set for yourself? You're good at calculating calories!

P: I eat in such a way that I avoid feeling sick, or swollen or . . .

T: Yes, but that's very subjective. How do you set organized limits?

P: If, for example, there's a pastry or piece of cake, I'll eat half of it. With pasta, I eat a bit less than other people do . . .

T: Well, help me understand this. The past fifteen days, you've followed what we might call a normal diet, except for the fact that it was reduced?

P: Yes, reduced in terms of the quantity of food, but I ate some of everything . . .

T: How did the people around you react to this situation?

P: They seemed a bit suspicious. They didn't know whether to ask me how it was going. That's what I thought, or maybe I was imagining . . . I don't know.

T: Suspicious of what?

P: When I went to the bathroom, they seemed to be trying to figure out whether I was going there to vomit; or, they noticed what I was eating. That was my impression, but I don't know . . .

T: Was your husband able to avoid talking about it?

P: We never talked about it.

T: Did you feel like talking about it?

P: Sometimes. For example, on the day I vomited . . . I would have liked to have said something then . . . I don't know . . . But I didn't say anything . . . because I feel as if . . . I'm weighing him down, so if I don't talk about it . . .

T: Did you miss it?

P: No.

T: You didn't miss that special moment . . .

P: No, because I had a lot of work, three conferences, things like that. I didn't feel like it. I was exhausted from other things.

Investigating the patient's eating habits

T: Good. What do you eat, on the average, in the course of one day? Can you describe the phases?

P: I eat in a disorderly way because I work office hours. When I get home, I put my daughter to bed for her nap. I eat erratically most times . . . just junk food . . .

T: Like what?

P: Nutella, snacks, biscuits, cereal . . .

T: You glutton!

P: In the evenings, if I'm not full, I'll have something . . .

T: Otherwise you skip dinner, and just watch your husband eat?

P: Yes.

T: Is that what's been happening, mostly, the past fifteen days, or did you mostly stay with him?

P: Oh, I always sit at the table in any case.

T: Did you eat?

P: Yes, a little. I always sat with them.

T: Did you always eat the food that was on the table?

P: Yes.

T: Is that because you were less attracted to junk food during the day?

P: Yes.

T: Did you eat less of it?

P: Yes. I can't go without a piece of chocolate, but if I [just] eat one, I can eat pasta . . .

T: In the past few days, did you eat less chocolate?

P: Yes, except for one day . . . on Easter Monday.

T: So the food you ordered usually ended up as leftovers?

P: Yes, because my mother prepared a lot of it.

First prescription: continue the food list, including favourite foods and specifying quantities

T: Now you have to become an expert at this . When you write the list, you must also write down the quantity. But we'd also like you to mostly include your junk food . . . You have to order the things you like to eat.

P: It doesn't need to be cooked. Everything I've been eating is prepackaged.

T: The things that you really like to eat, and that you like to eat and vomit. You have to be precise about the quantities, OK? Since you'll find the junk foods anyway, you don't need to go and look for them. They'll be there, with the usual note. You can eat them and vomit them, or you can eat and not vomit them, or you can not eat them . . . it's your problem! All right?

P: All right.

Second prescription: one small thing per day, "as if" the problem were gone

T: Another little piece of special homework. In the morning, around the same time that you were doing your fantasy exercise, you should now ask yourself a more concrete question: "What would I do differently today, if I no longer had this problem of eating and vomiting? *As if* it were gone? How would I organize my day differently? What different things would I do?" Among the things that come to mind that you would do differently as if the problem were gone, choose the smallest one, every day, and put it into practice. It has to be something different every day.

P: That's difficult!

T: One small thing every day, as if the problem weren't there . . .

P: And I have to do it?

T: And you have to do it. Something different every day. Bring the list, OK?

P: That's difficult. I don't know if I can do it!

T: Who knows? Who knows if you're good enough!

P: We'll see.

Session three

Report on the past week

CoT: How's it going? How have you been these past two weeks?

P: It's been bad, because I was sick, my daughter was sick, and I was able to do some things around the house and in the garden, [but] couldn't do what I had planned . . .

T: But still, you did some other things?

P: Yes, but insignificant things: gardening, housecleaning . . .

CoT: What about the list of things to eat?

P: Yes, I have it here.

T: How did it go?

P: Pretty well. Only one day, a Sunday, my mother wasn't there, so she didn't ask me the question. That day I ate and vomited.

Redefining the effects of the manoeuvres

T: Did you eat and vomit on other days?

P: I ate a little and never vomited.

T: How odd! You mean to tell us that in the past two weeks, you only ate and vomited once?

P: Only last Sunday.

T: The morning your mother didn't ask you . . .?

P: Yes, the same day, but not because of that . . .

T: We didn't say that. No one is making that interpretation.

P: Also because I was at home alone. I can't stand those kinds of days.

T: And you never performed the rituals on the other days, when you made the list and chose the tastiest things, the "junk"? Did you eat everything, or was there some left?

P: There was some left. Sometimes I ate less of it, sometimes I ate it all.

T: That Sunday, you were home alone . . .

P: Yes. I had cooked. I was alone, so I started . . .

T: Your husband wasn't there?

P: No, he plays soccer on Sundays, and the girl was sleeping. She had an earache, so I couldn't go out . . .

Reiterating the pleasurable aspect of the ritual

T: So you told yourself, "Let's at least have this small satisfaction . . ."

P: Yes. Actually, it wasn't premeditated. I started without noticing it. Later I felt swollen and nauseous, without inducing it . . .

T: What did you eat that time? Something you had cooked, or something you had ordered the previous days?

P: For lunch, I ate something I had cooked. In the afternoon, I started with a snack, some potato chips, and anything that was at hand.

T: How long did the whole thing last?

P: An hour and a half. I waited an hour. I was unsure whether I should vomit, because I felt bad about it. I had a headache, and knew that the effort of vomiting might make it worse. Then I said to myself, "OK, let's get rid of this weight!"

T: Did you wait to decide?

P: I don't know, I smoked . . .

T: Didn't you feel like going straight away?

P: No, I felt bad about it.

Investigating the dominant system of perceptions and reactions

T: Did you vomit because you were afraid of getting fat, or for other reasons?

P: Because I felt swollen and sick. I shouldn't have eaten all those things. I had been good the whole week, and then . . .

T: After that episode, were you good anyway for the rest of the week?

P: Yes.

T: Do you make an effort to "be good", or does it come naturally?

P: This week I had to, because I skipped some meals. I had to take my daughter to the hospital and several other things, so I couldn't . . .

T: Would you have done it otherwise?

P: I don't think so. I wasn't in the mood for it. I was neither depressed nor . . .

T: The week before, did you have to make an effort or did it come effortlessly?

P: No, because instead of sitting and eating, I did other things: planted flowers, cleaned the windows . . .

T: Do you feel this is a sign of improvement or not?

P: I think so. I was surprised, because I was expecting . . . I'm usually more determined: I go to the bathroom, stick my hand down my throat and it's all over. Instead, that day I noticed I was taking my time, smoking a cigarette . . .

T: Do you feel that your improvement consists of that episode, not having vomited as soon as you had binged, or in having managed to eat little during the whole week and not eating excessively?

P: I think the improvement lies in having limited my food intake, up to a point . . .

T: Enjoying what you ate?

P: Yes, because I was hungry.

T: Did you enjoy what you ate because you had the food ready?

P: Yes, all the things that I like.

T: What "junk" was that? Did you make a list?

P: Yes. Do you want to see it?

T: We're curious! (*Reads*): sandwiches, baked pasta, etc.

CoT: That's not junk food! They're very good foods!

P: Some of the sandwiches had a lot of mayonnaise on them.

T: (*Keeps reading*): toast, pudding, popsicles That's junk food! And did the people around you notice this change?

P: Actually they didn't ask me . . .

T: Do you think they noticed?

P: I don't know.

T: Last time, they were doubtful. Do you remember?

P: Yes, I think they still are, but they haven't asked me anything.

T: That's just as well!

CoT: Does your husband continue his silence?

P: Yes, and that bothers me.

CoT: Do you feel like talking to him?

P: Maybe this time, if he asks, I can say it went well.

T: He's respecting our instructions to keep a conspiracy of silence. How was your mood this past week?

P: Furious, every day, because several things happened at work, and my daughter . . . a lot of things all together, so I was nervous. Not depressed—nervous.

Redefining the effects of the "as if" prescription

T: What were some of the most curious things you thought of when you thought about things to do *as if* the problem were gone?

P: For example, I've been wanting to have my ear pierced again for about three years now, and I wanted to have my daughter's ears pierced. I went to several jewellery stores, and no one wanted to pierce our ears. My daughter's too young, and they didn't want to do a second piercing on me, but I tried! I also wanted to go to the beach, but my daughter wakes up from her nap at 4.30 p.m., and . . .

First prescription: food list

T: We're impressed by what you've told us, so let's proceed along the same lines. We'd like you to keep writing a detail list of "junk food". After that, it's up to you to choose whether to eat, not to eat, or eat as much as you want.

Second prescription: one "as if" action every day

T: Every morning, we'd like you to ask yourself the same question: "What would I do differently from what I usually do, if the problem were gone". Then choose the smallest thing that comes to mind, and do it. If, as I hope, your illnesses are over, you'll be able to do some things you planned, not "recycled" activities in the garden.

Third prescription: ninety-minute interval between eating and vomiting

T: We're pleased by what you've just told us, because it's something that we were going to prescribe. We're pleased that you anticipated us. If you happen to binge like you did last Sunday, and start eating, and eating and eating, we want you to avoid trying to hold back. You should do it. When you feel the food's up to here, stop, take an alarm clock, set it to sound an and a half hour later, and wait an hour and a half before you vomit. As soon as the alarm sounds, not a minute before or a minute later, run and vomit. OK?

P: That way, after an hour and a half, it will all come out.

T: Every time it happens, OK? Not a minute earlier or later. During that hour and a half, you must avoid putting any food in your mouth.

P: So how should I vomit?

T: As you usually do it, with your fingers in your mouth, but without eating or drinking anything else. All right? Ninety minutes later. We're pleased with you. With no illusions, but pleased.

P: What does that mean?

T: We'll explain later.

P: Should I keep bringing the list?

T: Of course, of the things done as if the problem were gone.

P: All right.

Session four

T: How have things been going?

P: Not bad! (*She hands over the food list*)

T: What does that mean?

P: Well, I managed to control myself pretty well. My moods weren't too bad. I vomited once. I set the alarm, like you told me. That hour felt like it lasted for ever!

Redefining the effects of the interval between eating and vomiting

T: One thing at a time. This is the list of things you ate or planned to eat. Did you only vomit once in the past fifteen days?

P: Yes, last Thursday.

T: How was that day different from the other fourteen days?

P: I couldn't control myself, I ate more. I felt that I had eaten too much, so I set the alarm, and then . . .

T: What did you do during that hour?

P: I played with my daughter, and smoked three or four cigarettes.

T: Why did you say it seemed to last forever?

P: I kept looking at the clock.

T: Did it bother you to have to stay there?

P: Yes. I'd have liked to have gone straight away, so I wouldn't have to think about it any more.

T: So you wouldn't have to think about it any more or so you wouldn't have to keep that food inside you?

P: No, it's because I knew I had to do it. Whenever I know I have to do something, it always bothers me to wait. I'm like that in everything. That day, I was with my daughter, watching the clock and waiting to go. But that hour was long!

T: When you vomited, did it work as usual or was it harder? Was it more of a struggle or was everything perfect?

P: It went well, because everything came out at the first attempt! How shameful!

T: It all came out at the first attempt?

P: Yes. I didn't have to struggle. Usually, when I wait, it all comes out. If I go straight away, the food hasn't reached the stomach yet, so . . .

T: So it came out better . . . Did you like it better?

P: I relieved myself immediately. I didn't have to do it two or three times. I felt the weight come off at the first try.

T: How were your moods?

P: I was very busy with work and other things. It went well. I was very sleepy . . .

T: Sleepy? How come?

P: Because I worked a lot . . . then there was housework, my daughter, those kinds of things, always in a rush. One gets tired.

T: How did the people around you react when they saw that you only vomited once?

P: They don't know. My husband asked me "How many times did you vomit?" I said "Once, on Thursday."

T: How did he react?

P: I didn't look at him. We were in the car, and I was afraid he'd say "See, it's not working".

Redefining the effects of the "as if" exercise

T: We gave you another task too, right?

P: Yes, to do one thing a day.

T: As if the problem were gone. Did you do that?

P: Yes.

T: What came to mind?

P: Almost every time it was going out with my daughter. We went to the zoo, to the playground, and so on. Of course, one can't do anything very extravagant with a child!

T: Would you like to do something extravagant?

P: No . . . Going out at night with my friends . . . It must have been a year since I went out with a woman friend, and one morning I thought "That's what I could do differently today."

T: And did you?

P: Yes, and I enjoyed it!

T: Did you do anything else that you hadn't done for a while?

P: I went to the zoo. I went shopping, because I don't get out of the house very much. My daughter wakes up from her nap at five . . .

Emphasizing the importance of the change that has occurred

T: Why did you think your husband might say it isn't working, or that he would be unsatisfied with you? A month ago, you were vomiting much more often.

P: Yes, it used to happen several times a day.

T: Twice in a month is a remarkable improvement!

P: Yes, but he doesn't know . . .

T: Didn't he know how much you used to vomit before?

P: Yes, he has some idea, but maybe now that I'm coming here he expects me not to do it at all.

T: Twice in a month . . .

P: That's good for me!

T: That's right. It's definitely very little!

P: Yes, I'm happy because I can . . .

T: Did it take a great effort to keep from doing it, or not?

P: If I had a lot of things to do, it wouldn't take any effort at all. If I worked in a mine, I would never vomit.

T: Anorexia doesn't exist in India, because if a daughter doesn't eat, the father will gladly eat her plate of rice. And people in Africa don't suffer from agoraphobia, because they have to run around the whole day.

P: Right. But last Thursday I had nothing to do, and we had nothing planned. We were all there, at home . . .

T: On days like that, you can't find anything that might create a bit of enthusiasm in you?

P: Not last Thursday, also because I'm very lazy, and don't feel like moving. On days like that I feel ugly, and stay at home.

T: Do you often feel ugly?

P: It happens on some days. On those days, I stay home and tend not to move.

First prescription: continue with the food list

T: Let's proceed. I want you to continue writing the food list for me.

Second prescription: two "as if" things per day, or one that may count as two

T: I want you to do two things as if the problem were gone to become two, instead of just one. The smallest things you can think of, but two each day. Or one that's a little bigger, which counts as two. So, every morning, ask yourself: "How would I behave differently today, if I didn't have this problem any more?" and choose the two smallest things, or one big one that counts as two.

P: That's difficult. I don't know what to do . . .

T: You've been good the past fifteen days.

P: But I don't do anything special.

T: I'm not asking for anything strange . . . just small things.

Third prescription: two-hour interval between eating and vomiting

T: Now let's talk about the most difficult thing: when you feel like vomiting, after eating, you must set the alarm to sound two hours later.

P: Meanwhile, I'll have finished two packs of cigarettes.

T: Do whatever you like, but set the alarm to sound two hours later, and when it sounds, not one minute earlier or one minute later, run and vomit.

P: That's OK. I set it at an hour and a half before.

T: Now it's two hours.

P: Last time you said "we have no illusions", and I didn't understand what you meant.

T: It means that I'm happy about the way things are going with you, but I'm not deceiving myself. I'm optimistic, but without illusions.

Session five

CoT: How did it go?

P: We had the flu. I did everything you told me.

T: Two hours?

P: Yes, two hours. Once. I didn't vomit anything. It didn't come. I had already digested the food.

T: Only once? So in fifteen days you only tried to vomit once. You waited two hours, and then you couldn't do it.

P: No.

T: How did you feel about that?

P: It bothered me, because I wasn't able to get rid of everything I had eaten.

CoT: Did you have a great binge?

P: No, not an extravagant one, but I had some very calorie-rich foods.

T: What?

P: Peanuts . . . shall I give you the list?

T: Let's see. When did it happen? On Sunday?

P: No, on Monday.

T: So we've changed the day?

P: Yes.

CoT: Did you write a list of the small things you did as if the problem were gone?

P: Yes.

T: Yes, it's written down here. You've been great! (*The therapist reads from the list:*) Visiting a friend, shopping with the daughter, etc. So what exactly happened on Monday? How did it start?

P: I got home from work as usual. I was alone there; my daughter was sleeping. I didn't feel like doing anything in the house. I stayed there, doing nothing. After eating, I lay down on the bed with my daughter and set the alarm. After two hours, I went.

T: And when you didn't succeed?

P: I didn't eat anything more until the next day.

T: So you compensated?

P: Yes, well . . .

T: Was it hard?

P: Not eating?

T: Yes.

P: No.

T: You punished yourself that way?

P: Yes.

T: Good. How come it didn't happen on Sunday?

P: I don't know.

T: Did you have a more enjoyable Sunday than usual?

P: No, I worked. We're organizing a congress, and I work at home too.

T: So you were busier than usual that Sunday.

P. Yes.

T: I wonder what will happen tomorrow when you're not so busy!

P: No, my boss called, and I'll have to work at least two hours.

T: What's your assessment of the situation?

P: I don't know. I was hoping I wouldn't vomit this time; instead, it happened again.

T: We told you it would happen at least once.

P: Well, that's what you said. I was hoping it wouldn't.

Further investigation on the patient's dominant system of perceptions and reactions

T: I told you that you'd be doing it at least once. What's the most serious problem, from your point of view? That you ate, and felt like vomiting? Would it have been as terrible if you had eaten but not felt the need to vomit? What is it that you can't forgive yourself, the binge or . . .

P: Eating more than usual.

CoT: And not vomiting?

P: Yes.

T: What I'm about to say may sound strange, but you must be prepared for that by now, right?

P: Everything you make me do is strange!

Redefining the effects of the "as if" exercise

T: I have two questions about the things you did "as if" the problem were gone. Did you always have to make an effort to find them? Was it hard, or did they come to mind easily?

P: I did things I was supposed to do anyway. But I don't think about vomiting much. I never do it when I'm busy.

T: Good. Has your mood been better, worse, or the same during the past two weeks?

P: I was a bit nervous because I had to stay in the house with the baby.

T: Because she was sick?

P: Yes.

First prescription: three-hour interval between eating and vomiting, and avoid fasting

T. OK. I'll just say that when you have to vomit (and it will happen after a binge) you must now wait three hours, not one minute less, not one minute more.

P: That means not vomiting!

T: That's not all. If we take away the vomiting solution and replace it with fasting, we're not changing anything. So if you eat, you may vomit after three hours, but you have to avoid fasting. You must eat regular meals.

P: It's so difficult.

T: I warned you. That's not all. The most interesting thing is another.

Reframing: the "small disorder that keeps order"

T: I believe that in order to teach you not to feel the need to transgress whenever you have nothing to do, we need to teach you the art of the "small disorder that maintains order". In nature, all the most stable balances are maintained by the fact that there's a small disorder that maintains the order. If a certain balance lacks a small imbalance, it becomes rigid, and dies, or breaks.

Second prescription: one small eating transgression a day

T: So, between now and the next time we meet, we want you to allow yourself one small eating transgression every day. A very small one, for example a biscuit or a piece of chocolate . . .

P: I always do that.

T: We want it to be separate from what you usually eat, and we want you to write it down. So, "if I allow myself this, I can do without it; if I don't allow it, it will be irresistible" and if you binge, you wait three hours before vomiting. You decide whether to vomit or not.

P: Can I decide this time?

Reframing by using an aphorism

T: Yes, but you may not decide to fast. All right? Again, "if I allow myself to do it, I can also do without it; if I don't allow it, it will be irresistible". It's OK to let yourself binge once in a while!

P: Yes, I know, but . . .

T: But?

P: Not me.

T: Why not you?

P: Because it bothers me.

T: Why does it bother you?

P: It bothers me because I'm afraid I'll get fat, and it bothers me to feel swollen. Even if I just have two glasses of water, I feel swollen.

T: It's useless for me to explain something you know as well as I do, and that is that if a person keeps balanced eating habits during the week, it's all right to transgress once a week . . .

P: Yes, nothing will happen . . .

T: It's useless for me to repeat it. The problem lies in the mental associations that you make between having a full stomach and immediately feeling like a "disgusting ball of fat".

P: More or less.

T: We need to help you change this idea. You can allow yourself a binge. Vomit three hours later. You may choose whether to vomit or not, but stick to a regular diet. And we want one small transgression every day.

P: I have no problem with that.

Third prescription: taking her measurements

T: One last thing. We want you to take your measurements as if you were a top model, this evening, and again before coming here. We'll see if you're like an accordion.

P: Fine (*laughs*).

T: And you'll learn to look at yourself, not in the mirror but with something a bit more reliable. You may alternate the scale and the mirror.

P: I never weigh myself.

T: But you look at yourself.

P: Yes.

T: And you see yourself immediately expanding?

P: No. I watch myself in profile and look at my belly.

T. Right. Measurements. OK . . .

Session six

Redefining the effects of the manoeuvre

CoT: How's it going?

P: I never vomited!

T: Oh!

P: Never set the alarm!

CoT: No bingeing?

P: No, I always controlled myself.

CoT: And the small transgression?

P: Yes. I wrote it down.

T: (*reads*) Two meatballs with bread and mayonnaise . . .

P: I was having a hypoglycaemic crisis.

T: A sandwich with nutella . . . various biscuits . . . chocolate . . . scampi . . .

P: I never fasted. I always ate small quantities of food. That's how I regulated my eating.

Complimenting the patient for what she's been able to do

T: You did very well. Then, here are the things you did *as if:* went out with Lisa, cleaned the house . . . Great! Two every day.

P: Even more than two per day.

T: Good. Now, what does that mean, in your opinion?

P: Well . . . There's something was different, because I controlled my food intake and all that. Not just the food. I felt a need to make order. I'm not usually like that. I'm actually disastrously messy. I feel comfortable in my own mess, but . . .

T: Did you notice something strange? You've been eating, eating different things, maybe even slightly forbidden things. You transgressed, and you're one centimetre slimmer!

P: Yes, but maybe water retention, swelling . . .

T: Your weight, too . . .

P: Yes, but I always vary between fifty and fifty-two kilos.

T: Yes, but to vary two kilos less, having eaten more, with transgressions, without vomiting . . .

P: It was worth it!

T: Ah! That's what I want to hear! What did the people around you notice?

P: They noticed that I was a bit more nervous. I felt as if I was practicing abstinence. I smoked twice as much as usual. They noticed I was a bit tense. And I was rather tense . . .

T: But what did they say when they saw you eating the chocolate and things like that?

P: I don't know if they saw me, because I'm always alone in the afternoons. The baby sleeps and . . .

T: So these things all happened while you were alone?

P: Yes.

T: When was it most difficult to avoid bingeing and vomiting?

P: Never. I never felt the need to.

T: Not even on Sundays?

P: No.

CoT: You mentioned that there was some control involved?

P: Yes. I tend to binge when I start feeling a bit swollen. Then I eat something extra and vomit everything. This time, instead, I stopped before getting that feeling. It wasn't so hard.

T: So it didn't take a lot of effort to control yourself?

P: No.

T: Did it happen spontaneously after a while, or did you always have to make an effort?

P: No, I didn't have to make an effort. It wasn't hard. I had a thousand things to do. I always do something right after [eating]: work, the baby, and so on. I didn't even think about it.

T: What made you nervous? Did you say "abstinence"?.

P: Yes. I think I controlled myself, but I was always thinking: "I'm scared of having to vomit, and not being able to make it."

T: You knew you had to wait several hours, and that . . .

P: No. You said I could choose this time.

T: Yes, yes. I said "You can do it, or not do it."

P: Yes, but I was careful. It wasn't a huge burden, but I knew I had to control myself.

T: Was it hard not to fast?

P: No, because I was hungry at dinnertime, since I hadn't been bingeing.

T: And when you ate the transgressive things, like sweets, how did you feel afterwards?

P: I felt good, because I wouldn't eat a whole eclair, but always a limited amount. But I didn't have a craving for sweets, or for anything in particular.

T: Good. I think you've been pretty good.

P: I think so, too.

More incentives to use her personal abilities, through provocation

T: It's true. You're definitely good, but we don't know how good you're going to be.

Prescriptions: (1) four-hour interval

T: For now, if things keep working, I don't thing we need to add anything else. So let's keep exactly the same prescriptions, with just one variation: if you feel the need to vomit, wait one more hour. So, if you need to do it, wait one more hour. That'll help you avoid doing it.

P: Yes. After four hours, I'll already have digested the food, so I won't be able to vomit even if I stick a spoon this long in my throat. Nothing will come out.

(2) Taking her measurements

T: And we'd like you to write down your measurements again for next time.

(3) One eating transgression a day, and avoid fasting

T: We want one transgression a day, and avoid anything that's even close to fasting.

(4) "As if" for the whole day

T: Ask yourself, "What would I do today if the problem were gone?" We'd like you to think about your whole day, not just one or two things. So ask yourself repeatedly: "How would I live if I didn't have to think in function of this problem? What would I do differently?"

P: After doing one thing I have to think of another?

T: That's right. For example, when anything comes to mind: "Could I do it as if I didn't have this problem, or not?" When in doubt, ask yourself, "How would I behave if I didn't have this problem?"

P: I wanted to tell you something. It's probably irrelevant. Almost every night, I dream about eating.

T: That's not so irrelevant, considering how long you've been doing this.

P: I eat a lot of chocolate. In the morning I wake up afraid I really did it.

T: Do you dream that you eat, or that you eat and vomit?

P: I dream that I eat.

T: Without vomiting?

P: Yes, but I wake up thinking I need to vomit, thinking "God, what did I do?" because I ate too much.

T: You feel guilty, and that you have to vomit.

P: Yes.

Reframing the utility of food-related dreams

T: It's the same with children. When children have dreams about the werewolf, or the dead, the ghosts in the night, it's very important, because that emotional discharge saves them from having fears during the day. So if you're able to move some things to the night, that helps us. So I'm very happy.

Clinical case example (vomiting 3)

P was referred to our centre in Arezzo by a colleague who, after a few sessions, felt that the therapy was proceeding with difficulty and asked for a consultation.

Session one

T: You're from M.

P: (*nods*)

T: You've been seeing Dr . . ., is that right?

P: Yes.

T: Well, of course I have the information pertaining to your case, but . . .

P: Of course!

T: . . . But as we always say in these cases, it's as if I didn't know anything about it, because what we have is one point of view, and we want to get the other point of view. OK?

P: Yes, I understand. I can give you a partial outline.

T: So, what's the situation?

P: The situation is . . . First of all, I had the honour of hearing you speak in M. last Thursday.

T: Oh, thank you.

P: Dr . . . suggested that I go there. That evening, you described the problems of anorexia, bulimia, and vomiting. I don't know exactly where to place myself among those categories, because my case has some peculiarities, some nuances . . . Let me put it this way. I go through long periods of not eating, then throw myself on the food, and vomit. This problem is creating a lot of unbalance for me. I can't understand the reason behind the problem. It's been going on for many years now—about ten. I've always tried to break away from this problem, but I've failed. I mean, I've even tried to avoid it by staying out at night, but I just can't avoid it.

Analysing the solutions attempted by the previous therapist

T: Now, the question I'm most interested in, before we start focusing on the present, is the following. Obviously, I've heard Dr . . .'s point of view with respect to the work you've been doing together. What I'd like to hear now is your own perspective on that work. How well have things been going, if they've been going well, or how badly have they been going if they've not been going well.

P: Well, I've had four or five sessions with Dr . . . . We were well into the therapy, and he was prescribing some things for me to do. At the fifth session, I told him that I didn't have the letters that I was supposed to write with me. I had written them, but didn't have them with me. The doctor got angry, and I told him I didn't have them with me because I didn't believe in his method. I mean, I had no faith in the success of the therapy. That may have been because he repeated several times that if the problem isn't solved by the tenth session, it's goodbye. I got a bit fixated on that, because after meeting five times with him, and his giving me things to do, I still get home at night and things are still the same for me. Nothing has changed inside.

T: Were you always able to apply his tasks to the letter, or not?

P: Yes, also because all the told me was to write some letters. He didn't ... We started out with my parents, with their collaboration, which meant that we were supposed to get together in the evening, after work, and they were supposed to dedicate thirty minutes of silence to ...

T: Right, OK.

P: But that was a complete failure, because my parents are unable to keep silent, so there were some rather ... furious, exasperating arguments. Then we got to the conspiracy of silence. My parents aren't supposed to intervene, or make any comments. They did that until a week ago. By the beginning of this week, they started to tell me to eat again ...

T. And what were the instructions on food?

P: There weren't any. All he told me with respect to food was "don't try to change anything because you won't succeed". He tried to pass off my crazy way of eating as ... I mean, he tried to pass me off as a crusader, because I have a younger brother who was born with some health problems, and since my parents are very focused on this problem, the doctor suggested that my problem might be playing a strategic role in alleviating my parents' anxiety about my brother and transferring those anxieties on to me, like some kind of buffer. At the beginning he asked me to concentrate on this idea, to try and see if I could assimilate it, but (and I wrote this in my letters) the whole idea is decidedly absurd. At first, he also tried to interpret my problem from a sexual point of view. He said: "Whenever you're trying to vomit, try to imagine that you're having sexual intercourse, like a quickie with a man. Yes, clearly ... but that didn't have any effect either, because, as you were saying the other evening, after the failure of my latest relationship, I haven't been able to have any other relationships. That's totally out of the question for me. Maybe because I realize that having a relationship with a man would just ... create another problem, because I can't get rid of this problem. I mean the thing that's foremost in my mind is food. I try to avoid it, but inevitably ...

T: Did this start after you broke up with that person, or while you were together?

P: No, the problem started before. It started many years ago.

Defining the current state of the problem

T: So what is the present problem? How does it manifest itself these days?

P: I leave the house in the morning and go to work. I don't eat lunch, I just drink.

T: What do you do? May I call you by your first name?

P: Yes, of course. I work in the commercial department of a company.

T: Good. So you drink, and don't eat.

Investigating the patient's system of family and social relationships

P: I don't eat. I get home at night, and find an increasingly intolerant environment. At the moment my parents aren't pestering me about this problem, but of course it's always in the air. I've noticed, especially in the past few months, that there's no dialogue between us. If I need to talk about something, they don't understand. I have to explain it in twenty different ways, I mean, I'm noticing that they're becoming prematurely senile. I think it's truly alarming.

T: How old are you?

P: Almost twenty-eight.

T: OK, so you get home in the evening . . .

P: Yes. I go from a work environment where I'm required to understand things quickly, and where I always have to be on top of things and understand whatever problem comes up, to an environment where I feel I'm talking to some idiots. I get mad at them because of that. I get irritated, and things always end up the same way.

T: OK . . .

P: I start eating. I don't binge. I eat normally, I mean, I think it's a normal amount, and then I vomit, and don't want to eat any more.

T: During the day, do you ever eat and not vomit?

P: Yes.

T: When?

P: Occasionally when I feel that I'm losing all my strength I'll eat something. After that, I might be busy, have things to do or people to see, maybe an appointment. Clearly then there's no time for . . .

T: No time for what, for vomiting? Otherwise you would do it?

P: No . . . I mean, there are other times when I'm having a better day . . . I don't know how to put it . . . I feel calmer. Maybe I've had some personal satisfaction, some imperceptible, really minimal thing that made my day. In that case . . .

T: So you're a person who's quick at feeling enthusiasms and equally quick at getting depressed?

P: Yes, but I'm not that sensitive to compliments. I mean, they don't move me that much. I feel it much more if I get criticized. Sometimes I make up my own criticisms. I'm really destructive towards myself, mentally . . .

T: Tell me, how do you spend your time, apart from going to work and fighting with your parents?

P: I volunteer in a museum near my home town.

T: What kind of museum is it?

P: A biology museum. It's being restructured. We're working on the archives and organizing things. I also sing in a choir, and that's something I enjoy a lot. Lately I've been given some responsibilities within the choral group. From April to June, I'm in a theatre group with some other young people. We do comedies, in the popular theatre genre.

T: Very well.

P: But although I feel I have an expressive personality, I get to a certain point, and then I'm blocked. I don't know. I feel as if people can look through me and see that I have this problem, and at that point I shut down and become shy. I get scared, and run away.

T: Well, I've finished with my questions. (*To the co-therapist*) Do you have any questions to ask?

CoT: Yes. May I call you by your first name?

P: (*nods*)

CoT: You've told us that this experience has been going on for ten years . . . that you're involved in several social activities, you have a job, you're in a choir, help in a museum, and you're involved in theatre. Who knows about your problem?

P: Apart from my family, there's one girl who pretended to be my good friend. Later I discovered that she had the same problem, although hers was increased to the *n*th degree, because she had a lot of other problems. She betrayed me by telling a group of people that we were friends with.

CoT: Do you still see her often?

P: No, because after I stopped living with my ex-boyfriend, I distanced myself from all those people, partly for the reason I just told you, because by then I knew that they knew about my problem, and I felt a kind of shame that made me want to leave them.

CoT: So only your parents know about it at the moment?

P: Yes.

CoT: You told us about your days that start in the morning, when you drink something, and don't eat anything until dinnertime. Except that sometimes you happen to eat something. But you don't usually eat anything until dinnertime?

P: (*nods*)

CoT: So you wait until the evening. Do you usually have dinner with your parents?

P: Yes.

CoT: Since you all eat together, do you have a favourite food or do you eat whatever is on the table?

P: My mother usually prepares something different for me. It's a habit, because I like fish and they don't. I eat a lot of vegetables, I like fruit, and I don't share their passion for meat, fat, and things like that.

CoT: So she knows what you like, and makes a special dinner for you.

P: Yes, well, I eat the same vegetable dish as everyone else, but I don't eat meat, or any of those elaborate dishes . . .

CoT: Do you vomit systematically during the week, every time you eat with them?

P: (*nods*)

CoT: When you eat out with your friends . . . do you ever eat out with your friends?

P: Rarely.

CoT: When you do, do things follow the same process, or not?

P: No.

CoT: So it only happens at home, and only in the evening?

P: Yes.

CoT: What happens after dinner? How much time goes by before you perform this rite of yours?

P: After dinner I do housework, and within an hour I'm in the bathroom.

CoT: Do you usually have dinner at the same time?

P: Yes, at 7 p.m.

CoT: OK, so dinner is at seven at your house. How do your parents feel about your coming to dinner, and about what happens after dinner? What's going on in your family?

P: Well, I don't know if they're pretending they're daft or what, in the sense that lately they've been leaving me alone more. They used to get on my case a lot, and try to keep me under control, to check what I did.

CoT: Could you give me an example of that control?

P: After dinner, I used to leave the table and go and vomit somewhere, and inevitably someone would follow me, trying to spy on me, saying "But what are you doing?"

CoT: Do you feel that the present situation with your parents is contributing to your problem, as you've described it?

P: Yes, I think so.

CoT: How?

P: In the sense that when I get home, I'm usually famished, naturally, and when I find myself in that amorphous environment, where my needs aren't being understood . . . what am I saying? Even the most elementary things are being misunderstood. I mean, if I tell them about something that happened during the day, I have to repeat it to my father because he didn't hear me. My mother understands something completely different. All that contributes to making me more nervous and irritable. Add that to the stress of being hungry, and eating and vomiting becomes a kind of outlet, because after having vomited I feel kind of relaxed, without strength.

T: OK. So it sounds like you get home in the evening with some expectations of being understood, of being around people who are at your own level, and instead you find people who are at a different level and don't understand you. Right?

P: I mean, they're on a different planet.

Reframing by a metaphorical image of the patient's family circumstances

T: I was just thinking about that. From what you've told us, to use a metaphor, you're a seagull that flies home every night, but instead of having its own little island with a cliff, its home is in the water, and it expects to go under water with the fish. Or worse, it expects the fish to fly, when in the best of circumstances the most they can do is dart out of the water. Or a fish and a seagull might meet at the water surface, but one's under water and the other's outside. As long as the seagull expects the fish to fly, it will always be frustrated and disappointed.

P: Frustrated, that's it, because then I get rude to them and feel guilty . . .

T: A feeling of guilt.

P: It's atrocious. Then I want to punish myself, because I don't deserve anything, really.

T: On the other hand, the fish can't expect the seagull to swim under water. It would drown. All it can do is dive and come out again. You know, nature plays some bad tricks sometimes: some fish might give birth to a seagull. Maybe that's what happened to you. So waging this struggle, expecting them to fly like you do, is the worst thing you can do to yourself. You're trying to change people who can't change. As I said, the most they can do is dart out of the water, but that's not flying, it's jumping. If you want someone who's at your same level, you've got to find them among the flyers, not the swimmers.

Metaphorical reframing of the patient's failed sentimental relationship

T: I gather that you thought you had found him once, but it turned out he wasn't a seagull either. Maybe he was kind of a shark who tried to devour you.

P: (*laughs*) Yes, that's it.

T: So you're very scared, and it's much more reassuring to stay under the surface and hope that the fish will become seagulls, rather than to fly high where you might find falcons, eagles, and larger birds of prey.

P: That more or less describes the conflict I'm experiencing, because within my family I feel that I am someone, because . . .

T: Because you can fly and they can't. That's obvious.

P: But outside my home, I feel as if a thousand eyes were watching me.

T: There are birds that can fly better than you, that are stronger than you, that have claws, and beaks . . .

P: I fly low.

T: You fly low, and they can eat you up. Well, well, well.

P: Yes, but I can't fly in mid-air. When I go up, I feel bad, and when I go down I feel bad too.

T: Maybe it's a matter of teaching you, of leading you as you learn to fly, to trust in your own resources, to avoid the dangerous birds, to defend yourself from danger. Well, well, well. So, based what you've told us, I think for now we'll just make one suggestion that may sound banal, but that we consider very important . . .

P: No problem.

T: You told us earlier that there are moments when, strangely, you eat and don't vomit, because something went . . . Let's put it this way: it's those moments when you fly without fear.

P: (*nods*)

T: Perhaps you don't notice that there are other, dangerous birds around, or that there are hunters who even shoot at seagulls.

P: I don't see them in those moments.

First prescription: find exceptions to the problem

T: From now until we meet again, we'd like you to notice those moments. In practice, we want you to do what comes spontaneously, without making any particular effort. But be careful to notice when you happen to be flying without being afraid, and in what circumstances. When did it happen, what were you doing, what weren't you doing, what went through your mind. We want to hear those kinds of observations. That'll help us take a step in the direction of teaching you to fly without fear, avoid hunters, birds of prey, and not to expect fish to fly. All right?

P: OK.

T: We can see you once a week or once every two weeks. What do you prefer?

P: Once every two weeks.

T: Very well. We'll see you in two weeks.

Session two

P: For the past two weeks, I was supposed to write about the good moments. There weren't any. I've had two horrible, nightmarish weeks.

Redefining the effects of the prescription

CoT: Can you tell me exactly what you remember us asking you?

P: Yes. You asked me to write about the happy moments. If I experienced any happy moments, I was supposed to write my reasons for being happy, and describe the situation, but it didn't happen. On the contrary, some things happened that perplexed me, made me even more insecure, even more traumatized. A series of things . . .

CoT: Very important things?

P: What worries me most is my family situation. There's no dialogue any more. Now I feel that my parents are afraid, that they're avoiding me. When I get home at night, maybe they're afraid of interfering somehow, of creating some unbalance, so they leave and go to sleep, and leave me there alone. I really feel that they're avoiding me. They avoid talking to me, because as soon as we start to talk, I inevitably get nervous, because I can tell they're not following what I'm saying. So now they just say hello, and then "We're going now. We're going downstairs." So I don't know how they're feeling and they don't know how I'm feeling.

The young woman also said she had received an interesting work offer. She was very insecure as to making a decision. Her indecision seemed to be based both on the amount of work and effort that the new job would require, and on her fear that the person who had offered her the job (a very rich and distinguished man) might be interested in her from a personal point of view. She said this situation was particularly difficult for her because thought of herself as "unbalanced", and feared that the man, whom she described as "psychologically very strong" might notice her weaknesses and take advantage of her.

T: Listen, this matter has strongly influenced your heart, right?

P: Yes.

T: And it's taken from you even more . . .

P: Yes. There hasn't been one evening without vomiting. I mean eating and vomiting.

CoT: Despite the fact that you didn't have a chance to speak with your parents, because they were avoiding you.

P: Right.

Redefining the parents' role in the manifestation of the symptom

CoT: So you ate alone, but without any arguments connected with the food . . .

P: Exactly. I realized that the two things weren't connected.

T: Great! You've done big chunk of work for us!

P: Oh, I'm glad.

CoT: We've reduced the variables a bit.

P: I've noticed this development: ever since that professional thing happened to me, ever since I made that contact, I've been feeling more self-assured from the professional point of view. I feel more confident and have more self control at work. I used to let people dominate me; now I've built my own space. It's just that when I'm not in a work environment it's as if my mask fell. I'm me again, and my personality changes completely.

Reframing the patient's relationship with her emotions through the narration of a story

T: Dr Jekyll and Mr Hyde. Or like in an even more terrible movie . . . I don't remember its name . . . *China Blue*, I think. A very nice movie, starring a very young Katherine Turner. She played the role of a very successful architect. During the day, she did wonderful things. She worked in an office, designing villas for millionaires. Alone at night, she went home, put on a wig, changed into very vulgar clothes, and transformed herself into a prostitute.

P: Wow.

T: In her case, the movie presented the hypothesis that her problem derived from her dissatisfaction, from her inability to have a balanced relationship with the opposite sex. She could only let herself go in perverse situations, where she was unrecognizable. So she could only be herself from a physical point of view when she wearing a mask, as if being herself physically were something shameful, as if being female all the way were something shameful, inappropriate for such a perfectly efficient, balanced person.

P: I see.

T: So that evening you went home and did *China Blue* your own way.

P: My own version.

T: Your own version.

P: So is it related to something sentimental, then?

T: Not necessarily. It's more complex than that. It's emotional, physical, relational.

P: Actually, I've never been able to understand my body.

T: We hadn't realized that. Thanks! (*He laughs*)

P: I mean, I never feel at ease, I'm always tense . . .

More reframing of the fact that the symptom is not connected to the patient's relationship with her parents, but rather with her difficulty in managing her own emotional and physical reactions

T: There's something I'd like to understand. Two sessions ago, you told us about your hypothesis that it was your parents, your family. In the past two weeks, you've changed your focus and realized that's not true. On the contrary, your parents stayed out of the picture this week . . .

P: I know!

T: There's been an external disturbance, as you described—a great satisfaction from the professional point of view, but a risk at the personal level. "This man's a lady-killer. I wonder what he wants from me . . ."

P: Exactly.

T: "I wonder what he really wants in the end. Maybe I wouldn't be able to control him; maybe I'd even like this to happen, but I don't know if I can afford it."

P: Well, no. I wouldn't like it, because I don't find his type attractive at all, but the position is attractive.

T: Yes. When we're talking about transgression, sometimes it's not the participant's beauty that counts. It's the act in itself.

P: But considering that right now I'd find it disgusting . . .

Redefining the pleasure of eating and vomiting

T: . . . Otherwise, how can we say that eating and vomiting is beautiful? If we tell that to ordinary people, they'll say "She's crazy!" However, if you repeat something a number of times, it may become intensely pleasurable. From the outside, it looks disgusting.

P: I know.

T: So perhaps you might construct something like that with the lady-killer. But there's one thing I'm curious about: when you had your evening appointment with eating and vomiting, was it a more intense experience this time? Was it more pleasurable, more compulsive, more irresistible?

P: Let me think. It think it was more like an outlet. I mean . . .

T: You couldn't control it, right? It was irresistible . . .

P: Absolutely. The more I try to control it (I eat, and then tell myself "Let's wait. Let's see"), the stronger it gets. I mean, it's something that starts from the inside. I really can't stop myself. I've tried to do what you suggested at that conference in M, trying to wait five minutes every evening, and then longer and longer . . .

T: Why do you always have do things by yourself?

P: No, I just thought "let me try". But then I couldn't do it.

T: It's too strong. Well, well.

P: I feel a bit like a guinea pig.

T: We're two guinea pigs too, because you're testing us, right?

P: But I . . .

T: And you don't like this, because you've always got to have everything under control, right? If you're not in control, it's a crisis.

P: Exactly. So I don't feel comfortable right now.

T: I can believe that. On the other hand, that's . . .

P: The price to be paid!

Logical explanation[38] of the dynamics that maintain the problem

T: . . . One of the fundamental things that maintain your problem is that you need to keep everything under your control. But since that would be impossible for anyone, you've constructed a situation where you can let yourself go completely, without involving other people, which is what you care most about, because you've already paid once for a personal involvement, and that's something you can't deal with.

P: I really don't trust anybody.

Reframing through a metaphoric image (the armour)

T: So, in fact, you're always wearing an armour.

P: A heavy one, too.

T: If anyone gets through the armour, it's a huge problem, because you're very fragile. And you're easy to take advantage of, from all points of view, am I right?

P: (*nods*)

T: Well, well, well.

P: Stop saying "well, well, well" all the time. If you don't stop . . .

T: (*To the co-therapist*) What do you think?

CoT: I'd like to know if she's prepared to extend the disorder created by that moment of total physical and emotional involvement. My question also refers to an emotion . . . the feeling you have after carrying out your gesture is one of relaxation. An outlet, you said. Last time, you told us that you feel relaxed after vomiting . . .

P: Yes, mainly from a physical point of view, since I have no strength left.

CoT: You're exhausted, without strength, just like when we have an intense bodily experience, because vomiting causes quite a contraction in your body, I think. Now, would you be prepared to transfer some of that disorder into other sectors, other contexts of your life?

P: You mean letting myself go?

CoT: No, no, no. Not letting yourself go. I think it's too early for that. We mustn't go too fast.

P: I don't understand your question.

CoT: That's because I haven't asked it yet. I'm wondering about the situation you're considering, from a professional point of view as well. Any change entails a new situation, learning to control a new situation. But there are some variables missing. You don't know exactly which variables you'll need to control, and you don't know whether you'll be able to control them, OK? This indecision increases the tensions you take home at night, and that you get rid of by vomiting. We're starting to take some risks, we've reached some kind of order, we're in control of our job, and guess what? We're being pressed to change, and now we have to face a new adventure.

P: That's exactly it.

T: To what point are you prepared to take some small risks, to let yourself go?

P: I don't understand.

T: Maybe this is what we're curious about: is having everything under control what you need most right now, or are you ready to apply your ability to let go (which you have, at night) to other things, in other contexts?

P: I'd like to know in what other contexts.

T: In your case, there seems to be only one alternative context. Your life consists of your job, eating and vomiting. It seems to me that you don't have anything else in your life, right? The third level is your family, which you've tried to use as the supposed cause of your problem until now, but in the end, when we analyse causes, we always end up facing our personal responsibilities. So this is my question, or my doubt: to what extent are you prepared to take a risk? To risk letting go?

P: Nothing. I'm too scared.

T: So your armour is irremovable, right? You can't take it off, even for just ten seconds?

P: No.

T: What kind personal abuse are you mostly afraid of? If you took off your armour—if you imagine that, by magic, you walk out of here and we two wizards have taken your armour away, so you're without an armour, what would be the first risks that you'd have to face?

P: Physical, against my will.

T: What does that mean?

P: An abuse of my person, physically, against my will, in case I didn't want it I mean physically, with a sexual act.

T: But in this case your armour is represented by your ritual, and your avoidance of situations where something might happen. But this fear means that you'd probably be easily available for that.

P: Yes.

T: So the main thing is that you don't trust yourself.

P: Yes, because I don't like myself.

T: What don't you like about yourself, your tendency to be a bit too physical?

P: Yes.

T: Your tendency to let your feelings prevail over reason?

P: Well, yes, that too, but basically there's my fear of showing what I've got inside. I try to compensate with my external image, but it never satisfies me. It's like being chained up.

T: I can believe that, but what is this thing you have inside, that you fear others will see?

P: My feelings, my ideas.

T: Your feelings. In what sense?

P: My ideas in general.

T: Your ideas . . . so we're talking about the mind, about thought. I think that, on the contrary, the biggest problem you have is with your feelings and emotions, not your thoughts. You're good at thinking.

P: In what . . . I don't . . .

T: I mean that you're very good at managing your thoughts, at planning, organizing. When you say "If the sorcery worked, and you took my armour away, I'd be afraid that someone might abuse me physically" this means that you might be available to being abused, and that means that you're afraid of your own reactions, of your own tendencies. So if I understand this correctly, there are two opposite tendencies in you.

Reframing through metaphorical images (the good fairy and the witch)

T: There's a rather strong tendency towards intense emotions, feelings, transgression, and an opposite tendency towards being impeccable . . .

a good little fairy. OK? So the armour's there to keep that witch locked in. So there are fairies and witches fighting inside you, and you're very scared of the witch, which is actually you. So you're being distrustful because you distrust yourself. Well, well.

P: (*nods*)

Reframing through aphorism

T: You know, when I hear this kind of thing, it reminds me of an aphorism that says "If you allow it, you can renounce it; if you don't allow it, it will become irresistible."

P: I've heard that . . .

T: Nobody wants you to actually start behaving lasciviously, to give space to the witches. But until you manage to get the witches and fairies inside you to work together, you'll remain a victim of the witch to a much greater degree than you think. The witch will influence you much more than you think.

P: Yes, I understand that, but I don't know what to do about it.

T: Well, that's why you're here. We're working on it.

P: I know there's this contrast.

Further clarification as to how the persistence of the problem is linked to her conflict with her parents

T: Meanwhile, you've shown us a completely different situation today than what transpired fifteen days ago. We've got rid of the notion that there was a family pathology. If there was one, it would have been in the past years. At the moment, it's uninfluential with respect to the persistence of your problem.

P: Yes, but whenever I speak to my parents, I still get angry and upset.

T: But that's obvious. You need to find a different enemy to fight. Don't fight this one. They're much too scared. We're all very good at constructing this kind of self-deception, to shift our attention to something less painful, in order to hide what's most painful. Today we've focused on where the problem really lies, and now we have to work on that problem.

P: (*nods*)

First "as if" prescription: one small thing per day (using the metaphor of the witch)

T: So we want you to do just one thing, a very small, simple, voluntary thing, along the lines of what P [the Cotherapist] was asking you. Between now and when we see you again, every day, we'd like you do one tiny, minimal, absolutely insignificant, not risky, but concrete thing, letting the witch guide your action, not the fairy. But just one tiny thing a day—something truly minimal. It mustn't entail any risk, it shouldn't expose you. Just the bare minimum. In the morning, think: "If I let the witch loose, and she gets going, what would I feel like doing?"

P: You mean, this is not something I have to do in public, it's . . .

T: Yes, yes, let me explain myself better. In the morning, you ask yourself: "If I released the part of my nature that I'm repressing with my armour", or "If I freed the imprisoned witch today, what would she make me do—or rather, what would I do?" You'll think of some big things first, then smaller and smaller things. Every day, we want you to choose the smallest thing that the witch might make you do, and put it in practice. But it has to be something different every day.

P: Hum.

T: OK. That's all we want.

P: Yes, I understand.

T: And if you want some advice regarding the offer you've received . . .

P: Yes, that would be great.

T: Take your time. Tell them that you're tempted by this offer, but that you also feel apprehensive about it; that you'd like to accept, but there are some things that need to be settled. Postpone your decision. That way we'll also see how much that lady-killer really wants you. OK? At the moment, any decision would seem wrong, because it would expose you either to your own disappointment with yourself, or to an excessive risk. Take your time, OK?

P: Very well.

T: We'll see you in fifteen days.

P: OK.

Session three

CoT: Do you have an escort today?

P: No.

CoT: You managed to get here alone?

P: (*smiling*) Yes.

CoT: How are things going? What happened?

Redefining the effects of the "as if" prescription

P: Now, for homework I was supposed to . . . choose something every day and "let the witch loose", right? So, the first few days were full of intense mental activity, because I'd think of something that I thought would be the most appropriate thing to let the witch loose on, right? And . . .

CoT: On what basis did you decide what was most appropriate?

P: If I felt a wish to keep that particular thing under control, to keep it in order, and see that it was done in a certain way. So I tried to counteract that tendency, but . . . as soon as I let the witch loose on that issue, something else would happen that seemed more appropriate. So in the beginning, the first two or three days, there was this conflict. Then as the days went by, I found something every day to let the witch loose on. But then, I don't do so many things every day, so I was running out of things, but I had to let go on something different every day . . . So I had to broaden my horizons a bit, and let go a bit on my job. That good-girl image that I want everyone to see in me. . . . I thought about it . . . I took my time in some situations where I realized I had to go against my own wishes, and asserted myself a bit, and that made me feel good, and . . . I felt as if I had expressed myself. I discovered that it's a self-reinforcing chain, in the sense that it's a pleasant feeling, and I noticed that, day after day, I was able to open up to people. Before, I always wanted to keep my distance from everyone else, from the group in general. Yes, maybe my indifference towards other people is gradually changing. I'm even able to look people straight in the eye, and have a dialogue with them without feeling inferior or seeking their approval, their benevolence. On my last two trips here, I isolated myself from the other passengers in my train compartment by taking out my crossword book, but this time I actually started a conversation with some people who seemed, well, banal at first. Each of us told their own story, and I heard some things that shocked me . . . well, in a good way, because they made me see my so-called problem in a different light . . .

CoT: Who do you think contributed most to that experience, the witch or the good fairy, as we've called them? Did you make them work together, or did you let one work more than the other?

P: I don't think it was either of them.

CoT: OK, so something new has turned up!

P: Me, as a person.

CoT: That's something new, considering how things have been for a while, isn't it?

Reframing by using an analogy to present the possibility of making the good fairy and the witch coexist within the same person

T: You know, when we have two opposites fighting each other, we need a third thing to in order to solve the conflict. It could be a synthesis of the two, or something completely different from both, something that we might call an emerging quality. Water is composed of oxygen and hydrogen molecules, but it has nothing to do with oxygen or hydrogen. You, too, can be an emerging quality of the witch and the good fairy, something completely different from either the fairy or the witch, even though it retains some of their characteristics.

CoT: This series of positive events that have occurred, step by step, by small steps—this virtuous, no longer vicious, circle or chain, as you have called it—what effects has this had on the different areas of your life? You said it was positive at the professional level, positive in your social life because you're able to look people in the eye a bit more, and you're able to talk, to have a dialogue . . . Have any other areas benefited?

P: Yes . . . I don't know . . . A kind of growing vitality that I've been feeling has made me meet someone, a man that I've been seeing for a week and . . . I'm watching my steps very carefully, but . . . This new thing is perplexing, and scares me a bit, but it's something I'd like to face . . .

T: I suppose it makes you feel enthusiastic!?

P: Yes.

T: And you've actually become a couple?

P: No! We're still . . .

T: You're still negotiating!

P: Yes. We've been seeing each other for a week, and . . . it's a beautiful relationship, I think! Because I've always made a dive for everything, but with this relationship, I'm still evaluating . . . Maybe also because he's a man of a certain age. He's six years older than I am. I'm not dealing with boys any more . . . I mean, he's a more mature kind of person, with ideas . . . And the main thing is that, with other men, I've always tried to hide my problem; I've been able to confide in him. I don't know how . . . I mean, it felt completely natural, in the sense that I felt no fear or shame. Yes, I'm often ashamed of my feelings. Instead, I just told him, just like that. I thought he wouldn't want to see me again after the first time, but instead . . .

CoT: Excuse me . . . you mentioned "your problem". Could you tell us exactly what you confessed to him?

P: My difficulties in establishing relationships with others in general, and my eating problems, but I didn't exactly tell him everything. I told him I have some problems with food.

Analysing the current state of the eating problem

CoT: And what exactly have you been doing regarding "the food problem", as you've defined it?

P: Well, it happened, but less. It happened in three instances when I felt a kind of emptiness inside, because of some resolutions I wasn't able to keep, because of my laziness and my inconstant character . . . So I felt this kind of internal void and . . . I don't know . . . like an outlet . . . It made me vomit.

T: How many times, did you say? Three times?

P: Yes.

CoT: In fifteen days?

Positive redefinition of the decreased symptom

T: That's a massive decrease.

P: Drastic.

T: You used to do it every night.

P: Yes.

T: And now only three times!

P: Yes.

T: How do you explain this change?

P: Well, I don't know. I've no idea. A similar thing happened with my parents. After not seeing each other for three days, we had had a good talk, and I started seeing them in a different light. I mean, they've laid down their arms, if they ever really had any . . . I'm not sure. In any case, they told me everything depends on me, and they can't do anything about it. If I want to, I'll get out of this, otherwise . . . otherwise I'll stay bogged down. They told me they're not going to try to intervene in any way, so the now the choice . . .

T: And how did they react when they saw that you had stopped doing it, except for three times?

P: I don't think they realized it.

T: You didn't tell them?

P: No.

Gratifying the patient for her abilities ("intellectual seduction")

T: Good. I think it's important that you avoid telling them, because this is your thing. It's completely your own achievement.

P: I don't know if they'd even believe me . . .

T: Oh!

P: That's right.

CoT: What have you discovered that you can, seeing that for fifteen days you've managed not to do what you used to?

P: Well, a lot of things. I bought myself a computer, so I spent my time at home becoming more familiar with this new tool.

T: So you'll be even better at your job!

P: I'm doing it for personal reasons; the programmes I have at home are completely different from the ones I . . .

T: So you'll do even better in general!

P: I'm not doing it to get better. It's just something I'm interested in.

CoT: You'll be more competent, in any case. It's an additional skill.

P: Yes, I think I'll be able to use what I'm learning.

T: What about that new job offer? How did you manage to postpone your decision?

P: Well . . . that evening I was . . . I was splendid! (*She laughs*)

T: Well . . . You've been fantastic for the past two weeks!

P: No, no! I faced the question head-on. I called him. It was a forty-five minute call, and the salesman had just returned from the US . . .

CoT: You called him?

P: Yes, because that was our agreement.

CoT: Oh, OK.

P: And . . .

CoT: When he got back from the States . . .

P: I called him and told him that if he needed someone in the short term, I couldn't consider his offer because there were some things I needed to figure out and organize, both on my job and outside, and that . . . yes, unfortunately, if he needed an answer quickly, I could only say no. And there I got a surprise, because I thought that would be the end of that. Instead, he told me: "No, if it's a matter of waiting two or three months, I can wait, as long as you let me know whatever you decide, and call me . . ." So it was left open.

T: You felt very capable when you did that, right?

P: Yes.

T: We might say "you rode on the tiger's back".

P: Yes, because . . . I don't know. Right then, it didn't seem so important to project a certain image for his benefit, or to try to make him like me somehow . . . to seem professional, or . . . I mean, I was simply being me. I told him what I thought, and that gave me a good feeling, because I usually try to be obliging. I always try to seem more than what I am. Instead, I just told him: "I'm sorry, but if you need someone immediately . . ."

Scale technique

T: Good. Before suggesting anything else, we'd like an evaluation ... a kind of number grade from you. You've told us about a great number of changes in the past fifteen days. We consider these changes important and substantial. You were the first to point them out. Now, if we put down a zero for the way things were when you first came here, and a ten for when you might tell us "we've solved all my problems—all of them", how many points would you give yourself today?

P: Today? Eight points. The problem is that I don't know if I can keep it up!

T: You'd give yourself an eight today?

P: Yes. After this morning, certainly.

T: Wait. I'm wondering: what needs to happen for you to be able to say that you've reached ten? What would be the point at which you could say: "I've reached ten. I don't need you any more", or "I need you just so I can keep it up?"

P: Oh ... yes ...

T: What concrete pieces of evidence would make you say that?

P: Let me say that an eight is a very good evaluation. I mean, I don't even aspire to a ten, because I'm fine the way I am now. What's still missing for it to become constant ... well, that's an unknown variable for me too! Also because I'm very perplexed about the roots of all this.

T: See, you're thinking about the roots ... You're looking back. I asked you to look forward.

P: Hum.

First prescription: think about what would make her say she's reached ten on the evaluation scale

T: What needs to happen, or what do you need to do, or what would you need to feel, to make you say we've reached a ten? I don't want an answer now. That's one of the prescriptions for the next fifteen days.

P: A ten would certainly mean independence ... leaving home ...

T: Yes, but I'd like you to think about this every day. OK? Every day, you must say to yourself: "OK, I'm at eight. At what point might I say

I'm at ten? What would be the point before that, a nine? What needs to happen for me to be able to tell those two that I've reached ten, or nine?" [To the co-therapist] Would you like to add something?

Reframing by narrating a story

CoT: Yes. I was struck by how firmly you said: "OK, everything is at a splendid eight, but there's a problem: I don't know if I'll be able to keep it up, and I don't know what else I need to do in order to keep it up." On the other hand, you don't know what's going to happen in the next few days . . . None of us knows. I remember a little story about a snail that found itself under a cherry tree. The snail started climbing up the tree. There were birds all around, and the birds were watching the snail, who was obviously making an enormous effort, climbing very, very slowly. One of the birds says: "Hey stupid, what are you climbing this tree for now?" (It was still early in the year, February or March) "Can't you see there aren't any cherries? You won't find anything up there!" And the snail says: "Yes, but by the time I get to the top, there will be cherries!"

P: I understand.

CoT: That's something you might think about in the next few days. Try to think about the opportunities you might take, about what would enable you to proceed towards something that you decide is valuable in the next few days, something that would automatically take you from an eight to a ten, or would enable you to proceed calmly, so that you can consolidate our eight first. It wouldn't be very efficient to reach a ten, not knowing whether the eight is sufficiently consolidated.

P: Yes. The fact is, nothing bad happened in the past fifteen days. On the contrary, everything was perfect.

T: Was it magic, in your opinion, or did you contribute to the construction of this new reality?

P: That's what I'm trying to figure out! It would be nice to know that I've created it, in a sense. Or to be able to see it from another . . .

Reframing through aphorism

T: You know, it's a known fact by now, even in the so-called "exact sciences", that true discoveries do not consist of discoveries of new substances, but of a change of perspective in the mind of the observer. It seems to us that, in that sense, you're making some new discoveries.

What we're concerned about now is that you continue this voyage of discovery, which doesn't mean seeing new worlds, but "changing your eyes", as Proust wrote. All right?

P: (*nods*)

T: We'll see you in three weeks.

The patient returned after three weeks reporting that everything was well, both in her rapport with food and in her personal relationships

Conclusions

At the end of this long and perhaps tiring journey inside the difficult universe of eating disorders, we would like to point out few but essential topics. Actually, even if these pathologies are severe and incapacitating, it is possible to build up models of therapy that are really effective and efficient. That means that it is possible to avoid the pessimism and resignation that psychiatric text-books utilize to describe such very resistant pathologies. Don D. Jackson (1964) used to say that there are no difficult patients, but often there are ineffective therapists and therapies. This is true only if therapies, in the way they are built up, are suitable and fit the problem, rather than the opposite. Moreover, as the psychic disorders evolve accordingly with the evolution of individuals and society, therapies must evolve too, to follow this process. That means that therapies that were effective years ago, are not suitable any more. Nietzsche, however, said: "In this world of images created by ourselves, we invent ourselves like a unit, like something that remains constant through the change" (1965, p. 151). As we already pointed out, in other works on the subject of brief therapy focused on specific disorders, probably some readers will be skeptical and doubtful about the results we declare. Probably these readers will think accordingly with their background and theories that it is impossible to rapidly solve complicated and involving problems, but, remembering Occam: "All the things that can be done with little, in vain are often done with a lot."

NOTES

1. According to other researchers, the relationship between sexual abuse and food disorders is extremely variable. As reported in Schwartz and Cohen (1996) and Caruso and Manara (1997), the presence of sexual abuse as a factor in food disorders goes from twenty-six per cent in Lacey and Evans (1986) and Manara, Caruso, and Mariotto (1996) to forty per cent in Hall, Tice, Beresford, Wooley, and Hall (1992), to fifty-eight per cent in Kearney-Cooke (1988), sixty per cent in Waller (1992), up to 69–70% in Oppenheimer, Howells, Palmer, and Chaldwel (1985) and Folsom and Krahn (1993).
2. The construct of "attempted solutions" is fundamental to the strategic approach to therapy. For more detailed descriptions of this orientation, see Fisch, Weakland, & Segal, 1982; Nardone, 1991, 1993, 1995a,b; Nardone & Watzlawick 1990, 2000; Watzlawick, 1977, 1981; Watzlawick, Weakland, & Fisch, 1974.
3. By *perceptive–reactive system* we mean an individual's redundant modalities of perception and reaction towards reality. These are expressed in the functioning of the three independent fundamental typologies of relationship: between Self and Self, Self and others, and Self and the world (Nardone, 1991).
4. The term "autopoiesis" refers to an organization that computes its own organization. It is the typical organization of living beings, as

autonomous units, capable of continuously producing themselves, of nourishing themselves and self-constructing through their own internal dynamics. "In the autopoietic unit, doing produces being, and this constitutes its peculiar organizational modality" (Maturana & Varela, 1980).

5. We should not underestimate the concrete pathologizing power of psychopathological and psychiatric labelling (Nardone, 1994; Pagliaro, 1995; Watzlawick, 1981), i.e., the "self-fulfilling prophecy" produced by the diagnosis in the person who receives it and the persons around him. Diagnostic labels, being performative linguistic acts (Austin, 1962), eventually create the reality that they are supposedly describing. Moreover, in the field of eating disorders, we also have the problem of the enormous popular diffusion of psychodiagnostic constructs, which has led to a growing emphasis on these disorders. The great interest and alarm that these disorders produce, due to their continuous publication, have made the symptom an important attention-getting vehicle for the persons who suffer from it.
6. In the case of phobic–obsessive disorders (agoraphobia, panic attacks, compulsive fixations and hypochondria), for example, we observed a series of specific and redundant dysfunctional attempted solutions: the tendency to avoid fear-laden situations, constant requests for help and protection from relatives and friends, attempts to control one's spontaneous physical reactions as well as the surrounding environment. The relationship with self, others, and the world of those persons who suffer from these disorders appears to be completely based on the above mentioned mechanisms of perception and reaction.
7. See Chapter Two for a more extensive discussion of our methodology.
8. This diagnostic classification is freely drawn from *DSM-IV* (APA, 1994).
9. Normal weight is generally calculated based on body mass index (BMI), which is calculated as the ratio of weight expressed in kilograms and the squared height expressed in metres, with a minimum limit of BMI less than or equal to 17.5 kg/m^2.
10. As a consequence, we use the label "bulimia" to denote all cases that are classified in psychiatric literature as "bulimia nervosa without purging behaviour", and some cases of psychogenic obesity.
11. The American Psychiatric Association reports that approximately fifty per cent of cases of anorexia nervosa evolve into bulimia nervosa (i.e., the disorder that we define as vomiting) (Costin, 1996).
12. See Chapter Two for data on the efficacy and effectiveness of our interventions.

13. For more detailed presentations this approach, see Nardone and Watzlawick (2000); Watzlawick (1981); Watzlawick, Weakland, and Fisch (1974); Weakland and Ray (1995).
14. Our treatment protocols for phobic–obsessive disorders obtained surprising results: eighty-seven per cent of cases were solved in an average of eleven sessions (Nardone, 1993; Sirigatti, 1994). In most of these cases (eighteen per cent) the remission of symptoms occurred within the first five sessions; among the latter, the symptoms disappeared after only one session (Nardone & Watzlawick, 2000).
15. Specific international literature on the results of psychotherapy shows a variability of positive results from a minimum of forty per cent to a maximum of seventy per cent (Garfield & Bergin, 1978; Luborsky, Singer, & Luborsky, 1975; Sirigatti, 1988, 1994). Even below a seventy per cent efficacy rate, we would therefore still be within the range of most therapies. Below fifty per cent, the same results can be obtained by placebos.
16. "Intervening variables" are all factors outside the researcher's control that can induce changes in the variable object of study. In our specific case, "intervening variables" are all the events in a subject's life that may influence the evolution of the disorder in the patient independently of the therapy.
17. We also include in this category so-called "bulimic anorexics".
18. Referring to group theory and the theory of logical types, Watzlawick, Weakland, and Fisch (1974) draw a distinction between two types of changes that can occur in a system. The first (change one) occurs within a system, leaving the system itself unchanged; the second (change two) is introduced from the outside and changes the system itself. Only a change two, which is effected on the solutions adopted by the person in order to produce a change one, leads to a concrete solution of the problem, requiring a leap to a different level of logic (i.e., going outside the system).
19. Our results for bulimia include those for binge eating (ten cases). We consider binge eating to be a specific form of evolution of bulimia.
20. See Agras et al., 1989, 1992; Fairburn et al., 1991; Garner et al., 1991; Mitchell et al., 1990 (cited in Wilson & Fairburn, 1993, p. 239)
21. For the sake of clarity, we will often refer to anorexics, bulimics, and vomiters as "her" or "the young woman". By doing this we do not intend to exclude male subjects with these problems from our discussion.
22. Selvini Palazzoli, Cirillo, Selvini, and Sorrentino (1998, p. 23) also report a decrease in anorexics (strictly defined) from sixty per cent in

the years 1971–1987 to 42.3% in the years 1988–1996, and a corresponding significant increase of bulimic anorexics (we consider this problem among the vomiting disorders).

23. On this subject, see Haley (1973, 1985); Nardone (1991, 1993); Nardone and Watzlawick (1990); Selvini Palazzoli (1963); Selvini Palazzoli, Boscolo, Cecchin, and Prata (1975); Watzlawick, Beavin, and Jackson (1967); Watzlawick, Weakland, and Fisch (1974)
24. The reframing through metaphor gives an analogical representation of the problem and its functional characteristics, and marks the passage from the stage of studying the persistence of the problem to the stage of intervention: the metaphors we use generally contain a narrative key to a solution that later evolves into direct prescriptions.
25. See Watzlawick and Nardone (1997).
26. The communication technique of speaking the patient's language, which is the basic rule of Strategic Therapy, has been defined as "tracing" technique by Bandler and Grinder (1975). For further information on this topic see Nardone (1991); Nardone and Watzlawick (1990); Watzlawick (1977).
27. Avoiding negative sentences during therapeutic conversation is a specific technique of Brief Strategic Therapy. See Nardone (1991) and Nardone and Watzlawick (1990).
28. Anonymous (1990).
29. By the term "bulimia", we refer only to subjects who compulsively eat large quantities of food without eliminating it through vomiting. When vomiting is present, we prefer to use the terms "vomiting" or "vomiting syndrome". Thus, our usage of the term "bulimia" includes some cases of psychogenic obesity and corresponds only partly to the disorder classified as "bulimia nervosa without purging" in *DSM IV*.
30. For a more efficient exposition, we will present our treatment method for bulimia within a single protocol, specifying at each stage how different manoeuvres are applied for particular variants of the disorder.
31. The *granting of pleasure* technique is not appropriate for "artichokes", with whom it is essential to shift the focus from pleasure-seeking through food to the patient's interpersonal relationships. Indeed, concentrating on the patient's relationship with food would only encourage the "artichoke's" attempted solution, and therefore go against our treatment goals.
32. Generally speaking, with almost all "artichokes" and "yo-yos".
33. We use this reframing manoeuvre not only when fasting is present, but in all cases characterized by rigid eating restrictions.

34. Many authors have noted the analogy between eating disorders and obsessive-compulsive disorders (Caruso & Manara, 1997).
35. As for bulimia, we will present a single protocol of treatment for vomiting. As we describe the different stages of treatment, we will illustrate how manoeuvres vary according to the different forms of the disorder.
36. This prescription is usually given to the mother because, in most cases, she is the member of the family most deeply involved in maintaining the disorder, her daughter's main accomplice.
37. We are referring to those manoeuvres that can have decisive effects on the pathogenous perceptive–reactive system of the disorder, i.e., the provocative representation of eating and vomiting as an erotic perversion, the technique of the interval, and the amplification of the pursuit of pleasure.
38. The use of rational explanation seems to be particularly effective with this patient, who is used to being appreciated for her intellectual abilities and always being in control of the situation. We are performing an "intellectual seduction" that gratifies the patient and stimulates her will to collaborate.

REFERENCES

AA.VV. (1980). *Handbook of Daily Readings*. Los Angeles: Overeaters Anonymous.

Abraham, S. F., Mira, M., & Llewellyn-Jones, D. (1983). Bulimia: a study of outcome, *International Journal of Eating Disorders*, 2: 175–180.

American Psychiatric Association (APA) (1994). *Diagnostic and Statistical Manual of Mental Disorders, IV*. Washington, DC: The American Psychiatric Association.

Anonymous (1990). *I 36 stratagemmi: l'arte cinese di vincere*, Naples: Guida Editori.

Arcuri, L. (1994). Giudizio e diagnosi clinica: analisi degli errori, *Scienze dell'Interazione, 1*(1): 107–116.

Austin, J. L. (1962). *How to Do Things with Words*. Cambridge, MA: Harvard University Press.

Bandler, R., & Grinder, J. (1975). *Patterns of the Hypnotic Techniques of Milton H. Erickson M.D.* Palo Alto, CA:. Meta Publications.

Bateson, G., Jackson, D. D., Haley, J., & Weakland, J. H. (1956). Toward a theory of schizophrenia, *Behavioral Science, 1*: 251–264.

Bergman, J. S (1985). *Fishing for Barracuda. Pragmatics of Brief Systemic Therapy*. New York: Norton.

Bernasconi, U. (1988). *Parole Alla Buona Gente*.

Canetti, E. (1996). *La Rapidità dello Spirito: Appunti da Hampstead (1954–1971)*. Milan: Adelphi.

Caruso, R., & Manara, F. (eds.) (1997). *I disturbi del comportamento alimentare*. Milan: Angeli.

Cioran, E. (1984). *La Tentazione di Esistere*. Milan: Adelphi.

Costin, C. (1996). *The Eating Disorder Sourcebook*. Los Angeles, CA: Lowell House.

Da Costa, N. (1989a). On the logic of belief. *Philosophical and Phenomenological Research, 2*: 413–446.

Da Costa, N. (1989b). The logic of self-deception. *American Philosophical Quarterly, 1*: 178–197.

Dalla Grave, R. (1996). *Anoressia Nervosa: i fatti*. Verona: Positive Press.

de Shazer, S. (1985). *Keys to Solution in Brief Therapy*. New York: Norton.

de Shazer, S. (1988). *Clues: Investigating Solutions in Brief Therapy*. New York: Norton.

de Shazer, S. (1994). *Words Were Originally Magic*. New York: Norton.

Elster, J. (1979). *Ulysses and the Sirens*. Cambridge: Cambridge University Press.

Elster, J. (ed.) (1985). *The Multiple Self*. Cambridge: Cambridge University Press.

Faccio, E. (1999). *Il disturbo alimentare. Modelli, ricerche e terapie*. Rome: Carocci editore.

Fiorenza, A., & Nardone, G. (1995). *L'intervento strategico nei contesti educativi. Comunicazione e problem-solving per i problemi scolastici*. Milan: Giuffrè.

Fisch, R., Weakland, J. H., & Segal, L. (1982). *The Tactics of Change: Doing Therapy Briefly*. San Francisco: Jossey Bass.

Folsom, V., & Krahn, D. (1993). The impact of sexual and physical abuse on eating disordered and psychiatric symptoms: a comparison of eating disordered and psychiatric inpatients. *International Journal of Eating Disorders, 13*: 249–258.

Garfield, S. L. (1981). Psychotherapy. A 40 years appraisal. *American Psychologist, 2*: 174–183.

Garfield, S. L., & Bergin, A. E. (eds) (1978). *Handbook of Psychotherapy and Behavior Change: An Empirical Analysis* 2nd edn. New York: Wiley.

Garfinkel, E., & Garner, D. M. (1985). *Handbook of Psychotherapy for Anorexia and Bulimia Nervosa*. New York: Guilford Press.

Grana, N. (1990). *Contraddizione e incompletezza*. Naples: Liguori.

Haley, J. (1973). *Uncommon Therapy: The Psychiatric Techniques of Milton H. Erickson, M.D.* New York: Norton.

Haley, J. (1985). *Conversation with Milton Erickson M.D.* Vol. I: *Changing Individuals;* Vol. II: *Changing Couples;* Vol. III: *Changing Families and Children*. Washington: Triangle Press.

Hall, R. C., Tice, L., Beresford, T. P., Wooley, B., & Hall, A. K. (1992). Sexual abuse in patients with anorexia nervosa and bulimia. *Psychosomatics, 30*: 73–79.

Heisenberg, W. (1958). *Physics and Philosophy*. New York: Harper.

Hsu, L. K. G. (1987). Outcome and treatment effects. In: P. S. V. Beumont, G. D. Burrows, & R. C. Casper (eds), *Handbook of Eating Disorder, Part I: Anorexia and Bulimia Nervosa*. Amsterdam: Elsevier Science.

Jackson, D. D. (1964). *Myths of Madness: New Facts for Old Fallacies*. New York: Macmillan.

Kearney-Cooke, A. (1988). Group treatment of sexual abuse among women with eating disorders. *Women ad Therapy, 6*: 5–22.

Keel, P. K., & Mitchell, J. E. (1997). Outcome in bulimia nervosa. *American Journal of Psychiatry, 154*(3): 313–321.

Laborit, H. (1982). *L'elogio della fuga*. Milan: Mondadori.

Lacey, J. H., & Evans, D. H. (1986). The impulsivist. A multi-impulsive personality disorder. *British Journal of Addiction, 81*: 641–649.

Lewin, K. (1946). Action research and minority problems. *Journal of Social Issues, 2*: 34–46.

Lichtenberg, G. C. (1981). *Libretto di Consolazione*. Milan: Rizzoli.

Luborsky, L., Singer, B., & Luborsky, L. (1975). Comparative studies of psychotherapies: is it true that everyone has won and all must have prizes? *Archives of General Psychiatry, 132*: 995–1004.

Madanes, C. (1981). *Strategic Family Therapy*. San Francisco: Jossey-Bass.

Madanes, C. (1984). *Behind the One-way Mirror*. San Francisco: Jossey-Bass.

Madanes, C. (1990). *Sex, Love and Violence*. New York: Norton.

Malenbaum, R., Herfog, D., Eisenthal, S., & Wyshak, G. (1988). Overeaters Anonymous: impact on bulimia. *International Journal of Eating Disorders, 7*: 139–143.

Manara, F., Caruso, R., & Mariotto, S. (1996). Sexuality and menstruation of women with eating disorders. *Abstract VII New York International Conference on Eating Disorders*, New York.

Maturana, H. R., Varela, F. J. (1980). *Autopoiesis and Cognition. The Realization of the Living*. Dordrecht: Reidel.

Nardone, G. (1991). *Suggestione → Ristrutturazione = Cambiamento. L'approccio strategico e costruttivista alla psicoterapia breve*. Milan: Giuffrè.

Nardone, G. (1993). *Paura, Panico, Fobie*. Milan: Ponte alle Grazie. English translation: *Brief Strategic Solution-Oriented Therapy of Phobic and Obessive Disorders*. Northvale, NJ: Aronson, 1996.

Nardone, G. (1994). *Manuale di sopravvivenza per psicopazienti*. Milan: Ponte alle Grazie.

Nardone, G. (1995a). Brief strategic therapy of phobic disorders: a model of therapy and evaluation research. In: J. H. Weakland & W. A. Ray (eds), *Propagations: Thirty Years of Influence from the Mental Research Institute* (Chapter 4). New York: Haworth Press.

Nardone, G. (1995b). Conoscere un problema mediante la sua soluzione: i sistemi percettivo-reattivi patogeni e la psicoterapia strategica. In G. Pagliaro & M. Cesa-Bianchi (eds), *Nuove prospettive in psicoterapia e modelli interattivo-cognitivi*. Milan: Angeli.

Nardone, G. (1997). Il linguaggio che guarisce: la comunicazione come veicolo di cambiamento terapeutico. In: P. Watzlawick & G. Nardone (Eds.), *Terapia Breve Strategica* (pp. 69–83). Milan: Cortina.

Nardone, G. (1998). *Psicosoluzioni*. Milan: Rizzoli.

Nardone, G., & Watzlawick, P. (1990). *L'Arte del Cambiamento: manuale di terapia strategica e ipnoterapia senza trance*. Milan: Ponte alle Grazie. English translation: *The Art of Change. Strategic Therapy and Hypnotherapy Without Trance*. San Francisco: Jossey-Bass.

Nardone, G., & Watzlawick, P. (eds), (2000). *Advanced Brief Therapy*. Northvale, NJ: Aronson.

Nietzsche, F. (1965). *La Gaia Scienza* (translated from the German original, *Die Höhliche Wissenchoff*. Milan: Adelphi.

Oppenheimer, R., Howells, K., Palmer, R. L., & Chaldwel, D. A. (1985). Adverse sexual experiences in childhood and clinical eating disorders: a preliminary description. *Journal of Psychiatric Research, 19*: 157–161.

Pagliaro, G. (1995). La mente discorsiva e la psicoterapia interattivo-cognitiva. In: G. Pagliaro & M. Cesa-Bianchi (eds), *Nuove prospettive in psicoterapia e modelli interattivo-cognitivi* (pp. 15–21). Milan: Angeli.

Paguni, R. (1993). *La ricerca in psicoterapia*. Rome: Armando.

Pascal, B. (1670). *Pensées*. Paris: Guillaume Depriez.

Popper, K. R. (1972). *Objective Knowledge*. London: Oxford University Press.

Rosenthal, R., & Jacobson, L. (1968). *Pygmalion in the Classroom: Teacher Expectation and Pupil's Intellectual Development*. New York: Rinehart & Winston, Holt.

Salvini, A. (1988). Pluralismo teorico e pragmatismo conoscitivo: assunti metateorici in psicologia della personalità. In: E. Fiora, I. Pedrabissi, & A. Salvini (eds.), *Pluralismo teorico e pragmatismo conoscitivo in psicologia della personalità* (pp. 11–15). Milan: Giuffrè.

Salvini, A. (1993). Introduzione a G. Nardone, *Paura, Panico, Fobie*. Ponte alle Grazie, Milano; English translation: Preface. In: G. Nardone, *Brief Strategic Solution-Oriented Therapy of Phobic and Obessive Disorders*, Northvale, NJ: Aronson, 1996.

Schopenhauer, A. (1896). *The Art of Controversy & Other Posthumous Papers*. London: Swan Sonnenschein & Co.

Schwartz, M., & Cohen L. (1996). *Sexual Abuse and Eating Disorders*. New York: Brunner/Mazel,.

Selvini Palazzoli, M. (1963). *L'Anoressia mentale*. Milan: Feltrinelli.

Selvini Palazzoli, M., Boscolo, L., Cecchin, G. F., & Prata, G. (1975). *Paradosso e controparadosso*. Milan: Feltrinelli. English translation: *Paradox and Counterparadox*, New York: Aronson, 1978.

Selvini Palazzoli, M., Cirillo, S., Selvini, M., & Sorrentino, A. M. (1988). *Ragazze anoressiche e bulimiche. La terapia familiare*, Milan: Cortina.

Sirigatti, S. (1988). La ricerca valutativa in psicoterapia: modelli e prospettive. In: G. Nardone, (ed.), *Modelli di psicoterapia a confronto*. Rome: Il Ventaglio.

Sirigatti, S. (1994). La ricerca sui processi e i risultati della psicoterapia. *Scienze dell'Interazione, 1*(1): 117–130.

Stolzenberg, G. (1978). Can an inquiry into the foundations of mathematics tell us anything interesting about mind? In: G. A. Miller & E. Lenneberg, (Eds.), *Psychology and Biology of Language and Thought*. New York: Academic Press.

Thom, R. (1990). *Parabole e catastrofi*. Milan: Il Saggiatore.

Tridenti, A., & Bocchia, S. (1993). *Il fenomeno anoressico-bulimico. Un tentativo di comprensione unitaria dei disturbi del comportamento alimentare*. Milan: Masson.

Varela, F. J. (1981). The creative circle. Sketches on the natural history of circularity. In P. Watzlawick (ed.), *The Invented Reality*. New York: Norton.

von Foerster, H. (1973). On constructing a reality. In: W. F. E. Preiser (ed.); *Environmental Design Research* Vol. 2 (pp. 35–46). Stroudsburg: Hutchinson & Ross: Dowden.

von Foerster, H. (1987). *Sistemi che osservano*. Rome: Astrolabio.

von Glasersfeld, E. (1981). An introduction to radical constructivism. In: P. Watzlawick (Ed.), *The Invented Reality* (pp. 17–40). New York: Norton.

von Glasersfeld, E. (1995). *Radical Constructivism*. London: The Falmer Press.

Waller, G. (1992). Sexual abuse and the severity of bulimic symptoms. *British Journal of Psychiatry, 161*: 90–93.

Walsh, B. T., Hadigan, C. M., Devlin, M. J., Gladis, M., & Roose, S. P. (1991). Long-term outcome of antidepressant treatment for bulimia nervosa. *Archives of General Psychiatry, 148*: 1206–1212.

Watzlawick, P. (1977). *Die Möglichkeit des Andersseins: zur Technick der therapeutischen Kommunikation*, Bern: Verlag Hans Huber. English translation: *The Language of Change*, New York: Basic Books, 1978.

Watzlawick, P. (ed.) (1981). *Die erfundene Wirklichkei*, Munich: Piper. English translation: *The Invented Reality*, New York: Norton.

Watzlawick, P. (1990). Therapy is what you say it is. In: J. K. Zeig, & S. G. Gilligan (eds), *Brief Therapy: Myths, Methods and Metaphors* (pp. 55–61). New York: Brunner/Mazel.

Watzlawick, P., Beavin, J. H., & Jackson, D. D. (1967). *Pragmatics of Human Communication. A Study of Interactional Patterns, Pathologies and Paradoxes*. New York: Norton.

Watzlawick P., & Nardone, G. (Eds.) (1997). *Terapia Breve Strategica*. Milan: Cortina.

Watzlawick P., Weakland J. H., & Fisch, R. (1974). *Change: Principles of Problem Formation and Problem Solution*. New York: Norton.

Weakland, J. H., & Ray, W. A. (eds) (1995). *Propagations: Thirty Years of Influence from the Mental Research Institute*. New York: Haworth Press.

Weakland, J. H., Fisch, R., Watzlawick, P., & Bodin, A. M. (1974). Brief therapy: focused problem resolution. *Family Process, 13*(2): 141–168.

Whitehead, A. N., & Russel, B. (1910–1913). *Principia Mathematica*, Cambridge: Cambridge University Press.

Wilson, G. T., & Fairburn, C. G. (1993). Cognitive treatments for eating disorders. *Journal of Consulting and Clinical Psychology, 61*(2), 216–269.

Zerbe, K. J. (1993). *The Body Betrayed*. Washington, DC: American Psychiatric Association Press.

Zuckerman, M. (1987). Biological connection between sensation seeking and drug abuse. In: J. Engel & L. Oreland (eds.), *Brain Reward Systems and Abuse* (pp. 165–176). New York: Raven Press.

INDEX